2023

Mittlerer Schulabschluss

Original-Prüfungsaufgaben und Training

Nordrhein-Westfalen

Englisch 10. Klasse

STARK

Bildnachweis

Deckblätter
S. 1: © Africa Studio. Shutterstock; S. 31: © 123rf.com; S. 163: © wavebreakmedia. Shutterstock

Hörverstehen
S. 37: © HelenSTB/flickr.com, lizenziert unter CC BY-SA 2.0; S. 38: © 57044. Shutterstock; S. 39: © Ajb110 | Dreamstime.com; S. 41: © Jody Ann. Shutterstock; S. 43: © Steffen Foerster. Shutterstock; S. 45: © Nikol Senkyrikova | Dreamstime; S. 46: © 123rf.com; S. 48: © mbfoley – Fotolia.com; S. 50: © Can Stock Photo/djpadavona; S. 52: © Nationaal Comité 4 en 5 mei

Leseverstehen
S. 62: Hintergrund © 123rf; Kiwi © Isselee Eric Philippe/123rf; S. 63: © Woraphon Banchobdi | Dreamstime.com; S. 65: Pincarel. Shutterstock; S. 66: © Can Stock Photo Inc./Jag_cz; S. 68: Schild © Becky Stares. Shutterstock; Niagarafälle © Chawalit S. Shutterstock; S. 70: © Amiami3, lizenziert unter CC BY-SA 3.0; S. 71: Backpacker © Odua | Dreamstime.com; Volunteer © Can Stock Photo Inc./4774344sean; S. 73: gemeinfrei; S. 76: Studio 8. Pearson Education Ltd; S. 77: © Gualtiero Boffi | Dreamstime; S. 80: © Cameron Pashak/www.istockphoto.com

Grammatik
S. 103: © Landd09 | Dreamstime.com; S. 104: © Multiart61 | Dreamstime.com; S. 106: © Paul Jenkinson; S. 108: © Everett Historical. Shutterstock; S. 109: © Luminis | Dreamstime.com; S. 111: Kletterer © Olivier Tuffé – Fotolia.com; Windsurfer: © Can Stock Photo Inc./3355m; Reiterin © Krzyssagit | Dreamstime.com; S. 112: Hintergrund „Party Night" © Janski/www.photocase.de; S. 114: Pokal © zentilia/123RF; Teddybär © AM-STUDIO. Shutterstock

Schreiben
S. 125: © mandy godbehear/123RF; S. 128: © flydragon. Shutterstock; S. 130: © Dana Rothstein | Dreamstime.com; S. 132/133: © Can Stock Photo Inc./asabii; S. 133: Golden Gate Bridge © Jay Beiler | Dreamstime.com; Cable Car © Minyun Zhou | Dreamstime.com

© 2022 Stark Verlag GmbH
16. neu bearbeitete und ergänzte Auflage
www.stark-verlag.de

Das Werk und alle seine Bestandteile sind urheberrechtlich geschützt. Jede vollständige oder teilweise Vervielfältigung, Verbreitung und Veröffentlichung bedarf der ausdrücklichen Genehmigung des Verlages. Dies gilt insbesondere für Vervielfältigungen, Mikroverfilmungen sowie die Speicherung und Verarbeitung in elektronischen Systemen.

Inhalt

Vorwort
Häufige Fragen zum mittleren Schulabschluss
Länderporträts zu den Bezugskulturen

Kurzgrammatik		1
1	Besonderheiten einiger Wortarten	3
1.1	Adjektive und Adverbien – *Adjectives and Adverbs*	3
1.2	Artikel – *Article*	6
1.3	Pronomen – *Pronouns*	8
1.4	Präpositionen – *Prepositions*	9
1.5	Konjunktionen – *Conjunctions*	10
1.6	Modale Hilfsverben – *Modal Auxiliaries*	11
2	Finite Verbformen	12
2.1	Zeiten – *Tenses* ▶	12
2.2	Passiv – *Passive Voice* ▶	18
3	Infinite Verbformen	19
3.1	Infinitiv – *Infinitive*	19
3.2	Gerundium (-*ing*-Form) – *Gerund*	21
3.3	Infinitiv oder Gerundium? – *Infinitive or Gerund?*	22
3.4	Partizipien – *Participles*	23
4	Der Satz im Englischen	25
4.1	Wortstellung – *Word Order*	25
4.2	Bedingungssätze – *Conditional Sentences* ▶	26
4.3	Relativsätze – *Relative Clauses*	27
4.4	Indirekte Rede – *Reported Speech* ▶	29
Hinweise, Tipps und Übungsaufgaben zu den Kompetenzbereichen		31
1	Hörverstehen	33
1.1	Strategien zum Bereich „Hörverstehen"	33
1.2	Häufige Aufgabenstellungen im Bereich „Hörverstehen"	35
1.3	Übungsaufgaben zum Bereich „Hörverstehen"	37
	Listening Test 1: Robben Island	37
	Listening Test 2: The News	38
	Listening Test 3: Apple and Rain	39
	Listening Test 4: Grey Owl	41
	Listening Test 5: The Art of Being Normal	42
	Listening Test 6: The California Gold Rush	43
	Listening Test 7: The Stolen Generations	45
	Listening Test 8: Couchsurfing or Wilderness?	46

Inhalt

    Listening Test 9: Inventing Elliot 47
    Listening Test 10: Sandringham 48
    Listening Test 11: The Super Bowl 50
    Listening Test 12: Sundae Girl 51
    Listening Test 13: Mary Robinson 52
    Listening Test 14: New Zealand Tips 54

2 Leseverstehen 55
2.1 Strategien zum Bereich „Leseverstehen" 55
2.2 Häufige Aufgabenstellungen im Bereich „Leseverstehen" 55
2.3 Übungsaufgaben zum Bereich „Leseverstehen" 59
    Reading Test 1: The Kiwi – New Zealand's Iconic Bird 59
    Reading Test 2: Young Refugees Learn about U.S.
    on the Soccer Field 63
    Reading Test 3: The History of Halloween 66
    Reading Test 4: Getting to Know Canada 68
    Reading Test 5: Volunteering in Australia 71
    Reading Test 6: "We May Be 'Born Free', but …" 73
    Reading Test 7: School Life Abroad 76
    Reading Test 8: The Double Life of Cassiel Roadnight 77
    Reading Test 9: Boot Camps for Teenagers 80
    Reading Test 10: Bog Child 83

3 Wortschatz – Verfügbarkeit sprachlicher Mittel 87
3.1 Strategien zum Bereich „Wortschatz" 87
3.2 Häufige Aufgabenstellungen im Bereich „Wortschatz" 90
3.3 Übungsaufgaben zum Bereich „Wortschatz" 92
    Aufgaben zum Grundwissen 92
    Prüfungsähnliche Aufgaben 98

4 Grammatik – Sprachliche Korrektheit 102
4.1 Strategien zum Bereich „Grammatik" 102
4.2 Übungsaufgaben zum Bereich „Grammatik" 103

5 Schreiben 115
5.1 Strategien zum Bereich „Schreiben" 115
5.2 Häufige Aufgabenstellungen im Bereich „Schreiben" 117
5.3 Hilfreiche Wendungen für den Bereich „Schreiben" 119
5.4 Allgemeine Übungsaufgaben zum Bereich „Schreiben" 125
5.5 Spezielle Übungen zu textgebundenen Schreibaufgaben 135

6 Anhang: Hörverstehenstexte 144

DEIN COACH ZUM ERFOLG!

Dein ActiveBook auf MySTARK:

Du kannst auf alle digitalen Inhalte (Prüfung 2022, Hördateien, interaktive Aufgaben, Videos, „MindCards") online zugreifen. Registriere dich dazu unter **www.stark-verlag.de/mystark** mit deinem **persönlichen Zugangscode:**

C4M8-W6G9-T6Q5

Die Inhalte dieser Auflage stehen bis 31.7.2024 zur Verfügung.

Das ActiveBook bietet dir:

- Viele interaktive Übungsaufgaben zu prüfungsrelevanten Kompetenzen
- Tipps zur Bearbeitung der Aufgaben
- Sofortige Ergebnisauswertung und detailliertes Feedback
- „MindCards" und Lernvideos zum gezielten Wiederholen zentraler Inhalte

MySTARK

DEIN COACH ZUM ERFOLG!

So kannst du interaktiv lernen:

Interaktive Aufgaben

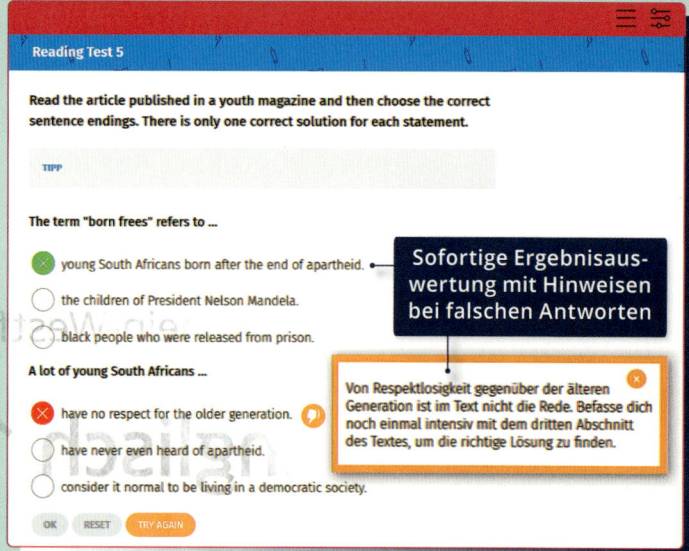

Tipps zur Bearbeitung der Aufgaben

Sofortige Ergebnisauswertung mit Hinweisen bei falschen Antworten

Lernvideos

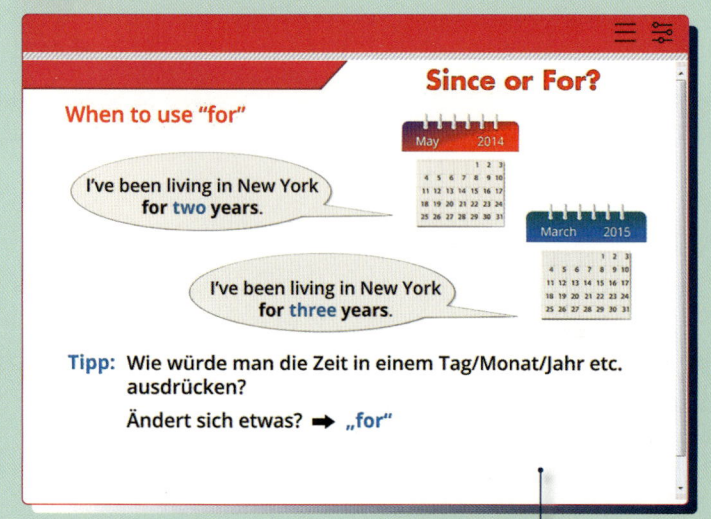

Anschauliche Erklärungen zur Grammatik und Tipps zum Vokabellernen

Web-App „MindCards"

Nützliche Wendungen mit Übersetzung

Individuelles Lernen nach dem Karteikartensystem

Systemvoraussetzungen:
- Mindestens 1024×768 Pixel Bildschirmauflösung
- Chrome, Firefox oder ähnlicher Webbrowser
- Internetzugang
- Adobe Reader oder kompatibler anderer PDF-Reader

Speaking

Writing

Inhalt

Original-Aufgaben der zentralen Prüfung in NRW 163
Mittlerer Schulabschluss 2017 2017-1
Mittlerer Schulabschluss 2018 2018-1
Mittlerer Schulabschluss 2019 .... 2019-1*
Mittlerer Schulabschluss 2021 2021-1

> **Mittlerer Schulabschluss 2022** .... www.stark-verlag.de/mystark
> Sobald die Original-Prüfungsaufgaben 2022 freigegeben sind, können sie als PDF auf der Plattform MyStark heruntergeladen werden (Zugangscode vgl. Farbseiten vorne im Buch).

* Wegen des Corona-Virus wurden 2020 die Zentralen Prüfungen in Klasse 10 durch Prüfungsarbeiten ersetzt, die dezentral von den Lehrkräften erstellt wurden. Für 2020 können daher keine Original-Aufgaben abgedruckt werden.

MP3-Dateien 🔊

Listening Test 1: Robben Island
Listening Test 2: The News
Listening Test 3: Apple and Rain
Listening Test 4: Grey Owl
Listening Test 5: The Art of Being Normal
Listening Test 6: The California Gold Rush
Listening Test 7: The Stolen Generations
Listening Test 8: Couchsurfing or Wilderness?
Listening Test 9: Inventing Elliot
Listening Test 10: Sandringham
Listening Test 11: The Super Bowl
Listening Test 12: Sundae Girl
Listening Test 13: Mary Robinson
Listening Test 14: New Zealand Tips
Hörverstehen 2017: Mama Africa
Hörverstehen 2017: Mamohato Children's Centre
Hörverstehen 2018: 67 Blankets for Mandela Day
Hörverstehen 2018: Teen Fiction
Hörverstehen 2019: Lighthouse Walk
Hörverstehen 2019: #YourChoice
Hörverstehen 2021: The Summer Plans of Danny Boyle
Hörverstehen 2021: Thomas Caffrey's Chocolate World
Hörverstehen 2022: Teil 1
Hörverstehen 2022: Teil 2

> **Hinweis:** Die MP3-Dateien kannst du ebenfalls über die Plattform MyStark abrufen.

Inhalt

Autorinnen und Autoren:
Patrick Charles, Walter Düringer, Paul Jenkinson, Brigitte Katzer, Sandra Klüser-Hanné, Elke Lüdeke, Martin Paeslack, Gerhard Philipp, Redaktion

Sprecherinnen und Sprecher der Hörtexte:
Daniel Beaver, Blair Galton, Esther Gilvray, Clare Gnasmüller, Daniel Holzberg, Rees Jeannotte, Daria Kozlova, Barbara Krzoska, Jennifer Mikulla, Benjamin Tendler, Roger Voight

Die **Hintergrundgeräusche** in den Tracks stammen aus folgenden Quellen: Freesound, Pacdv, Soundsnap

Sollten nach Erscheinen dieses Bandes noch wichtige Änderungen in der zentralen Prüfung 2023 vom Ministerium für Schule und Bildung bekannt gegeben werden, findest du aktuelle Informationen dazu auf der Plattform MyStark.

Vorwort

Liebe Schülerin, lieber Schüler,

dieses Buch eignet sich ideal zur selbstständigen und gezielten Vorbereitung auf Klassenarbeiten und den mittleren Schulabschluss.

- Die **Länderporträts** zu Neuseeland und Großbritannien liefern dir wertvolles Hintergrundwissen zu den **Bezugskulturen** der Prüfung 2023.
- In der **Kurzgrammatik** werden wichtige grammatische Themen knapp erläutert und an Beispielsätzen veranschaulicht.
- Zu einigen grammatischen Strukturen, mit denen erfahrungsgemäß viele Lernende Schwierigkeiten haben, gibt es zusätzlich **Lernvideos**.
  Ein weiteres Video zeigt dir außerdem, wie du mithilfe von **Lernstrategien** deinen **Wortschatz** erweitern und festigen kannst. Scanne mithilfe deines Smartphones oder Tablets den nebenstehenden QR-Code oder gib den folgenden Link ein – so gelangst du schnell und einfach zu den Lernvideos:
  http://qrcode.stark-verlag.de/lernvideos-englisch-1
- Jedes Kapitel in diesem Buch widmet sich einem **Kompetenzbereich**. Vorab erfährst du immer, welche Anforderungen auf dich zukommen können und wie du dich am besten darauf vorbereitest. Anhand der **Übungen** kannst du dann trainieren, wie man mit möglichen Aufgabenstellungen umgeht und sie erfolgreich löst.
- Neben vielen Aufgaben findest du das Symbol für „**interaktive Aufgabe**". Diese Übungen sind auch im ActiveBook enthalten, d. h., du kannst sie am Computer oder Tablet bearbeiten.
- Alle **Hörtexte** stehen dir als **MP3-Dateien** online zur Verfügung.
- Mit der Web-App „**MindCards**" kannst du am Smartphone **hilfreiche Wendungen** zu den Kompetenzen „Schreiben" und „Sprechen" wiederholen. Scanne dazu einfach die QR-Codes oder verwende folgende Links:
  https://www.stark-verlag.de/mindcards/writing-1;
  https://www.stark-verlag.de/mindcards/speaking-1
- Am Ende des Buches findest du eine Sammlung von **Original-Prüfungsaufgaben** der letzten Jahre. Anhand dieser Aufgaben kannst du testen, ob du für den „Ernstfall" gut gerüstet bist.

In einem separaten Band (Bestell-Nr. C05150L) gibt es zu allen Übungen dieses Buches und zu den Original-Prüfungsaufgaben ausführliche **Lösungsvorschläge** mit hilfreichen Hinweisen und Tipps.

Viel Spaß beim Üben und viel Erfolg in den Klassenarbeiten und in der Prüfung!

> Auf alle **digitalen Inhalte** (Prüfung 2022, MP3-Dateien, ActiveBook, Lernvideos und MindCards) kannst du online über die Plattform **MyStark** zugreifen. Deinen persönlichen **Zugangscode** findest du auf den Farbseiten vorne im Buch.

Lernvideos

MindCards „Writing"

MindCards „Speaking"

Häufige Fragen zum mittleren Schulabschluss

Wann findet die Prüfung statt?
Im Schuljahr 2022/2023 findet die zentrale Prüfung im Fach Englisch voraussichtlich am **9. Mai 2023** statt (Nachschreibtermin: 17. Mai 2023).

Aus welchen Teilen besteht die Prüfung?
Die schriftliche Prüfung besteht aus zwei Teilen: Im ersten Teil wird dein **Hörverstehen** überprüft. Im zweiten Teil musst du deine Kompetenzen in den Bereichen **Leseverstehen**, **Wortschatz** und **Schreiben** unter Beweis stellen. Welche Aufgabenformate und Textsorten dich genau in den einzelnen Prüfungsteilen erwarten, kannst du in den entsprechenden Kapiteln in diesem Buch unter „Häufige Aufgabenstellungen" nachlesen.

Gibt es inhaltliche Schwerpunkte?
Für die kommende Prüfung wurden **Großbritannien** und **Neuseeland** als Bezugskulturen ausgewählt. Du wirst also Aufgaben erhalten, die mit diesen beiden Regionen etwas zu tun haben. Auf den folgenden Seiten findest du **Länderporträts**, mit denen du dich über die wichtigsten Fakten informieren kannst. Auch die Texte und Aufgaben in diesem Buch vermitteln dir wertvolle Informationen (über Neuseeland z. B. in *Reading Test 1* und *Listening Test 14*). Auch wenn in der Regel keine landeskundlichen Details abgefragt werden, kann dir das Hintergrundwissen zu den beiden Bezugskulturen helfen, dich in der Prüfung schneller in den Texten und Aufgaben zurechtzufinden.

Wie viel Zeit habe ich für die Prüfung?
Du hast insgesamt **120 Minuten** Zeit. Dabei entfallen **20 Minuten** auf den ersten Teil (Hörverstehen) und **100 Minuten** auf den zweiten Teil der Prüfung (Leseverstehen – Wortschatz – Schreiben). Zusätzlich werden dir im zweiten Teil **10 Minuten Bonuszeit** und weitere **10 Minuten Auswahlzeit** gewährt, da du dich beim Schreiben zwischen zwei bis drei Teilaufgaben entscheiden musst.

Darf ich ein Wörterbuch verwenden?
Leider nein. Du wirst aber sehen, dass dies kein Problem ist, weil du auch unbekannte Begriffe gut aus dem Sinnzusammenhang erschließen kannst.

Wie setzt sich meine Note zusammen?
Deine Abschlussnote setzt sich aus der Prüfungsnote als Ergebnis deiner schriftlichen Prüfung und der Vornote zusammen. Diese Note beruht auf all deinen Leistungen seit Beginn des Schuljahres.

▶ Stimmen Vornote und Prüfungsnote überein, ist die Vornote auch die Abschlussnote. Bei einer Abweichung von einer Note entscheidet dein Fachlehrer oder deine Fachlehrerin zwischen beiden Noten.

▶ Falls Vornote und Prüfungsnote um zwei Noten abweichen, kannst du dich einer freiwilligen mündlichen Prüfung im Fach Englisch unterziehen.

▶ Weicht deine Prüfungsnote um mehr als zwei Notenstufen von der Vornote ab, ist die mündliche Prüfung für dich verpflichtend. Diese findet zwischen dem 5. und 13. Juni 2023 statt.

Länderporträts zu den Bezugskulturen

Some Aspects about the UK

The United Kingdom consists of the island of Great Britain (England, Scotland, Wales) and Northern Ireland. It is also informally referred to as "Britain" or "the UK". The British flag, the so-called **Union Jack**, is a combination of the English, Scottish and Northern Irish flags.

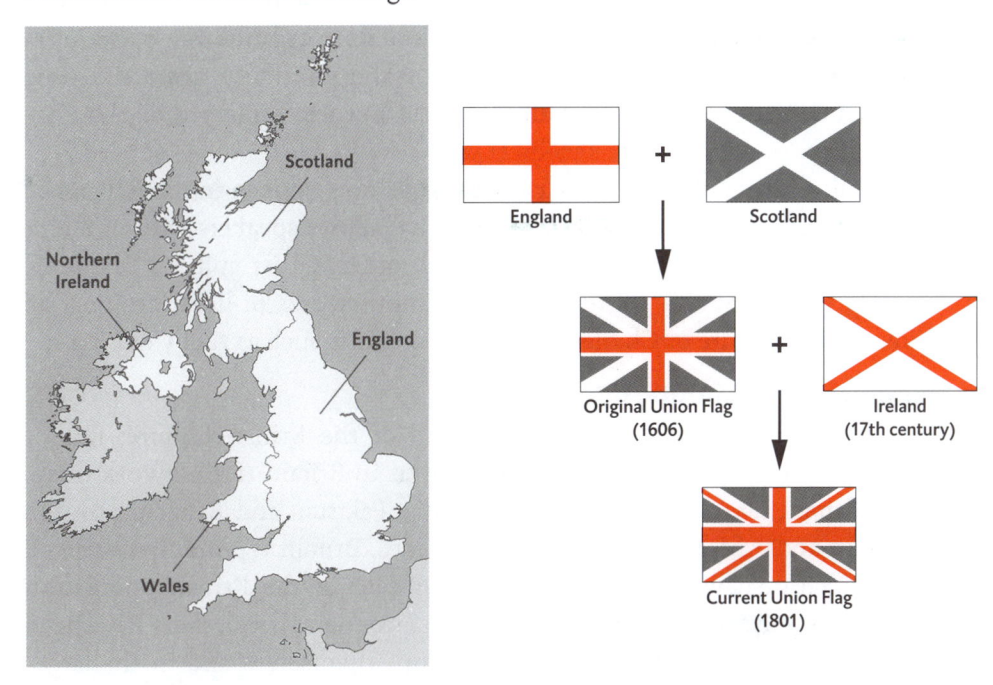

▶ **Political system:**

The UK is a parliamentary democracy with a constitutional monarch. The Queen is the official head of state, and although she has quite a few political functions, her role is mainly ceremonial. She and the rest of the **royal family** are important identification figures, however, as can be seen in the popularity of events such as royal weddings or the hype around the births of royal babies. Most of the actual political power in Britain lies in the hands of the **Prime Minister and his or her cabinet**, who have a relatively dominant position and can take far-reaching decisions. The work of the government is controlled by **Parliament**, which is made up of two chambers: the House of Commons (consisting of elected Members of Parliament/MPs) and the House of Lords (consisting of bishops or "peers" who either inherited their seat or were nominated by the monarch). MPs are elected by means of a **majority vote** or "first-past-the-post": The candidate who wins a simple majority of the votes in a constituency *(Wahlkreis)* becomes the MP for that district; the votes for the other candidates are ignored. This system tends to benefit big parties (such as the Conservatives or the Labour Party) and makes it relatively hard for smaller parties to win seats.

In 1998, some power was handed over from the central parliament in London to regional parliaments in Scotland, Wales and Northern Ireland, a process known as "**Devolution**".

Länderporträts zu den Bezugskulturen

▶ **From the Empire to the Commonwealth:**
For several centuries, Britain was an important imperial power that colonised and exploited other countries. At the beginning of the 20th century, the **British Empire** covered over a quarter of the world's surface. From the late 19th and early 20th century onwards, however, more and more countries wanted to break free from British rule, and after India gained its independence in 1947, the empire gradually came to an end. After decolonisation, a lot of former colonies maintained some ties with Britain and joined the so-called **Commonwealth of Nations**, a loose and voluntary organisation of 53 independent states. They cooperate economically and politically, share the same values (such as democracy and human rights) and are connected by the English language.

As a result of Britain's imperial past, English is now spoken in many parts of the world – it has become a **lingua franca** that allows speakers with different native languages to communicate with each other. Other cultural "exports" from Britain include its political system, famous works of literature (e.g. by William Shakespeare or Charles Dickens) and sports such as rugby or cricket.

▶ **Immigration and ethnic minorities:**
After the Second World War and the end of the British Empire, lots of people from the former colonies **immigrated** to Britain to find work there. Most of them came from Asia (mainly India, Pakistan and Bangladesh), the Caribbean and Africa. In the following decades, Britain repeatedly restricted its immigration laws. Today, about 13 per cent of the British population belong to an **ethnic minority group**. Ever since their arrival, there have been discussions (both within the minority groups themselves and in the larger society) whether they should keep their cultural traditions or rather adapt to a British lifestyle. Although most members of ethnic minorities are well-integrated, they still sometimes face discrimination, for example on the job market or in housing. Unfortunately, in recent years, prejudices and hate crimes against ethnic minority groups have increased, especially against people of Muslim faith.

▶ **Britain's relationship with the EU:**
Britain's relationship with the EU has been quite complicated. Britain joined the EEC in 1973 – however, just two years later, the first referendum was held about whether or not the UK should really stay in the EEC. Although a majority voted "yes" at the time, a lot of Britons never really identified with Europe. Many had the impression that the UK paid more to the EU than it got back or were worried that the European influence would grow too strong. **Euroscepticism** increased dramatically when more and more immigrants from Eastern Europe came to the UK in the early 2000s. In the European elections in 2014, the right-wing UK Independence Party won the most votes. It exploited people's fear of immigration and xenophobic prejudices and created a strongly anti-EU climate. In 2016, a referendum was held in which a very small majority of the British population voted in favour of leaving the European Union.

On 31 January 2020, the UK formally ended its EU membership, and in 2021, the new "Trade and Cooperation Agreement" *(Handels- und Kooperationsabkommen)* between the UK and the European Union came into effect. Interestingly, the majority of young Britons had voted to remain in the European Union and is not happy at all about Brexit. In some parts of the UK, such as Scotland or Northern Ireland, the majority of people would also have liked to remain in the EU. As a result, the wish to become independent from the UK might become stronger in these countries. Likewise, it is difficult to predict the economic consequences of Brexit but so far, they do not look good for the UK. A case in point is how many workers who had immigrated from Eastern European countries left the UK following Brexit. This had a domino effect: In autumn 2021, there was a lack of lorry drivers who would usually deliver food and fuel, leaving UK supermarket shelves empty and petrol stations in short supply.

▶ **Education system:**
British children have to attend school from the ages of 5 to 16. From 5 to 11, they attend primary school, later they go on to secondary school. Most pupils attend a **comprehensive school** which is open for pupils of all abilities. In some areas, however, there are also grammar schools and secondary modern schools. About 93 per cent of pupils go to a **state school**, which is free of charge; about 7 per cent attend an **independent** or **private school**, for which you have to pay a fee. The so-called **public schools**, such as Eton or Harrow, are the most expensive private schools and are usually attended by children from very wealthy families. At the age of 16, pupils take their **GCSEs** (which is roughly equivalent to the *Mittlerer Schulabschluss*). After that, they can decide whether they want to leave school, pursue further education that prepares them for the job market, or stay on and do their **A-levels** (roughly equivalent to the *Abitur*). Those who want to study at university have to pay very high tuition fees *(Studiengebühren)* – often more than £9000 per year. As a result, people from poorer families often can't afford to go to a top university or fall into huge debt to do so.

▶ **Teens and young adults:**
Teens in the UK enjoy most of the things teens in other countries do: They like to spend time on social media or playing online games, hanging out with friends, listening to music, playing sports, etc. Topics such as love, friendships, school pressure or worries about one's appearance are also concerns they share with teens elsewhere. Just like in other countries, lots of young people in Britain are worried about the effects of climate change and the corona pandemic. An increasing number of adolescents and young adults also fear that British society might become less tolerant after "Brexit".

Bildnachweis:
Karte Vereinigtes Königreich © NordNordWest, lizenziert nach CC BY-SA 3.0; Entwicklung des Union Jack: gemeinfrei; geteilte Flagge UK/EU © Tim Reckmann, lizenziert nach CC BY 2.0; Schulkinder © Jon Barlow. Pearson Education Ltd

Länderporträts zu den Bezugskulturen

Some Aspects about New Zealand

New Zealand is an island country in the southwest of the Pacific Ocean, about 1,600 kilometres southeast of Australia. It can be divided into two islands, the **North Island** and the **South Island**. These are sometimes referred to as "mainland" New Zealand. Apart from the two large islands there are **more than 700 smaller islands** which also belong to New Zealand.

▶ **Population and major cities:** Although New Zealand is slightly larger than the United Kingdom, only about 5 million people live there (compared to about 67 million in the UK). By far the most populous city in New Zealand is **Auckland**. New Zealand's capital city, however, is **Wellington**. Both cities are located on the North Island. **Christchurch** is the largest city on the South Island. The city suffered two severe earthquakes in September 2010 and February 2011. Thousands of buildings collapsed or were badly damaged, many people lost their lives. In 2019 Christchurch was the centre of a terrorist attack by a far-right extremist in which 51 people were killed. New Zealand's Prime Minister Jacinda Ardern described this tragedy as one of the darkest days in New Zealand's history.

▶ **Geography:** New Zealand is famous for its varied and spectacular landscapes. You can find long, sandy beaches, among which the Ninety Mile Beach is probably the most famous. The centre of the North Island is dominated by a volcanic plateau. The South Island is marked by the **Southern Alps**, a mountain range with many peaks more than 3,000 meters high. But New Zealand also has rain forests, fjords, glaciers, and much more. Peter Jackson's trilogy *Lord of the Rings* and *The Hobbit* were filmed in New Zealand and have made its stunning scenery more popular than ever before.

▶ **Plants and animals:** Because of its remote geographical position, there are many endemic plants and animals in New Zealand (which means they do not exist anywhere else in the world). The giant **kauri trees**, for example, are among the largest and oldest trees in the world. New Zealand is also famous for its birds, several of which are unable to fly. The most prominent example is the **kiwi**. It is a national symbol and in colloquial language New Zealanders are also often referred to as "kiwis". Other animals that can only be found in New Zealand are particular kinds of penguins, dolphins, sea lions and bats.

▶ **Key events in history:**

New Zealand is very far off. This is why it had been unpopulated for a very long time. At the end of the 13th century the **Polynesians** started to settle in the country. They were the ones to develop the traditional **Māori culture**. The first European to catch sight of New Zealand was the Dutch **Abel Tasman** in 1642. When his ship reached Golden Bay, a bloody encounter with the Māori came about, probably because of a misunderstanding. Four Dutch sailors were killed and Abel Tasman ended up never even setting foot on the island. It was not until 1769 that a new expedition arrived at the New Zealand coast, this time under the leadership of **James Cook**, a captain of the British Royal Navy. Cook made maps of New Zealand and for a long time, he was celebrated by many (mainly white) New Zealanders as an ancestor-like figure. In recent years, he has come to be seen in a more critical light. During the first encounter with the Māori, Cook's men killed at least nine indigenous people – a traumatic experience for the Māori.

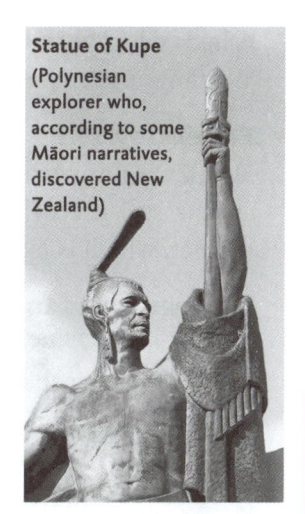

Statue of Kupe (Polynesian explorer who, according to some Māori narratives, discovered New Zealand)

After Cook, whale catchers, seal hunters and missionaries arrived in New Zealand, and the Māori and the European settlers began to exchange goods and establish **trading relations**. Because of the fact that firearms were traded, violent disorders became more frequent. In the first half of the 19th century, several Māori tribes fought each other in the so-called **Musket Wars**, in which more than 20,000 people were killed. The white settlers also brought new **diseases**, such as measles *(= Masern)*, and as a result many Māori died.

In 1840, the British and the Māori signed the **Treaty of Waitangi**. It is regarded as the founding document of New Zealand. The contract attached New Zealand to the British Crown and declared British sovereignty over the islands. Many Māori leaders signed the contract because they hoped that this would protect them against the French, who also had plans to colonise New Zealand. Moreover, the Māori leaders had been reassured by the British that they would keep ownership of their land and get the same rights as British subjects. However, as some parts of the treaty text were not translated accurately into Māori, there have been different interpretations of the contract. In the following years, a series of battles over land issues followed between government forces on the one hand and the Māori on the other. These are called the **New Zealand Wars (1845–1872)**. A lot of Māori unjustly **lost their land** to the British, which has been a source of pain ever since and can be seen as one of the reasons for the higher rate of poverty among the Māori.

In 1841, New Zealand became a **colony within the British Empire**. With the New Zealand Constitution Act in 1852 the country started to govern itself rather autonomously. Shortly afterwards, male Māori also got the right to vote and were able to have seats in parliament, and in the 1890s, New Zealand became the first country in the world to allow women to vote. In 1947 New Zealand finally gained **independence**. In the 1970s, a **Māori protest movement** was formed and the so-called **Waitangi Tribunal** was established, which allows Māori to complain about breaches against the treaty of Waitangi and claim compensation for their lost land.

▶ **Political system:**
New Zealand is part of the Commonwealth of Nations and the British monarch is still the official head of state. New Zealand has a parliament and a cabinet, which is led by the prime minister.

▶ **Demographics and religion:**
Today, about 70 per cent of New Zealanders are of European descent (in the Māori language they are called *Pākehā*), over 16 per cent are Māori, 15 per cent are Asian and 9 per cent Pacific Islanders. More than a quarter of New Zealanders were born outside the country. Nearly half of the population do not have a religion; about 37 per cent identify as Christians.

▶ **Economy:**
The economy in New Zealand has always relied to a large extent on agriculture. New Zealand is the biggest exporter of sheep meat and dairy products, for example. However, other sectors, such as tourism, also play an increasingly important role. The currency used is the New Zealand dollar.

▶ **Culture:**
New Zealand's culture is marked mainly by its Māori and European heritage as well as by cultural influences from other ethnic groups. Although most people speak English, about four per cent of the population also speak the Māori language *(Te Reo Māori)*. Further examples of Māori culture are its legends, artful tattoos, creative arts (such as weaving and carving), ritual dances (such as the *haka*) and many other customs (such as the *hongi*, a form of greeting by two people pressing their noses together).

▶ **Free time activities:**
Sports are of great importance in New Zealand. Rugby is the national sport and New Zealand's national team, the "All Blacks", are known around the world. Cricket is also very popular and further testifies to the British influence on the country. New Zealand is also one of the leading nations at sailing. Other widespread free time activities are netball, water sports, golf, tennis, skiing/snowboarding as well as extreme sports, such as bungee jumping.

greeting each other with a *hongi*

Māori women's rugby team performing a *haka*

Bildnachweis: Karte Neuseeland © danceyourlife/Shutterstock.com; Kauri-Baum © W. Bulach, lizenziert nach CC BY-SA 4.0; Kupe-Statue © Mike, lizenziert nach CC BY-SA 2.0; Hongi © Tim Rooke/Shutterstock.com; Haka © DANIEL POCKETT/EPA-EFE/Shutterstock.com

▶ **Kurzgrammatik**

Kurzgrammatik

Damit du die für Klassenarbeiten und sonstige Prüfungen relevanten Grammatikbereiche noch einmal wiederholen kannst, findest du hier die wichtigsten Grammatikregeln mit prägnanten Beispielen. Zu einigen Themen stehen dir zusätzlich Lernvideos ▶ zur Verfügung. Die mit * gekennzeichneten Bereiche der Grammatik musst du nicht aktiv beherrschen. Sie werden hier erklärt, damit du sie leichter verstehen kannst, falls sie einmal in einem Lese- oder Hörtext auftauchen sollten. Im Kapitel „Grammatik – Sprachliche Korrektheit" erhältst du weitere Tipps, wie du mit dieser Kurzgrammatik arbeiten kannst.

1 Besonderheiten einiger Wortarten

1.1 Adjektive und Adverbien – *Adjectives and Adverbs*

Bildung und Verwendung von Adverbien – *Formation and Use of Adverbs*

Bildung		
Adjektiv + *-ly*	glad →	gladly
Ausnahmen:		
• in mehrsilbigen Adjektiven wird *-y* am Wortende zu *-i*	easy → funny →	easily funnily
• stummes *-e* entfällt bei *due, true, whole*	true →	truly
• auf einen Konsonanten folgendes *-le* wird zu *-ly*	simple → probable →	simply probably
• *-ic* wird zu *-ically*	fantastic →	fantastically
Ausnahme:	public →	publicly
Beachte		
• Unregelmäßig gebildet wird:	good →	well
• Endet das Adjektiv auf *-ly*, so kann kein Adverb gebildet werden; man verwendet deshalb: *in a* + Adjektiv + *manner/way*.	friendly →	in a friendly manner
• In einigen Fällen haben Adjektiv und Adverb dieselbe Form.	daily, early, fast, hard, long, low, weekly, yearly	
• Manche Adjektive bilden zwei Adverbformen, die sich in der Bedeutung unterscheiden, z. B.:		

Adj./Adv.	Adv. auf *-ly*	
hard schwierig, hart	*hardly* kaum	The task is hard. (adjective) *Die Aufgabe ist schwierig.*
late spät	*lately* neulich, kürzlich	She works hard. (adverb) *Sie arbeitet hart.*
near nahe	*nearly* beinahe	She hardly works. (adverb) *Sie arbeitet kaum.*

Verwendung

Adverbien bestimmen

- Verben,

  She <u>easily</u> <u>found</u> her brother in the crowd.
  Sie fand ihren Bruder leicht in der Menge.

- Adjektive,

  This band is <u>extremely</u> <u>famous</u>.
  Diese Band ist sehr berühmt.

- andere Adverbien oder

  He walks <u>extremely</u> <u>quickly</u>.
  Er geht äußerst schnell.

- einen ganzen Satz

  näher.

  <u>Fortunately</u>, <u>nobody was hurt</u>.
  Glücklicherweise wurde niemand verletzt.

Beachte

Nach bestimmten Verben, die einen **Zustand** ausdrücken, steht nicht das Adverb, sondern das Adjektiv, z. B.:

to be	sein
to seem	scheinen
to stay	bleiben

Everything <u>seems</u> <u>quiet</u>.
Alles scheint ruhig (zu sein).

Nach manchen Verben kann entweder ein Adjektiv oder ein Adverb folgen (z. B. nach *to feel, to look, to smell, to taste*). Mit Adverb beschreiben diese Verben eine **Tätigkeit**, mit Adjektiv eine **Eigenschaft** des Subjekts.

Harry <u>looks</u> <u>happy</u>. (Eigenschaft)
Harry sieht glücklich aus.
↔ Harry <u>looks</u> <u>happily</u> at his cake. (Tätigkeit)
Harry schaut glücklich auf seinen Kuchen.

Steigerung des Adjektivs – *Comparison of Adjectives*

Bildung

Man unterscheidet:

- Grundform/Positiv (*positive*)

  Peter is y<u>oung</u>.

- 1. Steigerungsform/Komparativ (*comparative*)

  Jane is y<u>ounger</u>.

- 2. Steigerungsform/Superlativ (*superlative*)

  Paul is <u>the youngest</u>.

Steigerung auf -er, -est

- einsilbige Adjektive

  old, old<u>er</u>, old<u>est</u>
  alt, älter, am ältesten

- zweisilbige Adjektive, die auf -er, -le, -ow oder -y enden

  clever, cleve<u>rer</u>, cleve<u>rest</u>
  klug, klüger, am klügsten

  simple, simp<u>ler</u>, simp<u>lest</u>
  einfach, einfacher, am einfachsten

  narrow, narrow<u>er</u>, narrow<u>est</u>
  eng, enger, am engsten

  funny, funn<u>ier</u>, funn<u>iest</u>
  lustig, lustiger, am lustigsten

Beachte
- stummes *-e* am Wortende entfällt
- nach einem Konsonanten wird *-y* am Wortende zu *-i-*
- nach betontem Vokal wird ein Konsonant am Wortende verdoppelt

simp<u>l</u>e, simp<u>l</u>er, simp<u>l</u>est

funny, funn<u>i</u>er, funn<u>i</u>est

fi<u>t</u>, fi<u>tt</u>er, fi<u>tt</u>est

Steigerung mit *more ..., most ...*
- zweisilbige Adjektive, die nicht auf *-er, -le, -ow* oder *-y* enden
- Adjektive mit drei und mehr Silben

useful, <u>more</u> useful, <u>most</u> useful
nützlich, nützlicher, am nützlichsten

difficult, <u>more</u> difficult, <u>most</u> difficult
schwierig, schwieriger, am schwierigsten

Steigerungsformen im Satz – *Sentences with Comparisons*

Bildung
Es gibt folgende Möglichkeiten, Steigerungen im Satz zu verwenden:

- **Grundform:**
  Zwei oder mehr Personen oder Sachen sind **gleich oder ungleich**:
  (not) as + Grundform des Adjektivs + *as*

  Anne is <u>as</u> tall <u>as</u> John.
  Anne ist genauso groß wie John.

  John is <u>not as</u> tall <u>as</u> Steve.
  John ist nicht so groß wie Steve.

- **Komparativ:**
  Zwei oder mehr Personen oder Sachen sind **verschieden** (größer/besser/...):
  Komparativ des Adjektivs + *than*

  Steve is <u>taller</u> <u>than</u> Anne.
  Steve ist größer als Anne.

- **Superlativ:**
  Eine Person oder Sache wird **besonders hervorgehoben** (der/die/das größte/beste/...):
  the + Superlativ des Adjektivs

  Steve is one of <u>the</u> <u>tallest</u> boys in class.
  Steve ist einer der größten Jungen in der Klasse.

Steigerung des Adverbs – *Comparison of Adverbs*

Adverbien können wie Adjektive auch gesteigert werden.
- Adverbien auf *-ly* werden mit *more, most* bzw. mit *less, least* gesteigert.
- Adverbien, die dieselbe Form wie das Adjektiv haben, werden mit *-er, -est* gesteigert.

She talks <u>more</u> quickly than John.
Sie spricht schneller als John.

fast – fas<u>ter</u> – fas<u>test</u>
early – earl<u>ier</u> – earl<u>iest</u>

Unregelmäßige Steigerung – *Irregular Comparisons*

Unregelmäßig gesteigerte Formen muss man auswendig lernen. Einige wichtige Formen sind hier angegeben:

good – better – best
bad – worse – worst
well – better – best
badly – worse – worst
little – less – least
much – more – most

Die Stellung von Adverbien im Satz – *The Position of Adverbs in Sentences*

Adverbien können verschiedene Positionen im Satz einnehmen:

- Am **Anfang des Satzes**, vor dem Subjekt *(front position)*

  Tomorrow, he will be in London.
  Morgen [betont] wird er in London sein.

  Unfortunately, I can't come to the party.
  Leider kann ich nicht zur Party kommen.

- **Im Satz** *(mid position):*
  vor dem Vollverb

  She often goes to school by bike.
  Sie fährt oft mit dem Rad in die Schule.

  nach *to be*

  She is already at home.
  Sie ist schon zu Hause.

  nach dem ersten Hilfsverb

  You can even go swimming there.
  Man kann dort sogar schwimmen gehen.

- Am **Ende des Satzes** *(end position)*

  He will be in London tomorrow.
  Er wird morgen in London sein.

  Gibt es mehrere Adverbien am Satzende, so gilt die **Reihenfolge**:
  Art und Weise – Ort – Zeit
  (manner – place – time)

  The snow melts slowly in the mountains at springtime.
  Im Frühling schmilzt der Schnee langsam in den Bergen.

1.2 Artikel – *Article*

Der **bestimmte Artikel** steht, wenn man von einer **ganz bestimmten Person oder Sache** spricht.

The cat is sleeping on the sofa.
Die Katze schläft auf dem Sofa. [nicht irgendeine Katze, sondern eine bestimmte]

Beachte
Der bestimmte Artikel steht **immer** bei:
- **abstrakten Begriffen**, die näher erläutert sind

The agriculture practised in the USA is very successful.
Die Landwirtschaft, wie sie in den USA praktiziert wird, ist sehr erfolgreich.

Kurzgrammatik

- **Gebäudebezeichnungen**, wenn man vom Gebäude selbst spricht

The school should be renovated soon.
Die Schule (= das Schulgebäude) sollte bald renoviert werden.

- **Eigennamen im Plural** (z. B. bei Familiennamen, Gebirgen, Inselgruppen, einigen Ländern)

the Johnsons, the Rockies, the Hebrides, the Netherlands, the USA

- Namen von **Flüssen** und **Meeren**

the Mississippi, the North Sea, the Pacific Ocean

Der **unbestimmte Artikel** steht, wenn man von einer **nicht näher bestimmten Person oder Sache** spricht.

A man is walking down the road.
Ein Mann läuft gerade die Straße entlang.
[irgendein Mann]

Beachte
Der unbestimmte Artikel steht **häufig** bei:

- **Berufsbezeichnungen** und **Nationalitäten**

She is an engineer. *Sie ist Ingenieurin.*
He is a Scot(sman). *Er ist Schotte.*

- Zugehörigkeit zu einer **Religion** oder **Partei**

She is a Catholic. *Sie ist Katholikin.*

Es steht **kein Artikel** bei:

- **nicht zählbaren** Nomen wie z. B. **Stoffbezeichnungen**

Gold is very valuable.
Gold ist sehr wertvoll.

- **abstrakten Nomen** ohne nähere Bestimmung

Buddhism is widespread in Asia.
Der Buddhismus ist in Asien weitverbreitet.

- **Bezeichnungen für Gruppen von Menschen**, z. B. *man* (= der Mensch bzw. alle Menschen), *society*

Man is responsible for global warming.
Der Mensch ist für die Klimaerwärmung verantwortlich.

- **Institutionen**, z. B. *school, church, university, prison*

School starts at 9 a.m.
Die Schule beginnt um 9 Uhr.

- **Mahlzeiten**, z. B. *breakfast, lunch*

Dinner is at 8 p.m.
Das Abendessen ist um 20 Uhr.

- *by* + **Verkehrsmittel**

I went to school by bike.
Ich fuhr mit dem Fahrrad zur Schule.

- **Personennamen** (auch mit Titel) oder **Verwandtschaftsbezeichnungen**, die wie Namen verwendet werden

Tom, Mr Scott, Queen Elizabeth II, Dr Hill, Dad, Uncle Harry

- Bezeichnungen für **Straßen**, **Plätze**, **Brücken**, **Parkanlagen**

Fifth Avenue, Trafalgar Square, Westminster Bridge, Hyde Park

- Namen von **Ländern**, **Kontinenten**, **Städten**, **Seen**, **Inseln**, **Bergen**

France, Asia, San Francisco, Loch Ness, Corsica, Ben Nevis

1.3 Pronomen – *Pronouns*

Possessivbegleiter und -pronomen – *Possessive Determiners and Pronouns*

> „Possessiv" bedeutet **besitzanzeigend**. Man verwendet diese Formen, um zu sagen, **wem etwas gehört**.
>
> Man unterscheidet Possessivbegleiter, die mit einem Substantiv stehen, und Possessivpronomen (sie ersetzen ein Substantiv):
>
> | mit Substantiv | ohne Substantiv |
> |---|---|
> | my | mine |
> | your | yours |
> | his/her/its | his/hers/– |
> | our | ours |
> | your | yours |
> | their | theirs |

This is my bike.   –   This is mine.
This is your bike. –   This is yours.
This is her bike. –   This is hers.
This is our bike. –   This is ours.
This is your bike. –   This is yours.
This is their bike. – This is theirs.

Reflexivpronomen – *Reflexive Pronouns*

> Reflexivpronomen (*reflexive pronouns*), also **rückbezügliche Fürwörter, beziehen sich auf das Subjekt** des Satzes **zurück**:
>
> myself
> yourself
> himself / herself / itself
> ourselves
> yourselves
> themselves
>
> **Beachte**
> - Einige Verben stehen ohne Reflexivpronomen, obwohl im Deutschen mit „mich, dich, sich etc." übersetzt wird.
>
> - Einige Verben können sowohl mit einem Objekt als auch mit einem Reflexivpronomen verwendet werden. Dabei ändert sich die Bedeutung, z. B. bei *to enjoy* und *to help*.

I will look after myself.
You will look after yourself.
He will look after himself.
We will look after ourselves.
You will look after yourselves.
They will look after themselves.

I apologise …
Ich entschuldige mich …

He is hiding.
Er versteckt sich.

He is enjoying the party. (Verb mit Objekt)
Er genießt die Party.

She is enjoying herself. (Verb mit Reflexivpronomen)
Sie amüsiert sich.

He is helping the child. (Verb mit Objekt)
Er hilft dem Kind.

Help yourself! (Verb mit Reflexivpronomen)
Bedienen Sie sich!

Reziprokes Pronomen – *Reciprocal Pronoun* ("each other / one another")

each other/one another ist unveränderlich. Es bezieht sich auf **zwei oder mehr Personen** und wird mit „sich (gegenseitig)"/ „einander" übersetzt.	They looked at each other and laughed. *Sie schauten sich (gegenseitig) an und lachten.* oder: *Sie schauten einander an und lachten.*
Beachte Einige Verben stehen ohne *each other*, obwohl im Deutschen mit „sich" übersetzt wird.	to meet — *sich treffen* to kiss — *sich küssen* to fall in love — *sich verlieben*

1.4 Präpositionen – *Prepositions*

Präpositionen *(prepositions)* sind Verhältniswörter. Sie drücken **räumliche, zeitliche oder andere Arten von Beziehungen** aus.

The ball is under the table.
He came home after six o'clock.

Die wichtigsten Präpositionen mit Beispielen für ihre Verwendung:

- **at**
  Ortsangabe: *at home*
  Zeitangabe: *at 3 p.m.*

  I'm at home now.   *Ich bin jetzt zu Hause.*
  He arrived at 3 p.m.   *Er kam um 15 Uhr an.*

- **by**
  Angabe des Mittels: *by bike*

  She went to work by bike.
  Sie fuhr mit dem Rad zur Arbeit.

  Angabe des Verursachers (in Passivsätzen): *by a bus*

  Her car was hit by a bus.
  Ihr Auto wurde von einem Bus angefahren.

  Angabe der Ursache: *by mistake*

  He did it by mistake.
  Er hat es aus Versehen getan.

  Zeitangabe: *by tomorrow*

  You will get the letter by tomorrow.
  Du bekommst den Brief bis (spätestens) morgen.

- **for**
  Zeitdauer: *for hours*

  We waited for the bus for hours.
  Wir warteten stundenlang auf den Bus.

- **from**
  Ortsangabe: *from Dublin*

  Ian is from Dublin.
  Ian kommt aus Dublin.

  Zeitangabe: *from nine to five*

  We work from nine to five.
  Wir arbeiten von neun bis fünf Uhr.

- **in**
  Ortsangabe: *in England*

  In England, they drive on the left.
  In England herrscht Linksverkehr.

  Zeitangabe: *in the morning*

  They woke up in the morning.
  Sie wachten am Morgen auf.

- of
  Besitz/Zugehörigkeit/Teilmenge:
  owner of the house, north of the city, two days of the week, one bar of soap

  The village lies north of the city.
  Das Dorf liegt nördlich der Stadt.

- on
  Ortsangabe: *on the left, on the floor*

  On the left, you see the London Eye.
  Links sehen Sie das London Eye.

  Zeitangabe: *on Monday*

  On Monday, she will buy the tickets.
  (Am) Montag kauft sie die Karten.

- to
  Richtungsangabe: *to the left*

  Please turn to the left.
  Bitte wenden Sie sich nach links.

  Angabe des Ziels: *to London*

  He goes to London every year.
  Er fährt jedes Jahr nach London.

1.5 Konjunktionen – *Conjunctions*

Konjunktionen *(conjunctions)* verwendet man, um **zwei Hauptsätze oder Haupt- und Nebensatz miteinander zu verbinden**. Mit Konjunktionen lässt sich ein Text strukturieren, indem man z. B. Ursachen, Folgen oder zeitliche Abfolgen angibt.

Die wichtigsten Konjunktionen mit Beispielen für ihre Verwendung:

- after — nachdem

  What will you do after she's gone?
  Was wirst du tun, nachdem sie gegangen ist?

- although — obwohl

  Although she was ill, she went to work.
  Obwohl sie krank war, ging sie zur Arbeit.

- as — als (zeitlich)

  As he came into the room, the telephone rang.
  Als er ins Zimmer kam, klingelte das Telefon.

- as soon as — sobald

  As soon as the band began to play, …
  Sobald die Band zu spielen begann, …

- because — weil, da

  I need a new bike because my old bike was stolen.
  Ich brauche ein neues Rad, weil mein altes Rad gestohlen wurde.

- before — bevor

  Before he goes to work, he buys a newspaper.
  Bevor er zur Arbeit geht, kauft er eine Zeitung.

- but — aber

  She likes football but she doesn't like skiing.
  Sie mag Fußball, aber sie mag Skifahren nicht.

- either … or — entweder … oder

  We can either watch a film or go to a concert.
  Wir können uns entweder einen Film ansehen oder in ein Konzert gehen.

• in order to	– um ... zu, damit	Peter is in Scotland in order to visit his friend Malcolm. *Peter ist in Schottland, um seinen Freund Malcolm zu besuchen.*
• neither ... nor	– weder ... noch	We can neither eat nor sleep outside. It's raining. *Wir können draußen weder essen noch schlafen. Es regnet.*
• so that	– sodass	She shut the door so that the dog couldn't go outside. *Sie machte die Tür zu, sodass der Hund nicht hinausgehen konnte.*
• when	– wenn (zeitlich), sobald	Have a break when you've finished painting this wall. *Mach eine Pause, sobald du diese Wand fertig gestrichen hast.*
• while	– während (zeitlich)	He came home while I was reading. *Er kam nach Hause, während ich gerade las.*
	– während (Gegensatz)	Belle is beautiful while the Beast is ugly. *Belle ist schön, während das Biest hässlich ist.*

1.6 Modale Hilfsverben – *Modal Auxiliaries*

Im Englischen gibt es zwei Arten von Hilfsverben: *to be, to have* und *to do* können Hilfsverben sein, wenn sie zusammen mit einem anderen Verb im Satz vorkommen:

I have read the book. *Ich habe das Buch gelesen.*

Außerdem gibt es noch die sogenannten „modalen Hilfsverben". Zu den **modalen Hilfsverben** (*modal auxiliaries*) zählen z. B.:

can, may, must

Bildung
- Die modalen Hilfsverben haben für alle Personen **nur eine Form**, in der 3. Person Singular also kein -s.

I, you, he / she / it,
we, you, they } must

- Auf ein modales Hilfsverb folgt der **Infinitiv ohne to**.

You must look at my new bike.
Du musst dir mein neues Fahrrad ansehen.

- **Frage und Verneinung** werden nicht mit *do / did* umschrieben.

"Can you hear me?" – "No, I can't."
„Kannst du mich hören?" – „Nein, kann ich nicht."

Ersatzformen
Die modalen Hilfsverben können nicht alle Zeiten bilden. Deshalb benötigt man **Ersatzformen**. Diese können auch im Präsens verwendet werden.

- **can** (können)
  Ersatzformen:
  (to) be able to (Fähigkeit),
  (to) be allowed to (Erlaubnis)

  I can sing. / I was able to sing.
  Ich kann singen. / Ich konnte singen.

  You can't go to the party. /
  I wasn't allowed to go to the party.
  Du darfst nicht auf die Party gehen. /
  Ich durfte nicht auf die Party gehen.

  Beachte
  Im *simple past* und *conditional I* ist auch could möglich.

  When I was three, I could already ski.
  Mit drei konnte ich schon Ski fahren.

- **may** (dürfen) – sehr höflich
  conditional I: might
  Ersatzform: **(to) be allowed to**

  You may go home early. /
  You were allowed to go home early.
  Du darfst früh nach Hause gehen. /
  Du durftest früh nach Hause gehen.

- **must** (müssen)
  Ersatzform: **(to) have to**

  He must be home by ten o'clock. /
  He had to be home by ten o'clock.
  Er muss um zehn Uhr zu Hause sein. /
  Er musste um zehn Uhr zu Hause sein.

  Beachte
  must not / mustn't = „nicht dürfen"

  You must not eat all the cake.
  Du darfst nicht den ganzen Kuchen essen.

  „nicht müssen, nicht brauchen"
  = **not have to, needn't**

  You don't have to / needn't eat all the cake.
  Du musst nicht den ganzen Kuchen essen. /
  Du brauchst nicht … zu essen.

2 Finite Verbformen

2.1 Zeiten – *Tenses*

Simple Present

Bildung
Grundform des Verbs (Infinitiv)
Ausnahme: 3. Person Singular: Infinitiv + -s

I / you / we / you / they stand
he / she / it stands

Beachte
- Bei Verben, die auf einen Zischlaut (z. B. -s, -sh, -ch, -x und -z) enden, wird in der 3. Person Singular -es angefügt.

  kiss – he / she / it kisses
  rush – he / she / it rushes
  teach – he / she / it teaches
  fix – he / she / it fixes

- Bei Verben, die auf Konsonant + -y enden, wird -es angefügt; -y wird zu -i-.

  carry – he / she / it carries

Bildung von Fragen im *simple present*
(Fragewort +) *do / does* + Subjekt + Infinitiv

Where does he live? / Does he live in London?
Wo lebt er? / Lebt er in London?

Beachte

Die Umschreibung mit *do/does* wird nicht verwendet,
- wenn nach dem Subjekt gefragt wird (mit *who, what, which*),

Who likes pizza?
Wer mag Pizza?

What happens next?
Was passiert als Nächstes?

Which tree has more leaves?
Welcher Baum hat mehr Blätter?

- wenn die Frage mit *is/are* gebildet wird.

Are you happy?
Bist du glücklich?

Bildung der Verneinung im *simple present*
don't/doesn't + Infinitiv

He doesn't like football.
Er mag Fußball nicht.

Verwendung

Das *simple present* wird verwendet:
- bei Tätigkeiten, die man **gewohnheitsmäßig** oder häufig ausführt
Signalwörter: z. B. *always, often, never, every day, every morning, every afternoon*

Every morning, John buys a newspaper.
Jeden Morgen kauft John eine Zeitung.

- bei **allgemeingültigen** Aussagen

London is a big city.
London ist eine große Stadt.

- bei **Zustandsverben**: Sie drücken Eigenschaften/Zustände von Personen und Dingen aus und stehen normalerweise nur in der *simple form*, z. B. *to hate, to know, to like*.

I like science-fiction films.
Ich mag Science-Fiction-Filme.

Beachte

Das *simple present* kann sich auch auf die Zukunft beziehen. Siehe hierzu S. 17.

Present Progressive / Present Continuous

Bildung
am/is/are + *-ing*-Form (*present participle*)

read → am/is/are reading

Mehr zur Bildung des *present participle* siehe Kapitel 3.4 der Kurzgrammatik.

Bildung von Fragen im *present progressive*
(Fragewort +) *am/is/are* + Subjekt + *-ing*-Form

Is Peter reading? / What is he reading?
Liest Peter gerade? / Was liest er?

Bildung der Verneinung im *present progressive*
am not/isn't/aren't + *-ing*-Form

Peter isn't reading.
Peter liest gerade nicht.

Verwendung

Mit dem *present progressive* drückt man aus, dass etwas **gerade passiert** und **noch nicht abgeschlossen** ist. Es wird daher auch als **Verlaufsform** der Gegenwart bezeichnet.

Signalwörter: *at the moment, now*

Beachte

Das *present progressive* kann sich auch auf die Zukunft beziehen. Siehe hierzu S. 17.

At the moment, Peter is drinking a cup of tea.
Im Augenblick trinkt Peter eine Tasse Tee. [Er hat damit angefangen und noch nicht aufgehört.]

Simple Past

Bildung

Regelmäßige Verben: Infinitiv + *-ed*

walk	→	walked

Beachte

- stummes *-e* entfällt
- Bei Verben, die auf Konsonant + *-y* enden, wird *-y* zu *-i-*.
- Nach betontem Vokal wird der Schlusskonsonant verdoppelt.

hope	→	hoped
carry	→	carried
stop	→	stopped

Die *simple past*-Formen unregelmäßiger Verben muss man auswendig lernen. Einige wichtige Formen sind hier angegeben – weitere Beispiele sind z. B. in Wörterbüchern aufgeführt.

be	→	was / were
have	→	had
give	→	gave
go	→	went
say	→	said
see	→	saw
take	→	took

Bildung von Fragen im *simple past*

(Fragewort +) *did* + Subjekt + Infinitiv

Why did / Did he look out of the window?
Warum sah / Sah er aus dem Fenster?

Beachte

Die Umschreibung mit *did* wird nicht verwendet,

- wenn nach dem Subjekt gefragt wird (mit *who, what, which*),

Who paid the bill?
Wer zahlte die Rechnung?

What happened to your friend?
Was ist mit deinem Freund passiert?

Which boy cooked the meal?
Welcher Junge hat das Essen gekocht?

- wenn die Frage mit *was/were* gebildet wird.

Were you happy?
Warst du glücklich?

Bildung der Verneinung im *simple past*

didn't + Infinitiv

He didn't call me.
Er rief mich nicht an.

Kurzgrammatik

Verwendung
Das *simple past* beschreibt Handlungen und Ereignisse, die **in der Vergangenheit passierten** und **bereits abgeschlossen** sind.

Signalwörter: z. B. *yesterday, last week/year, two years ago, in 2012*

Last week, he helped me with my homework.
Letzte Woche half er mir bei meinen Hausaufgaben. [Die Handlung fand in der letzten Woche statt, ist also abgeschlossen.]

Past Progressive / Past Continuous

Bildung
was/were + *-ing*-Form *(present participle)*

watch → was/were watching

Verwendung
Die **Verlaufsform** *past progressive* verwendet man, wenn **zu einem bestimmten Zeitpunkt** in der Vergangenheit eine **Handlung ablief** bzw. wenn eine **Handlung** von einer anderen **unterbrochen** wurde.

Yesterday at 9 o'clock, I was still sleeping.
Gestern um 9 Uhr schlief ich noch.

I was reading a book when Peter came into the room.
Ich las (gerade) ein Buch, als Peter ins Zimmer kam.

Present Perfect (Simple)

Bildung
have/has + *past participle*

Zur Bildung des *past participle* siehe Kapitel 3.4 der Kurzgrammatik.

write → has/have written

Verwendung
Das *present perfect* verwendet man,
- wenn ein Vorgang **in der Vergangenheit begonnen** hat und **noch andauert**,
- wenn das Ergebnis einer vergangenen Handlung **Auswirkungen auf die Gegenwart** hat.

Signalwörter: z. B. *already, ever, just, how long, not ... yet, since, for*

Beachte
- *have/has* können zu *'ve/'s* verkürzt werden.

He has lived in London since 2008.
Er lebt seit 2008 in London.
[Er lebt jetzt immer noch in London.]

I have just cleaned my car.
Ich habe gerade mein Auto geputzt.
[Man sieht möglicherweise das saubere Auto.]

Have you ever been to Dublin?
Warst du schon einmal in Dublin?

He's given me his umbrella.
Er hat mir seinen Regenschirm gegeben.

Present perfect or Simple past?

Since or For?

- Das *present perfect* wird oft mit *since* und *for* verwendet, die beide „seit" bedeuten.
  - ***since*** gibt einen **Zeitpunkt** an:

    Ron has lived in Sydney <u>since 2007</u>.
    Ron lebt seit 2007 in Sydney.

  - ***for*** gibt einen **Zeitraum** an:

    Sally has lived in Berlin <u>for five years</u>.
    Sally lebt seit fünf Jahren in Berlin.

Present Perfect Progressive / Present Perfect Continuous

Bildung
have/has + been + -ing-Form (present participle)

write → <u>has</u>/<u>have</u> <u>been</u> <u>writing</u>

Verwendung
Die **Verlaufsform** *present perfect progressive* verwendet man, um die **Dauer einer Handlung** zu **betonen**, die in der Vergangenheit begonnen hat und noch andauert.

She <u>has been sleeping</u> for ten hours.
Sie schläft seit zehn Stunden.
[Sie schläft immer noch.]

Past Perfect (Simple)

Bildung
had + past participle

write → <u>had</u> <u>written</u>

Verwendung
Die Vorvergangenheit *past perfect* verwendet man, wenn ein Vorgang in der Vergangenheit **vor einem anderen Vorgang in der Vergangenheit abgeschlossen** wurde.

He <u>had bought</u> a ticket before he took the train to Manchester.
Er hatte eine Fahrkarte gekauft, bevor er den Zug nach Manchester nahm. [Beim Einsteigen war der Kauf abgeschlossen.]

Past Perfect Progressive / Past Perfect Continuous

Bildung
had + been + -ing-Form (present participle)

write → <u>had</u> <u>been</u> <u>writing</u>

Verwendung
Die **Verlaufsform** *past perfect progressive* verwendet man für **Handlungen**, die in der Vergangenheit **bis zu dem Zeitpunkt andauerten**, zu dem eine neue Handlung einsetzte.

She <u>had been sleeping</u> for ten hours when the doorbell rang.
Sie hatte seit zehn Stunden geschlafen, als es an der Tür klingelte. [Sie schlief bis zu dem Zeitpunkt, als es an der Tür klingelte.]

Will-future

Bildung
will + Infinitiv

buy → will buy

Bildung von Fragen im *will-future*
(Fragewort +) *will* + Subjekt + Infinitiv

What will you buy?
Was wirst du kaufen?

Bildung der Verneinung im *will-future*
will not / won't + Infinitiv

She won't come to our party.
Sie wird nicht zu unserer Party kommen.

Verwendung
Das *will-future* verwendet man, wenn ein Vorgang **in der Zukunft stattfinden** wird:
- bei Vorhersagen oder Vermutungen

The weather will be fine tomorrow.
Das Wetter wird morgen schön (sein).

- bei spontanen Entscheidungen

[doorbell] "I'll open the door."
„Ich mache die Tür auf."

Going to-future

Bildung
am / is / are + *going to* + Infinitiv

find → am / is / are going to find

Verwendung
Das *going to-future* verwendet man, wenn man ausdrücken will,
- was man für die Zukunft **plant** oder **zu tun beabsichtigt**,

I am going to work in England this summer.
Diesen Sommer werde ich in England arbeiten.

- dass ein **Ereignis bald eintreten wird**, da bestimmte **Anzeichen** vorhanden sind.

Look at those clouds. It's going to rain soon.
Schau dir diese Wolken an. Es wird bald regnen.

Simple Present und *Present Progressive* zur Wiedergabe der Zukunft – Using Simple Present and Present Progressive to Talk about the Future

Verwendung
- Mit dem *present progressive* drückt man **Pläne** für die Zukunft aus, für die bereits **Vorkehrungen** getroffen wurden.

We are flying to New York tomorrow.
Morgen fliegen wir nach New York.
[Wir haben schon Tickets.]

- Mit dem *simple present* wird ein zukünftiges Geschehen wiedergegeben, das **von außen festgelegt** wurde, z. B. Fahrpläne, Programme, Kalender.

The train leaves at 8.15 a.m.
Der Zug fährt um 8.15 Uhr.

The play ends at 10 p.m.
Das Theaterstück endet um 22 Uhr.

Talking about the Future

Future Progressive / Future Continuous*

Bildung
will + be + -ing-Form (present participle)

work → will be working

Verwendung
Die **Verlaufsform** *future progressive* drückt aus, dass ein **Vorgang** in der Zukunft zu einem bestimmten Zeitpunkt **gerade ablaufen wird**.

Signalwörter: z. B. *this time next week / tomorrow, tomorrow* + Zeitangabe

This time tomorrow, I will be sitting in a plane to London.
Morgen um diese Zeit werde ich gerade im Flugzeug nach London sitzen.

Future Perfect (Future II)*

Bildung
will + have + past participle

go → will have gone

Verwendung
Das *future perfect* drückt aus, dass ein **Vorgang** in der Zukunft **abgeschlossen sein wird** (Vorzeitigkeit in der Zukunft).

Signalwörter: z. B. *by then, by* + Zeitangabe

By 5 p.m. tomorrow, I will have arrived in London.
Morgen Nachmittag um fünf Uhr werde ich bereits in London angekommen sein.

▶ Active and Passive voice

2.2 Passiv – *Passive Voice*

Bildung
Form von *(to) be* in der entsprechenden Zeitform + *past participle*

The bridge was finished in 1894.
Die Brücke wurde 1894 fertiggestellt.

Zeitformen:
- simple present

  Aktiv: Joe buys the milk.
  Passiv: The milk is bought by Joe.

- simple past

  Aktiv: Joe bought the milk.
  Passiv: The milk was bought by Joe.

- present perfect

  Aktiv: Joe has bought the milk.
  Passiv: The milk has been bought by Joe.

- past perfect

  Aktiv: Joe had bought the milk.
  Passiv: The milk had been bought by Joe.

- will-future

  Aktiv: Joe will buy the milk.
  Passiv: The milk will be bought by Joe.

Aktiv → Passiv

- Das Objekt des Aktivsatzes wird zum Subjekt des Passivsatzes.
- Soll das Subjekt des Aktivsatzes im Passivsatz angegeben werden, wird es als *by-agent* angeschlossen.
- Stehen im Aktiv **zwei Objekte**, lassen sich zwei verschiedene Passivsätze bilden. Ein Objekt wird zum Subjekt des Passivsatzes, das zweite bleibt Objekt.

Beachte
Das indirekte Objekt (wem?) muss im Passivsatz mit *to* angeschlossen werden.

Passiv → Aktiv

- Der mit *by* angeschlossene Handelnde *(by-agent)* des Passivsatzes wird zum Subjekt des Aktivsatzes; *by* entfällt.
- Das Subjekt des Passivsatzes wird zum Objekt des Aktivsatzes.
- Fehlt im Passivsatz der *by-agent*, muss im Aktivsatz ein Handelnder als Subjekt ergänzt werden, z. B. *somebody, we, you, they*.

Aktiv: Joe [Subjekt] bought the milk [Objekt].
Passiv: The milk [Subjekt] was bought by Joe [by-agent].

Aktiv: They [Subjekt] gave her [ind. Obj.] a ball [dir. Obj.].
Passiv: She [Subjekt] was given a ball [dir. Obj.].

oder:
Aktiv: They [Subjekt] gave her [ind. Obj.] a ball [dir. Obj.].
Passiv: A ball [Subjekt] was given to her [ind. Obj.].

Passiv: The milk [Subjekt] was bought by Joe [by-agent].
Aktiv: Joe [Subjekt] bought the milk [Objekt].

Passiv: The match [Subjekt] was won.
Aktiv: They [(ergänztes) Subjekt] won the match [Objekt].

3 Infinite Verbformen

3.1 Infinitiv – *Infinitive*

Der **Infinitiv** (Grundform des Verbs) **mit *to*** steht z. B. **nach**:
- bestimmten **Verben**, z. B.:

to *decide*	(sich) entscheiden, beschließen
to *expect*	erwarten
to *hope*	hoffen
to *manage*	schaffen
to *offer*	anbieten
to *plan*	planen
to *promise*	versprechen
to *seem*	scheinen
to *try*	versuchen
to *want*	wollen

He decided to wait.
Er beschloss zu warten.

- bestimmten **Substantiven und Pronomen** (something, anything), z. B.:

attempt	Versuch
idea	Idee
plan	Plan
wish	Wunsch

  We haven't got anything to eat at home.
  Wir haben nichts zu essen zu Hause.

  She told him about her plan to go to Australia.
  Sie erzählte ihm von ihrem Plan, nach Australien zu reisen.

- bestimmten **Adjektiven** und deren Steigerungsformen, z. B.:

certain	sicher
difficult / hard	schwer, schwierig
easy	leicht

  Maths is often difficult to understand.
  Mathe ist oft schwer zu verstehen.

- **Fragewörtern**, wie z. B. *what, where, which, who, when, how* und nach *whether*. Diese Konstruktion ersetzt eine indirekte Frage mit modalem Hilfsverb.

  We knew where to find her. /
  We knew where we could find her.
  Wir wussten, wo wir sie finden konnten.

Die Konstruktion **Objekt + Infinitiv** wird im Deutschen oft mit einem „dass"-Satz übersetzt.

Sie steht z. B. **nach**:

- bestimmten **Verben**, z. B.:

to allow	erlauben
to get	veranlassen
to help	helfen
to persuade	überreden

  She allows him to go to the cinema.
  *Sie erlaubt ihm, dass er ins Kino geht. /
  … ins Kino zu gehen.*

- **Verb + Präposition**, z. B.:

to count on	rechnen mit
to rely on	sich verlassen auf
to wait for	warten auf

  She relies on him to arrive in time.
  Sie verlässt sich darauf, dass er rechtzeitig ankommt.

- **Adjektiv + Präposition**, z. B.:

easy for	leicht
necessary for	notwendig
nice of	nett
silly of	dumm

  It is necessary for you to study more.
  Es ist notwendig, dass du mehr lernst.

- **Substantiv + Präposition**, z. B.:

opportunity for	Gelegenheit
idea for	Idee
time for	Zeit
mistake for	Fehler

  Work experience is a good opportunity for you to find out which job suits you.
  Ein Praktikum ist eine gute Gelegenheit, herauszufinden, welcher Beruf zu dir passt.

- einem **Adjektiv**, das durch **too** oder **enough** näher bestimmt wird.

  The box is too heavy for me to carry.
  Die Kiste ist mir zu schwer zum Tragen.

  The weather is good enough for us to go for a walk.
  Das Wetter ist gut genug, dass wir spazieren gehen können.

3.2 Gerundium (-ing-Form) – *Gerund*

Bildung
Infinitiv + -ing

Beachte
- stummes -e entfällt
- nach kurzem betontem Vokal: Schlusskonsonant verdoppelt
- -ie wird zu -y

read → read<u>ing</u>

writ<u>e</u> → writing

sto<u>p</u> → stop<u>p</u>ing

<u>lie</u> → l<u>y</u>ing

Verwendung
Das *gerund* kann sowohl Subjekt als auch Objekt eines Satzes sein.

Subjekt: <u>Skiing</u> is fun.
Skifahren macht Spaß.
Objekt: He has given up <u>smoking</u>.
Er hat mit dem Rauchen aufgehört.

Manche Wörter ziehen die -*ing*-Form nach sich. Die -*ing*-Form steht z. B. nach:

- bestimmten **Verben**, wie z. B.:

to *dislike*	nicht mögen
to *enjoy*	genießen, gern tun
to *finish*	beenden
to *give up*	aufgeben
to *keep*	weitermachen
to *consider*	in Betracht ziehen

He <u>enjoys</u> <u>reading</u> comics.
Er liest gerne Comics.

My mother <u>keeps</u> <u>telling</u> me to study more.
Meine Mutter sagt mir ständig, dass ich mehr lernen soll.

- **Verb + Präposition**, wie z. B.:

to *believe in*	glauben an
to *dream of*	träumen von
to *look forward to*	sich freuen auf
to *talk about*	sprechen über

She <u>dreams</u> <u>of</u> <u>becoming</u> a lawyer.
Sie träumt davon, Anwältin zu werden.

- **Adjektiv + Präposition**, wie z. B.:

(be) *afraid of*	sich fürchten vor
famous for	berühmt für
good / bad at	gut / schlecht in
interested in	interessiert an

She is <u>good</u> <u>at</u> <u>playing</u> football.
Sie spielt gut Fußball.

- **einem Substantiv**, wie z. B.:

trouble	Schwierigkeiten
fun	Spaß

I have <u>trouble</u> <u>doing</u> my Maths homework.
Ich habe Schwierigkeiten, meine Mathehausaufgabe zu lösen.

- **Substantiv + Präposition**, wie z. B.:

chance of	Chance, Aussicht auf
in danger of	in Gefahr
reason for	Grund für

Do you have a <u>chance</u> <u>of</u> <u>getting</u> the job?
Hast du eine Chance, die Stelle zu bekommen?

- **bestimmten Präpositionen**, wie z. B.:
after	nachdem
before	bevor
by	indem; dadurch, dass
instead of	statt

Before leaving the room, he said goodbye.
Bevor er den Raum verließ, verabschiedete er sich.

3.3 Infinitiv oder Gerundium? – *Infinitive or Gerund?*

Einige Verben können sowohl **mit** dem **Infinitiv** als auch **mit der -*ing*-Form** stehen, **ohne** dass sich die **Bedeutung ändert**, z. B.
to love, to hate, to prefer, to start, to begin, to continue.

I hate getting up early.
I hate to get up early.
Ich hasse es, früh aufzustehen.

Bei manchen Verben **ändert sich** jedoch die **Bedeutung**, je nachdem, ob sie mit Infinitiv oder mit der -*ing*-Form verwendet werden, z. B.
to remember, to forget, to stop.

- *to remember* + Infinitiv:
  „daran denken, etwas zu tun"

  I must remember to post the invitations.
  Ich muss daran denken, die Einladungen einzuwerfen.

  to remember + -*ing*-Form:
  „sich erinnern, etwas getan zu haben"

  I remember posting the invitations.
  Ich erinnere mich daran, die Einladungen eingeworfen zu haben.

- *to forget* + Infinitiv:
  „vergessen, etwas zu tun"

  Don't forget to water the plants.
  Vergiss nicht, die Pflanzen zu gießen.

  to forget + -*ing*-Form:
  „vergessen, etwas getan zu haben"

  I'll never forget meeting the President.
  Ich werde nie vergessen, wie ich den Präsidenten traf.

- *to stop* + Infinitiv:
  „stehen bleiben, um etwas zu tun"

  I stopped to read the road sign.
  Ich hielt an, um das Verkehrsschild zu lesen.

  to stop + -*ing*-Form:
  „aufhören, etwas zu tun"

  He stopped laughing.
  Er hörte auf zu lachen.

3.4 Partizipien – *Participles*

Partizip Präsens – *Present Participle*

Bildung
Infinitiv + *-ing*

Beachte
- stummes *-e* entfällt
- nach betontem Vokal: Schlusskonsonant verdoppelt
- *-ie* wird zu *-y*

talk	→	talking
write	→	writing
stop	→	stopping
lie	→	lying

Verwendung
Das *present participle* verwendet man zur Bildung der Verlaufsformen, z. B.
- zur Bildung des *present progressive*,
- zur Bildung des *past progressive*,
- zur Bildung des *present perfect progressive*,
- zur Bildung des *future progressive**,

oder wie ein Adjektiv, wenn es vor einem Substantiv steht.

Peter is reading. *Peter liest (gerade).*

Peter was reading when I saw him. *Peter las (gerade), als ich ihn sah.*

I have been living in Sydney for 5 years. *Ich lebe seit 5 Jahren in Sydney.*

This time tomorrow I will be working. *Morgen um diese Zeit werde ich arbeiten.*

The village hasn't got running water. *Das Dorf hat kein fließendes Wasser.*

Partizip Perfekt – *Past Participle*

Bildung
Infinitiv + *-ed*

Beachte
- stummes *-e* entfällt
- nach betontem Vokal wird der Schlusskonsonant verdoppelt
- *-y* wird zu *-ie*
- Die *past participles* unregelmäßiger Verben muss man auswendig lernen. Einige wichtige Formen sind hier angegeben – weitere Beispiele sind z. B. in Wörterbüchern aufgeführt.

talk	→	talked
live	→	lived
stop	→	stopped
cry	→	cried
be	→	been
have	→	had
give	→	given
go	→	gone
say	→	said

Verwendung
Das *past participle* verwendet man zur Bildung der Perfektformen, z. B.
- zur Bildung des *present perfect*,

He hasn't talked to Tom yet. *Er hat noch nicht mit Tom gesprochen.*

- zur Bildung des *past perfect*,

  Before they went biking in France, they had bought new bikes.
  Bevor sie nach Frankreich zum Radfahren gingen, hatten sie neue Fahrräder gekauft.

- zur Bildung des *future perfect**,

  The letter will have arrived by then.
  Der Brief wird bis dann angekommen sein.

zur Bildung des Passivs

The fish was eaten by the cat.
Der Fisch wurde von der Katze gefressen.

oder wie ein Adjektiv, wenn es vor einem Substantiv steht.

Peter has got a well-paid job.
Peter hat eine gut bezahlte Stelle.

Verkürzung von Nebensätzen durch Partizipien – *Using Participles to Shorten Clauses*

Adverbiale Nebensätze (meist des Grundes oder der Zeit) und **Relativsätze** können durch ein Partizip verkürzt werden.

She watches the news, because she wants to stay informed.
→ Wanting to stay informed, she watches the news.
Sie sieht sich die Nachrichten an, weil sie informiert bleiben möchte.

Das Zeitverhältnis zwischen Haupt- und Nebensatz bestimmt die Form des Partizips:
- Das *present participle* verwendet man, um Gleichzeitigkeit mit der Haupthandlung auszudrücken.

  He did his homework listening to music.
  Er machte seine Hausaufgaben und hörte dabei Musik.

- *Having + past participle* verwendet man, um auszudrücken, dass die Nebenhandlung vor der Haupthandlung geschah.

  Having done his homework, he listened to music.
  Nachdem er seine Hausaufgaben gemacht hatte, hörte er Musik.

- Das *past participle* verwendet man auch, um einen Satz im Passiv zu verkürzen.

  Sally is a manager in a five-star hotel which is called Pacific View.
  → Sally is a manager in a five-star hotel called Pacific View.

Beachte
- Man kann einen Nebensatz der Zeit oder des Grundes verkürzen, wenn **Haupt- und Nebensatz dasselbe Subjekt** haben.

  When he was walking down the street, he saw Jo.
  → When walking / Walking down the street, he saw Jo.
  Als er die Straße entlangging, sah er Jo.

- Bei **Kausalsätzen** (Nebensätzen des Grundes) entfallen die Konjunktionen *as*, *because* und *since* im verkürzten Nebensatz.

  As he was hungry, he bought a sandwich.
  → Being hungry, he bought a sandwich.
  Da er hungrig war, kaufte er ein Sandwich.

- In einem **Temporalsatz** (Nebensatz der Zeit) bleibt die einleitende **Konjunktion** häufig erhalten, um dem Satz eine **eindeutige Bedeutung** zuzuweisen.

  When he left, he forgot to lock the door.
  → When leaving, he forgot to lock the door.
  Als er ging, vergaß er, die Tür abzuschließen.

  Tara got sick eating too much cake.
  Tara wurde schlecht, als/während/da sie zu viel Kuchen aß. [verschiedene Deutungen möglich]

- Bei **Relativsätzen** entfallen die Relativpronomen *who*, *which* und *that*.

I saw a six-year-old boy who played the piano.
I saw a six-year-old boy playing the piano.
Ich sah einen sechsjährigen Jungen, der gerade Klavier spielte. / … Klavier spielen.

Verbindung von zwei Hauptsätzen durch ein Partizip – *Using Participles to Link Clauses*

Zwei Hauptsätze können durch ein Partizip verbunden werden, wenn sie **dasselbe Subjekt** haben.

Beachte
- Das Subjekt des zweiten Hauptsatzes und die Konjunktion *and* entfallen.
- Die Verbform des zweiten Hauptsatzes wird durch das Partizip ersetzt.

He did his homework and he listened to the radio.
He did his homework listening to the radio.
Er machte seine Hausaufgaben und hörte Radio.

4 Der Satz im Englischen

4.1 Wortstellung – *Word Order*

Im Aussagesatz gilt die Wortstellung
Subjekt – **P**rädikat – **O**bjekt
(**s**ubject – **v**erb – **o**bject):
- Subjekt: Wer oder was tut etwas?
- Prädikat: Was wird getan?
- Objekt: Worauf / Auf wen bezieht sich die Tätigkeit?

Erklärungen und Beispiele zur **Bildung** des englischen **Fragesatzes** finden sich auch bei den verschiedenen Zeiten (vgl. Kap. 2.1) und bei den Modalverben (vgl. Kap. 1.6).

Beachte
- Orts- und Zeitangaben stehen oft am Satzende.
- Ortsangaben stehen vor Zeitangaben.

Cats catch mice.
Katzen fangen Mäuse.

We will buy a new car tomorrow.
Morgen werden wir ein neues Auto kaufen.
He moved to New York in June.
Er zog im Juni nach New York.

Conditional sentences

4.2 Bedingungssätze – *Conditional Sentences*

Ein Bedingungssatz (Konditionalsatz) besteht aus zwei Teilen: einem Nebensatz *(if-clause)* und einem Hauptsatz *(main clause)*. Im *if*-Satz steht die **Bedingung** *(condition)*, unter der die im **Hauptsatz** genannte **Folge** eintritt. Man unterscheidet drei Arten von Konditionalsätzen:

Bedingungssatz Typ I – *Conditional Sentence Type I*

Bildung

- *if*-Satz (Bedingung):
  simple present
- Hauptsatz (Folge):
  will-future

If you read this book,
Wenn du dieses Buch liest,

you will learn a lot about music.
erfährst du eine Menge über Musik.

Der *if*-Satz kann auch nach dem Hauptsatz stehen. In diesem Fall entfällt das Komma:

You will learn a lot about music if you read this book.
Du erfährst eine Menge über Musik, wenn du dieses Buch liest.

Im Hauptsatz kann auch
- ein modales Hilfsverb (z. B. *can*, *must*, *may*) + Infinitiv sowie

If you go to London, you must visit me.
Wenn du nach London fährst, musst du mich besuchen.

- die Befehlsform des Verbs (Imperativ) stehen.

If it rains, take an umbrella.
Wenn es regnet, nimm einen Schirm mit.

Verwendung

Bedingungssätze vom Typ I verwendet man, wenn die **Bedingung erfüllbar** ist. Man gibt an, was unter bestimmten Bedingungen **geschieht** oder **geschehen kann**.

Sonderform

Bedingungssätze vom Typ I verwendet man auch bei einer **generellen Regel**. Hierbei steht sowohl im Hauptsatz als auch im *if*-Satz das *simple present*.

If you mix blue and yellow, you get green.
Wenn du die Farbe Blau mit Gelb mischst, erhältst du Grün.

Bedingungssatz Typ II – *Conditional Sentence Type II*

Bildung
- *if*-Satz (Bedingung):
  simple past
- Hauptsatz (Folge):
  conditional I = would + Infinitiv

If I <u>went</u> to London,
Wenn ich nach London fahren würde,

I <u>would</u> <u>visit</u> the Tower.
würde ich mir den Tower ansehen.

Verwendung
Bedingungssätze vom Typ II verwendet man, wenn die **Bedingung nur theoretisch erfüllt** werden kann oder **nicht erfüllbar** ist.

Bedingungssatz Typ III – *Conditional Sentence Type III*

Bildung
- *if*-Satz (Bedingung):
  past perfect
- Hauptsatz (Folge):
  conditional II = would + have + past participle

If I <u>had gone</u> to London,
Wenn ich nach London gefahren wäre,

I <u>would have visited</u> the Tower.
hätte ich mir den Tower angesehen.

Verwendung
Bedingungssätze vom Typ III verwendet man, wenn sich die **Bedingung auf die Vergangenheit bezieht** und deshalb **nicht mehr erfüllbar** ist.

4.3 Relativsätze – *Relative Clauses*

Ein Relativsatz ist ein Nebensatz, der sich **auf eine Person oder Sache** des Hauptsatzes **bezieht** und diese **näher beschreibt**:
- Hauptsatz:
- Relativsatz:

The boy <u>who looks like Jane</u> is her brother.
Der Junge, der Jane ähnlich sieht, ist ihr Bruder.

The boy … is her brother.
… who looks like Jane …

Bildung
Haupt- und Nebensatz werden durch das Relativpronomen verbunden.
- Das Relativpronomen ***who*** bezieht sich auf Personen.

Peter, <u>who</u> lives in London, likes travelling.
Peter, der in London lebt, reist gerne.

- Das Relativpronomen **whose** bezieht sich ebenfalls auf Personen. Es gibt die Zugehörigkeit dieser Person zu einer anderen Person oder Sache an.

  Pari, whose parents are from India, is in my class.
  Pari, deren Eltern aus Indien stammen, ist in meiner Klasse.

  This is the boy whose mobile was stolen.
  Das ist der Junge, dessen Handy gestohlen wurde.

- Das Relativpronomen **which** bezieht sich auf **Sachen**.

  The film "Dark Moon", which we saw yesterday, was far too long.
  Der Film „Dark Moon", den wir gestern sahen, war viel zu lang.

- Das Relativpronomen **that** kann sich auf **Sachen** und auf **Personen** beziehen und wird nur verwendet, wenn die **Information** im Relativsatz **notwendig** ist, um den ganzen Satz zu verstehen.

  The film that we saw last week was much better.
  Der Film, den wir letzte Woche sahen, war viel besser.

Verwendung

Mithilfe von Relativpronomen kann man **zwei Sätze miteinander verbinden**.

London is England's biggest city. London is very popular with tourists.
London ist Englands größte Stadt. London ist bei Touristen sehr beliebt.

→ London, which is England's biggest city, is very popular with tourists.
 London, die größte Stadt Englands, ist bei Touristen sehr beliebt.

Beachte

Man unterscheidet zwei Arten von Relativsätzen:

- **Notwendige Relativsätze** (*defining relative clauses*) enthalten Informationen, die **für das Verständnis** des Satzes **erforderlich** sind.

  The man who is wearing a red shirt is Mike.
  Der Mann, der ein rotes Hemd trägt, ist Mike.

  Hier kann das Relativpronomen entfallen, wenn es Objekt ist; man spricht dann auch von *contact clauses*.

  The book (that) I bought yesterday is thrilling.
  Das Buch, das ich gestern gekauft habe, ist spannend.

- **Nicht notwendige Relativsätze** (*non-defining relative clauses*) enthalten **zusätzliche Informationen** zum Bezugswort, die für das Verständnis des Satzes nicht unbedingt notwendig sind. Dieser Typ von Relativsatz wird **mit Komma** abgetrennt.

  Sally, who went to a party yesterday, is very tired.
  Sally, die gestern auf einer Party war, ist sehr müde.

Kurzgrammatik 29

4.4 Indirekte Rede – *Reported Speech*

Reported speech

Bildung und Verwendung

Die indirekte Rede verwendet man, um **wiederzugeben, was eine andere Person gesagt** oder **gefragt hat**.

Dazu benötigt man ein **Einleitungsverb**. Häufig verwendete Einleitungsverben sind: to say, to think, to add, to agree, to tell, to answer

In der indirekten Rede verändern sich die Pronomen, in bestimmten Fällen auch die **Zeiten** und die **Orts-** und **Zeitangaben**.

- Wie die Pronomen sich verändern, hängt von der **Situation** ab.

direkte Rede		indirekte Rede
I, you, we, you	→	he, she, they
my, your, our, your	→	his, her, their
this, these	→	that, those

direkte Rede	indirekte Rede
Bob says to Jenny: "I like you."	Bob says to Jenny that he likes her.
Bob sagt zu Jenny: „Ich mag dich."	*Bob sagt zu Jenny, dass er sie mag.*

direkte Rede	indirekte Rede
Bob says, "I love dancing."	Bob says (that) he loves dancing.
Bob sagt: „Ich tanze sehr gerne."	*Bob sagt, er tanze sehr gerne.*
Bob said, "I love dancing."	Bob said (that) he loved dancing.
Bob sagte: „Ich tanze sehr gerne."	*Bob sagte, er tanze sehr gerne.*

- **Zeiten:**
Keine Veränderung, wenn das Einleitungsverb im *present tense*, im Futur oder im *present perfect* steht:

Die Zeit der direkten Rede wird in der indirekten Rede normalerweise **um eine Zeitstufe zurückversetzt**, wenn das **Einleitungsverb** im *past tense* oder *past perfect* steht:

simple present	→	simple past
simple past	→	past perfect
present perfect	→	past perfect
will-future	→	conditional I

Joe: "I like it."	Joe said he liked it.
Joe: "I liked it."	Joe said he had liked it.
Joe: "I've liked it."	Joe said he had liked it.
Joe: "I will like it."	Joe said he would like it.

direkte Rede	indirekte Rede
Jack: "I'll call her tomorrow."	Jack says (that) he will call her tomorrow. [Der Bericht erfolgt noch am selben Tag.]
	Jack said (that) he would call her the following day. [Der Bericht erfolgt z. B. eine Woche später.]

- **Zeitangaben** verändern sich, wenn der Bericht zu einem späteren Zeitpunkt erfolgt, z. B.:

now	→	then, at that time
today	→	that day, yesterday
yesterday	→	the day before
tomorrow	→	the following day
next week	→	the following week

- Welche **Ortsangabe** verwendet wird, hängt davon ab, wo sich der Sprecher im Moment befindet, z. B.:

  here → there

direkte Rede	indirekte Rede
Amy: "I was here when the accident happened."	Amy says (that) she was here when the accident happened. *[Der Bericht erfolgt noch an der Unfallstelle.]*
	Amy said (that) she had been there when the accident had happened. *[Der Bericht erfolgt z. B. am nächsten Tag an einem anderen Ort.]*

Bildung der indirekten Frage

Häufige Einleitungsverben für die indirekte Frage sind: to ask, to want to know, to wonder

- **Fragewörter** bleiben in der indirekten Rede **erhalten**. Die **Umschreibung** mit *do/does/did* **entfällt** in der indirekten Frage.

- Enthält die direkte Frage **kein Fragewort**, wird die indirekte Frage mit *whether* oder *if* eingeleitet:

direkte Rede	indirekte Rede
Tom: "When did they arrive?"	Tom asked when they had arrived.
Tom: „Wann sind sie angekommen?"	Tom fragte, wann sie angekommen seien.
Tom: "Are they staying at the youth hostel?"	Tom asked if/whether they were staying at the youth hostel.
Tom: „Übernachten sie in der Jugendherberge?"	Tom fragte, ob sie in der Jugendherberge übernachteten.

Befehle/Aufforderungen in der indirekten Rede

Häufige Einleitungsverben sind: to tell, to order, to ask

In der indirekten Rede steht hier **Einleitungsverb + Objekt + (not) to + Infinitiv**

direkte Rede	indirekte Rede
Tom: "Leave the room."	Tom told me to leave the room.
Tom: „Verlass den Raum."	Tom forderte mich auf, den Raum zu verlassen.

▶ Hinweise, Tipps und Übungsaufgaben zu den Kompetenzbereichen

1 Hörverstehen

Hörverstehenstexte und die dazugehörigen Aufgabenstellungen können sehr unterschiedlich sein. Die Aufnahmen, die du im Rahmen des MSA zu hören bekommst, können aus Sachtexten bzw. realen Sprechsituationen und aus literarischen Texten bestehen. Beide Arten von Texten können sowohl **monologisch** (nur eine Person spricht) als auch **dialogisch** angelegt sein (es gibt zwei oder mehr Sprecher*innen).

Im Bereich der **Sachtexte bzw. realen Sprechsituationen** wird dir beispielsweise ein Radiointerview, ein Podcast oder eine Rede vorgespielt. Bei den Aufnahmen kann es sich aber auch um scheinbar zufällig aufgeschnappte Situationen aus dem Alltag handeln, z. B. um ein Telefongespräch.

Bei den **literarischen Texten** wird dir in der Regel ein kurzer Auszug aus einer Erzählung oder einem Hörspiel vorgespielt. Die Texte können von mehreren Sprechern gesprochen sein – manchmal kommt es aber auch vor, dass ein einzelner Sprecher oder eine einzelne Sprecherin gleich in mehrere Rollen schlüpft. In diesen Fällen musst du beim Zuhören genau auf Änderungen in der Tonlage und Aussprache achten, um zu erkennen, welche Figur im Text gerade spricht.

Oft enthalten die Hörtexte auch **Hintergrundgeräusche** (wie Musik oder Special Effects). Diese machen es teilweise schwieriger, den gesprochenen Text zu verstehen – sie können dir aber auch wertvolle Hinweise auf den Inhalt geben (z. B. signalisiert ein Pausengong, dass die Situation in der Schule stattfindet).

1.1 Strategien zum Bereich „Hörverstehen"

Vorgehen in der Prüfung

In der Prüfung wird dir jeder Hörverstehenstext in der Regel **zweimal** vorgespielt.

Vor dem ersten Vorspielen des Textes hast du meist etwas Zeit, dir die **Aufgabenstellungen** auf dem Arbeitsblatt **anzusehen**. Lies sie dir sorgfältig durch und überlege genau, um welche Art von Aufgabe es sich handelt. Manchmal musst du die Gesamtaussage des Textes erfassen und manchmal sollst du Details aus dem Text herausfinden. Überlege schon vor dem Hören, auf welche Kerninformationen es in den Aufgaben ankommt. Darauf musst du dich dann während des Hörens ganz besonders konzentrieren. Zu den Aufgaben, die du nach dem ersten Hören bereits beantworten kannst, kannst du gleich die **richtige Lösung aufschreiben**.

Arbeitsschritt 1

Beim zweiten Hördurchgang kannst du zum einen deine Antworten noch einmal überprüfen und zum anderen die noch verbleibenden Aufgaben beantworten. Da du vor dem ersten Hören die Arbeitsaufträge lesen konntest, weißt du, welche **Detailinformationen** gefragt sind. Dies können z. B. bestimmte Wörter sein, die du in Lücken schreiben musst. In solchen Fällen lohnt es sich, während des Hörens **Notizen** zu machen.

Arbeitsschritt 2

Arbeitsschritt 3 Nach dem zweiten Hören hast du genügend Zeit, um jede Aufgabe auf deinem Arbeitsblatt noch einmal gründlich durchzulesen und zu **kontrollieren**. Hast du nach dem ersten Hören bereits einige Aufgaben beantwortet, so überprüfe sie jetzt noch einmal auf ihre Richtigkeit. Bei Detailinformationen, die innerhalb von einzelnen Aufgaben gefragt sind, solltest du zur Beantwortung deine Notizen heranziehen und die Antworten auf das Aufgabenblatt übertragen.

Einen Punkt solltest du immer beachten: Bei Aufgaben mit mehreren Fragen folgen diese in der Regel der Textchronologie, d. h., wenn du z. B. die Lösung zu einer der mittleren Fragen nicht weißt, dann passe beim zweiten Hören besonders gut in der Mitte der Aufnahme auf.

Tipp
- Vor dem ersten Hören: Worum geht es im Text? Lies die Aufgabenstellungen genau durch.
- Beim/nach dem ersten Hören: Trage die Lösungen zu den Aufgaben ein, die du schon beantworten kannst. Welche Informationen fehlen dir noch?
- Mache dir bei umfangreicheren Aufgabenstellungen Notizen über Details, die du für die Beantwortung der Fragen brauchst.
- Beim/nach dem zweiten Hören: Löse die restlichen Aufgaben. Überprüfe noch einmal die Aufgaben, die du bereits nach dem ersten Hören gelöst hast.

Vorgehen beim Üben

Zu Übungszwecken kannst du dir den Hörverstehenstext ruhig so oft anhören, wie du möchtest. Versuche, die Arbeitsaufträge nur durch Zuhören zu beantworten. Nur wenn du überhaupt nicht auf die richtige Lösung kommst, solltest du den Hörverstehenstext im Anhang lesen. Bei der Bearbeitung der Hörverstehensaufgaben in diesem Buch solltest du wie folgt vorgehen:

▶ Lies die Aufgabenstellungen genau durch. Hast du sie alle verstanden? Kläre unbekannte Wörter mithilfe eines Wörterbuches.

▶ Höre dir den entsprechenden Text einmal an, sodass du weißt, worum es darin geht. Höre dir anschließend den Text noch einmal an. Diesen Schritt kannst du so oft wiederholen, wie es für dich hilfreich ist.

▶ Höre dir den Text an und versuche dabei, die Aufgaben zu lösen.

▶ Wenn du alle Aufgaben bearbeitet hast, solltest du die Richtigkeit deiner Lösungen überprüfen, indem du dir den Text ein weiteres Mal anhörst.

▶ Anschließend überprüfst du deine Antworten anhand des Lösungsbuchs zu diesem Band. Wenn du viele Fehler gemacht hast, dann überlege genau, wie sie zustande gekommen sind. Hast du den Hörtext nicht genau verstanden? Hast du die Fragestellung falsch aufgefasst? Lies gegebenenfalls den Hörtext durch und wiederhole die gesamte Aufgabe in ein paar Wochen.

▶ Versuche, mit der Bearbeitung jeder weiteren Hörverstehensaufgabe in diesem Buch die Zahl der Hördurchgänge zu reduzieren, bis du bei der in der Prüfung üblichen Anzahl angelangt bist. Im MSA und in Klassenarbeiten werden dir die Texte meist nur zweimal, manchmal auch nur einmal, vorgespielt.

Neben der Arbeit mit diesem Buch gibt es noch weitere Möglichkeiten, um dein Hörverstehen zu trainieren. Sieh dir z. B. Filme oder Youtube-Videos auf Englisch an. Auf diese Weise wirst du mit dem Klang der Sprache besser vertraut und merkst, dass du nicht jedes einzelne Wort verstehen musst, um den Sinn des jeweiligen Films bzw. Clips zu erfassen.

1.2 Häufige Aufgabenstellungen im Bereich „Hörverstehen"

Multiple choice

Bei diesem Aufgabentyp wird dir ein Satzanfang vorgegeben und du musst ankreuzen bzw. abhaken, welches von mehreren Satzenden am besten dazu passt. Im MSA sind meist drei Auswahlmöglichkeiten vorgegeben, von denen aber nur eine richtig ist. Die Auswahlmöglichkeiten sind der Länge nach angeordnet. Es hat also wenig Sinn, zu überlegen, ob die erste Möglichkeit wirklich richtig sein kann, weil man bei der vorhergehenden Aufgabe schon das erste Satzende gewählt hat. Hier gibt es keine Regel.

Text: *(Beispiel)*
Reporter: Today we're broadcasting live from Glastonbury Festival. Most people think it's just music and concerts, but there are lots more things to do and see – theatre performances, dance, even poetry. Let's take a look behind the scenes …

Task (and solution):
Tick the correct box.

Glastonbury Festival is …
- [ ] for music lovers only.
- [ ] an important theatre and film event.
- [✓] an event with many different forms of art.

Filling in gaps

Bei diesem Aufgabenformat musst du entweder Lücken ausfüllen oder Sätze vervollständigen. Da hier detailgenaues Verstehen gefordert ist, ist es besonders wichtig, dass du die Aufgabenstellung vor dem Hören des Textes aufmerksam durchliest, damit du weißt, worauf du beim Hören achten musst. Arbeite ganz konzentriert, damit du die geforderte Information beim Hören nicht verpasst. Wenn du ein Wort nicht sofort verstehst, grüble nicht darüber nach, sondern versuche, die restlichen Lücken auszufüllen. Dieses eine Wort kannst du beim zweiten Hördurchgang nachtragen.

Text: *(Beispiel)*
Chill (a rapper): Rap and hip-hop started in the Bronx. The kids there have tough lives; there's no work, no money, and lots of gangs. Many hate what they're born into, but they can't change anything or get out of it. Rap is their voice – through it they can tell their stories.

Task (and solution):
Fill in the information.
Through rap music, young people in the Bronx gain a __voice__.

Answering questions / Giving examples

Manchmal musst du in der Prüfung auch kurze Fragen zum Hörtext beantworten oder Aspekte, die im Text erwähnt werden, nennen. Anhand der Arbeitsanweisung kannst du erkennen, wie viele Aspekte du angeben sollst. In der Regel reicht es, wenn du in Stichworten antwortest – du musst also keine vollständigen Sätze formulieren.

Beispiel

Text:

Presenter: Have you ever wondered how some YouTube stars can make a living from their videos? Well, the most common way is to allow companies to place ads at the beginning of their videos. However, some YouTubers also go as far as promoting certain products or companies in the video itself.

Task (and solution):
Write down the information needed.

There are different ways for YouTubers to earn money. Name **two**.
- ▶ placing ads at the beginning of the video
- ▶ promoting products / companies in the video itself

Matching

Während Multiple-Choice-Aufgaben, Lückensätze und Kurzantworten relativ häufig im MSA vorkommen, sind die sogenannten *Matching*-Aufgaben eher selten. Doch auch sie können dich prinzipiell in der Prüfung und natürlich in Klassenarbeiten und Tests erwarten. Die Aufgabenstellungen können dabei sehr unterschiedlich sein: Es kann z. B. sein, dass dir mehrere kurze Texte von verschiedenen Sprechern vorgespielt werden, denen du die jeweils passenden Aussagen zuordnen musst, oder aber du musst bestimmte Eigenschaften den richtigen Orten zuordnen etc.

Beispiel

Text:

Amelia: I think I'd like to see a lot more done for the environment. There's a lot of talking, but where's the action? And when something is suggested, like wind farms, then people start complaining that they spoil the view!

Ethan: If public transport was better, people would use their cars less and that would mean less pollution and cleaner air in our cities. It's the same with cycle tracks. If there were more car-free routes for bikes, more people would cycle.

Task (and solution):
Choose the correct statement for each speaker and write the letters in the boxes.

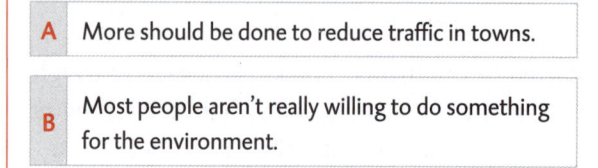

| A | More should be done to reduce traffic in towns. |

| B | Most people aren't really willing to do something for the environment. |

Amelia	B
Ethan	A

1.3 Übungsaufgaben zum Bereich „Hörverstehen"

Listening Test 1: Robben Island

Each week WorldRadio takes a look at a different country to help holidaymakers decide where to go for their summer holidays – this week, the subject is South Africa. The presenter and her guest are talking about Robben Island, where Nelson Mandela spent many years in prison.

▶ First read the tasks carefully for about 90 seconds.
▶ Then listen to the interview. While you are listening, tick (✓) the correct box or fill in the information needed.
▶ At the end, listen to the interview again. Check your answers and complete any missing sections.

1. To get to Robben Island visitors must make a …
   - [ ] 13-minute boat journey.
   - [ ] 30-minute boat journey.
   - [ ] 17-kilometre boat journey.

2. The tour guides have two roles. Give **one** example.
   _____

3. Some ex-prisoners still live on the island together with a few
   _____ .

4. The maximum-security prison was …
   - [ ] racially segregated.
   - [ ] for political prisoners.
   - [ ] for bank robbers and other criminals.

5. The leaders and the "normal" prisoners …
   - [ ] were not allowed to mix.
   - [ ] tried to avoid each other.
   - [ ] were often put in large 40-bed dormitories.

6. In the evenings the prisoners …
   - [ ] helped each other and talked a lot.
   - [ ] wrote messages to pass on to their leaders.
   - [ ] had long discussions with Nelson Mandela.

7. How and where could messages be passed on? Give **one** example.

8. Nelson Mandela never …
   ☐ argued with the prison guards.
   ☐ complained about the conditions in the prison.
   ☐ accepted anything the other prisoners wouldn't also get.

9. Escaping from the island was nearly impossible. Why? Give **one** example.

Listening Test 2: The News

You are going to hear two news items.

▶ First read the tasks.
▶ Then listen to the news items. While you are listening, tick (✓) the correct box.
▶ At the end, listen to the news items again and check your answers.

News Item 1: The Pardoning of the Thanksgiving turkey

1. Thanksgiving is celebrated to remember the …
   ☐ Pilgrims' first harvest.
   ☐ arrival of the first settlers.
   ☐ foundation of the new colonies.

2. Harry Truman was the first president who …
   ☐ was given a turkey as a present.
   ☐ spared a turkey on Thanksgiving.
   ☐ officially celebrated Thanksgiving.

3. The first official pardon was issued by …
   ☐ Ronald Reagan.
   ☐ John F. Kennedy.
   ☐ George Bush senior.

4. Oliver North …
   ☐ fought in the Iran War.
   ☐ wanted to become president instead of Reagan.
   ☐ was indirectly responsible for the first turkey pardoning.

News Item 2: What about a Batmobile?

1. Zac Mihajlovic …
   - [ ] is 29 years old.
   - [ ] lives in Austria.
   - [ ] was born in 1998.

2. He built his Batmobile …
   - [ ] to fight crime.
   - [ ] in his backyard.
   - [ ] with his grandfather.

3. The car is so special because …
   - [ ] it has a real car licence.
   - [ ] it has bullet-proof windows.
   - [ ] even a police escort cannot stop it.

4. Zac needed the police once because …
   - [ ] there were people blocking his way.
   - [ ] people took pictures of him in Sydney.
   - [ ] they helped him to fight some criminals.

Listening Test 3: Apple and Rain

You are going to hear an excerpt from the novel *Apple and Rain* by Sarah Crossan. The narrator, a girl called Apple, is talking to Pilar (her best friend), Donna, Hazel, and Mariah (three girls from her class).

▶ First read the tasks.
▶ Then listen to the text. While you are listening, tick (✓) the correct box or write down the information needed.
▶ At the end, listen to the text again and check your answers.

1. The scene takes place …
   - [ ] at the beach.
   - [ ] after a lesson.
   - [ ] during a lesson.

2. Donna is talking about …
   - [ ] a fun day out.
   - [ ] her new earrings.
   - [ ] some guys she likes.

3. Apple did not go swimming with the other girls because she ...
   - [ ] was not allowed to.
   - [ ] preferred to go to church.
   - [ ] did not know they were going.

4. Apple does not have lunch with Donna, Hazel, and Mariah because she ...
   - [ ] wants to lose weight.
   - [ ] feels they do not want her there.
   - [ ] is going to have lunch with Pilar.

5. Apple is ...
   - [ ] jealous of a boy.
   - [ ] afraid of losing her only friend.
   - [ ] not going to tell anyone about her feelings.

6. Apple is looking for ways to avoid going to drama lesson.
   Name **one** of her ideas.

   _____

After listening to the **whole** text, complete this task.

7. The text is about ...
   - [ ] disappointments in a friendship.
   - [ ] how teenagers spend their free time.
   - [ ] school problems and how to avoid them.

Listening Test 4: Grey Owl

Gina McGee is an author-illustrator of children's comics. For her next book she has been researching the story of Grey Owl. Cameron Jones talks to her about this man and what he achieved.

▶ First read the tasks.
▶ Then listen to the interview. While you are listening, tick (✓) the correct box or fill in the information.
▶ At the end, listen to the interview again and check your answers.
▶ Here is some vocabulary you might need:
First Nations, indigenous people – the original inhabitants of Canada

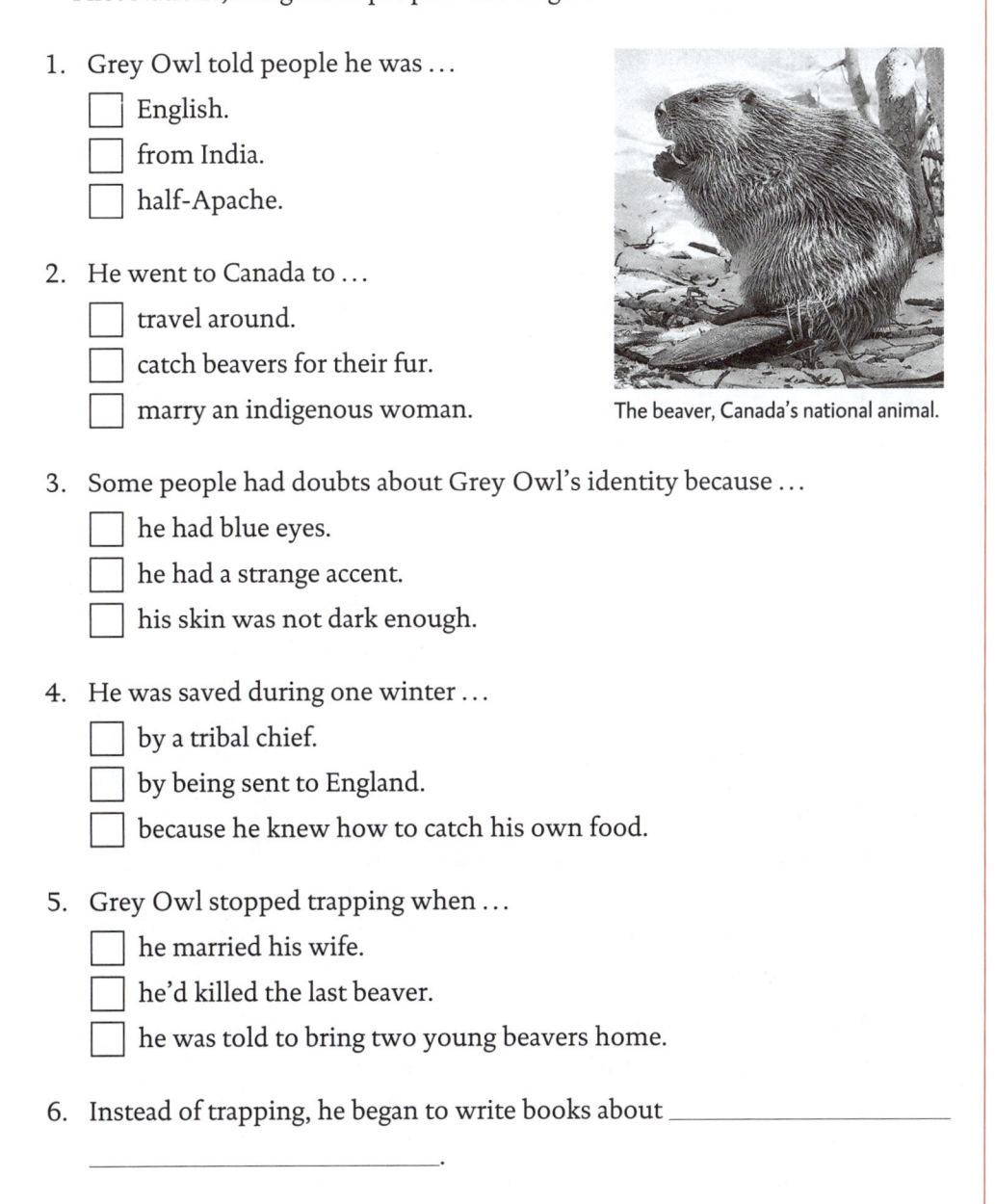

1. Grey Owl told people he was …
   - [ ] English.
   - [ ] from India.
   - [ ] half-Apache.

2. He went to Canada to …
   - [ ] travel around.
   - [ ] catch beavers for their fur.
   - [ ] marry an indigenous woman.

   The beaver, Canada's national animal.

3. Some people had doubts about Grey Owl's identity because …
   - [ ] he had blue eyes.
   - [ ] he had a strange accent.
   - [ ] his skin was not dark enough.

4. He was saved during one winter …
   - [ ] by a tribal chief.
   - [ ] by being sent to England.
   - [ ] because he knew how to catch his own food.

5. Grey Owl stopped trapping when …
   - [ ] he married his wife.
   - [ ] he'd killed the last beaver.
   - [ ] he was told to bring two young beavers home.

6. Instead of trapping, he began to write books about _____ .

7. As a result of his work, he …
   - [ ] soon became very rich.
   - [ ] was invited to talk to the Royal Family in Britain.
   - [ ] was hired to give tours of the Canadian national parks.

8. After he died, _____ discovered who Grey Owl really was.

9. Many people were angry with Grey Owl because …
   - [ ] he stopped the fur trade in Canada.
   - [ ] he hadn't told the truth about himself.
   - [ ] they didn't like his ideas about conservation.

Listening Test 5: The Art of Being Normal

You are going to hear an excerpt from the novel *The Art of Being Normal* by Lisa Williamson. The narrator, Leo Denton, is relatively new at Eden Park School. During one of the lessons, he has a conversation with two of his classmates.

▶ First read the tasks.
▶ Then listen to the text. While you are listening, tick (✓) the correct box.
▶ At the end, listen to the text again and check your answers.

1. The narrator, Leo, …
   - [ ] has already heard about Becky's party.
   - [ ] asks Alicia if she wants to go to the party with him.
   - [ ] is surprised to hear there will be a party at Becky's house.

2. Leo …
   - [ ] is keen on going to parties.
   - [ ] does not really like parties.
   - [ ] does not know yet whether he has time.

3. Most of the pupils at Eden Park School …
   - [ ] are friends with Leo.
   - [ ] are a bit afraid of Leo.
   - [ ] want Leo to come to their parties.

4. Leo seems to …
   - [ ] feel rather insecure.
   - [ ] hate the other pupils.
   - [ ] be a very popular guy.

5. Alicia tries to tell Leo that …
   - [ ] she understands what he feels like.
   - [ ] she is really disappointed with him.
   - [ ] her family is going to move to London.

6. Right now, Alicia …
   - [ ] feels like an outsider.
   - [ ] is looking for new friends on the internet.
   - [ ] seems well-integrated at Eden Park School.

7. Alicia wants to …
   - [ ] go to the party with Leo.
   - [ ] go to Becky's party alone.
   - [ ] bring her friend Ruby to the party.

8. In the end, Leo is …
   - [ ] too nervous to go to the party.
   - [ ] relieved because Alicia will go without him.
   - [ ] happy and excited because he will go to the party with Alicia.

Listening Test 6: The California Gold Rush

You are going to hear a report about the gold rush in California.

▶ First read the tasks.
▶ Then listen to the report. While you are listening, tick (✓) the correct box or fill in the information needed.
▶ At the end, listen to the report again and check your answers.

1. The first person to find gold was …
   - [ ] a settler.
   - [ ] an Englishman.
   - [ ] a Native American.

   a gold nugget

2. The gold nugget was discovered in …
   - [ ] a river.
   - [ ] a sawmill.
   - [ ] the hills of California.

3. How was the nugget tested to see if it was gold? Give **one** example.

   _____

4. The man knew the metal was gold because it was _____.

5. People in New York first learnt about gold in California …
   ☐ from stories about it.
   ☐ from a member of Congress.
   ☐ through a newspaper article.

6. People travelling west to seek gold …
   ☐ usually did not have a family.
   ☐ often had wrong expectations.
   ☐ knew they would have to work hard.

7. Van Valen's wife …
   ☐ had a very difficult life.
   ☐ only earned $ 500 in two years.
   ☐ moved to California to help her husband.

8. Most of the gold seekers …
   ☐ did not make a lot of money.
   ☐ returned home east after a few years.
   ☐ were successful enough to have comfortable lives.

9. One result of the gold rush was that California …
   ☐ joined the USA.
   ☐ became very rich.
   ☐ now appeared on maps.

Listening Test 7: The Stolen Generations

Jenny Green teaches history at the University of Sydney. Greg Masters, a radio presenter, has invited her into the studio to talk about Australia's "Stolen Generations".

Aboriginal child

▶ First read the tasks.
▶ Then listen to the interview. While you are listening, tick (✓) the correct box or fill in the information.
▶ At the end, listen to the interview again and check your answers.

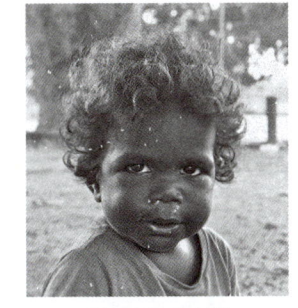

1. The so-called "Stolen Generations" were children taken away from their families up until about …
   - [ ] 1900.
   - [ ] 1917.
   - [ ] 1970.

2. The governments wanted Aboriginal children to _____ white culture.

3. The governments' purpose of taking Aboriginal children away was to …
   - [ ] wipe out the Aboriginal way of life.
   - [ ] create a culturally more diverse society.
   - [ ] allow white childless couples to have children.

4. Most children were put into homes …
   - [ ] near big cities.
   - [ ] close to their families.
   - [ ] far away from their parents.

5. The children had to …
   - [ ] watch anti-Aboriginal films.
   - [ ] take new names and speak English.
   - [ ] perform Aboriginal ceremonies in front of white people.

6. In the homes, Aboriginal children …
   - [ ] felt safe and protected.
   - [ ] received a good education.
   - [ ] were not looked after well.

7. National _____ Day began so that Australians would not forget the Stolen Generations and what happened to them.

8. During the Olympic Games in 2000, an Aboriginal athlete became famous for several reasons. Name **two**.

   ▶ _____

   ▶ _____

9. Nowadays, …

   ☐ the government does all it can to support Aboriginal families.

   ☐ the trauma of the "Stolen Generations" has finally been healed.

   ☐ a lot of Aboriginal children are still taken away from their parents.

Listening Test 8: Couchsurfing or Wilderness?

You are going to hear a radio programme. An interviewer is asking different people how they usually spend their holidays.

▶ First read the statements (A–G) and look at the list of speakers (0–5).
▶ Then listen to the programme. Choose the correct statement for each speaker and write the letters in the correct boxes. There is an example at the beginning (0).
▶ There is one more statement than you need.
▶ At the end, listen to the programme again and check your answers.

	Statements
A	I love being outdoors.
B	I like camping, but I don't want to sleep on the forest floor.
C	Couchsurfing is too risky.
D	I usually go on city trips.
E	**I want nature, silence and luxury.**
F	I don't want to be a tourist in the traditional sense.
G	We can't afford to stay at a hotel.

Speakers	Answers
0 – John (Example)	E
1 – Olivia	
2 – Hailey	
3 – Carter	
4 – Josh	
5 – Sara	

Hörverstehen | 47

Listening Test 9: Inventing Elliot

You are going to hear an excerpt from the novel *Inventing Elliot* by Graham Gardner.

▶ First read the tasks.
▶ Then listen to the excerpt. While you are listening, tick (✓) the correct box.
▶ At the end, listen to the excerpt again and check your answers.

1. One night, Elliot …
   - [ ] lay in his bed.
   - [ ] lay on the sofa.
   - [ ] sat in the living room.

2. Elliot's mother …
   - [ ] was on the phone.
   - [ ] talked to a neighbour.
   - [ ] talked about his father.

3. Elliot was feeling …
   - [ ] sad.
   - [ ] happy.
   - [ ] excited.

4. Elliot's father worked a lot. Elliot …
   - [ ] missed him a lot.
   - [ ] often talked to him on the phone.
   - [ ] was happy not to see him so often.

5. One night Elliot heard …
   - [ ] people talking in the garden.
   - [ ] unfamiliar voices under his bedroom.
   - [ ] someone laughing under his bedroom.

6. In the kitchen, there were …
   - [ ] two neighbours.
   - [ ] two police officers.
   - [ ] a doctor and a nurse.

7. They asked Elliot …
   - [ ] to get dressed.
   - [ ] to go back to bed.
   - [ ] to stay in the kitchen.

8. Elliot's father had been attacked …
   - [ ] in his office.
   - [ ] in front of the house.
   - [ ] walking back to his car.

9. His injuries were …
   - [ ] minor.
   - [ ] severe.
   - [ ] moderate.

10. His dad …
    - [ ] died.
    - [ ] had come home.
    - [ ] was still in hospital.

Listening Test 10: Sandringham

The podcast "A day out" has invited people to present their favourite places in Britain. Listen to John talking about the one he enjoys the most – Sandringham House, which is a private home of the British monarch, Queen Elizabeth II.

▶ First read the tasks.
▶ Then listen to the podcast. While you are listening, tick (✓) the correct box or fill in the missing information.
▶ At the end, listen to the podcast again and check your answers.

1. Sandringham House was bought for …
   - [ ] Queen Victoria.
   - [ ] the Royal Family.
   - [ ] one of Queen Victoria's children.

2. Visitors could not enter the house until _____.

3. The Queen owns Sandringham House together with …
   - [ ] her own fruit farm.
   - [ ] all the Norfolk coast.
   - [ ] a large part of the countryside near it.

4. After paying and entering the grounds, visitors …
   - [ ] can hire bikes to explore the estate.
   - [ ] have only a short walk to get to the house.
   - [ ] can enjoy the gardens before arriving at the house.

5. Visitors …
   - [ ] might run into one of the Royals.
   - [ ] get to see only a part of the house.
   - [ ] enter the house through the museum.

6. One vehicle in the museum was _____
   so that it could carry all the Royal luggage.

7. The Queen uses _____
   to return to London.

8. The Royal Family usually go to church at Sandringham …
   - [ ] in order to relax.
   - [ ] on Christmas Day.
   - [ ] on public holidays.

9. The ghost at Sandringham House …
   - [ ] does annoying things.
   - [ ] has scared many guests staying there.
   - [ ] has supposedly been seen many times.

Hörverstehen

Listening Test 11: The Super Bowl

Listen to Jeff and Chelsea talking about the Super Bowl and how it started.

▶ First read the tasks.
▶ Then listen to the interview. While you are listening, tick (✓) the correct box or fill in the information.
▶ At the end, listen to the interview again and check your answers.

1. The National Football League was …
   - [ ] founded in 1960.
   - [ ] owned by a group of businessmen.
   - [ ] the most important American football organisation until 1960.

2. Why did the National Football League and the American Football League decide to merge? Name **one** reason.
   _____

3. The word "super" in the name "Super Bowl" came from …
   - [ ] a kid's toy.
   - [ ] the players.
   - [ ] the owner of one of the leagues.

4. The word "bowl" had already been used in American football. For what? Give **one** example.
   _____
   _____

5. The first Super Bowl game was in the year _____.

6. When the first Super Bowl took place, …
   - [ ] not all the seats were sold.
   - [ ] it was difficult for fans to get to the stadium.
   - [ ] about 15 million people watched the game on TV.

7. The Super Bowl is always on …
   - [ ] a Monday.
   - [ ] 1st February.
   - [ ] the first Sunday in February.

8. Cities that want to host the Super Bowl have to fulfil certain criteria. Give **one** example.

   _____

9. The Super Bowl has grown to become ...
   - [ ] an official holiday in the USA.
   - [ ] the most watched sporting event in the USA.
   - [ ] the most famous sporting competition worldwide.

Listening Test 12: Sundae Girl

You are going to hear an excerpt from the novel *Sundae Girl* by Cathy Cassidy. The narrator is Jude Reilly from St Joseph's school.

▶ First read the tasks.
▶ Then listen to the excerpt. While you are listening, tick (✓) the correct box.
▶ At the end, listen to the excerpt again and check your answers.

1. Jude is worried about ...
   - [ ] a Maths test.
   - [ ] her bad marks.
   - [ ] Parents' Night at school.

2. Jude is ...
   - [ ] very tired.
   - [ ] enjoying the evening.
   - [ ] ashamed of her family.

3. Jude's mother now works as ...
   - [ ] a teacher.
   - [ ] an actress.
   - [ ] a hairdresser.

4. Jude's parents ...
   - [ ] live together.
   - [ ] are separated.
   - [ ] will marry soon.

5. Kevin Carter …
   - [ ] is selling tea.
   - [ ] is Jude's boyfriend.
   - [ ] is in Jude's English class.

6. Jude's dad is …
   - [ ] a teacher.
   - [ ] a comedian.
   - [ ] an Elvis impersonator.

7. Kevin Carter thinks that Kristina Kowalski is …
   - [ ] ugly.
   - [ ] pretty.
   - [ ] impolite.

8. Jude's grandfather is wearing …
   - [ ] a tie.
   - [ ] a hat.
   - [ ] sunglasses.

9. Kevin thinks the two elderly people look very …
   - [ ] normal.
   - [ ] friendly.
   - [ ] unusual.

10. Jude …
    - [ ] is proud of her grandparents.
    - [ ] pretends she is not related to them.
    - [ ] introduces her grandparents to Kevin.

Listening Test 13: Mary Robinson

Listen to Brenna talking about Mary Robinson for an Irish podcast.

- ▶ First read the tasks.
- ▶ Then listen to the podcast.
  While you are listening, tick (✓) the correct box or write down the information needed.
- ▶ At the end, listen to the podcast again and check your answers.

1. The podcast is about …
   - ☐ inspiring Irish personalities.
   - ☐ characters in Irish literature.
   - ☐ important figures in Irish history.

2. Mary Robinson …
   - ☐ won the Nobel Prize in Literature.
   - ☐ was president of the United Nations.
   - ☐ was the first female president of Ireland.

3. Mary Robinson has been fighting …
   - ☐ for the values of the Church.
   - ☐ for the rights of women, gay and lesbian people.
   - ☐ against censorship and discrimination in literature.

4. Which qualities does Brenna particularly admire about Mary Robinson? Give **two** examples.

   ▶ _____

   ▶ _____

5. The title of Mary Robinson's memoir is …
   - ☐ *A Matter of Faith*.
   - ☐ *Every Day Counts*.
   - ☐ *Everybody Matters*.

6. Mary Robinson …
   - ☐ is regarded as a moral authority.
   - ☐ is enjoying a relaxing retirement.
   - ☐ focuses on helping elderly people.

7. For Mary Robinson …
   - ☐ fighting poverty is the most pressing issue.
   - ☐ climate change and human rights are closely linked.
   - ☐ human rights should have priority over climate protection.

Listening Test 14: New Zealand Tips

Listen to the podcast about New Zealand.

▶ First read the tasks.
▶ Then listen to the podcast. While you are listening, tick (✓) the correct box or write down the information needed.
▶ At the end, listen to the podcast again and check your answers.

1. A lot of rivers in New Zealand …
   ☐ are protected.
   ☐ are used for tourism.
   ☐ have been sold to private companies.

2. Bungy jumping …
   ☐ is Jack's favourite hobby.
   ☐ originated in New Zealand.
   ☐ can be done from a bridge over Waikato River.

3. What is said about Waikato River?
   Name **one** fact.
   _____
   _____

4. August is a good time for …
   ☐ hiking.
   ☐ water sports.
   ☐ winter sports.

5. The "Lord of the Rings" guided tours …
   ☐ only take place in spring.
   ☐ take place throughout the country.
   ☐ have brought New Zealand's economy millions of dollars.

6. During an abseiling and cave experience, you will …
   ☐ experience complete darkness.
   ☐ be able to bungy jump into the cave.
   ☐ marvel at the beautiful surroundings.

7. This episode of the podcast mainly deals with…
   ☐ Māori cultural sites.
   ☐ eco-friendly tourism.
   ☐ sports and outdoor activities.

2 Leseverstehen

Es gibt viele verschiedene Arten von Lesetexten. Ebenso vielfältig können die Aufgabenstellungen dazu sein. Die wichtigsten Textsorten und Aufgabenstellungen, die dich in Klassenarbeiten und in der MSA-Prüfung erwarten können, werden wir dir hier vorstellen.

2.1 Strategien zum Bereich „Leseverstehen"

Je nachdem, welche Art von Lesetext oder welche Art von Aufgabenstellung du bearbeiten musst, unterscheidet sich die Vorgehensweise. Manchmal musst du die Gesamtaussage des Textes erfassen *(reading for gist)* und manchmal sollst du Details aus dem Text herausfinden. Du musst dann den Text nach den geforderten Informationen durchforsten *(skimming* oder *scanning)*.

Arbeitsschritt 1
Zunächst einmal ist es sinnvoll, den Text an sich ganz genau zu betrachten. Oft kannst du bereits am **Layout**, d. h. an der Gestaltung des Textes, erkennen, um welche **Textsorte** es geht. Wenn du weißt, ob der dir vorliegende Text ein Zeitungsbericht, ein literarischer Text oder ein Blogeintrag ist, dann bist du schon einen Schritt weiter.

Arbeitsschritt 2
Als Nächstes solltest du den **Text** einmal **genau lesen**. Die meisten unbekannten Wörter kannst du ganz leicht aus dem **Sinnzusammenhang erschließen**. Lass dich also nicht aus der Ruhe bringen, wenn dir das eine oder andere Wort unbekannt ist. Ganz entscheidend ist, dass du dir bei diesem Arbeitsschritt einen guten **Überblick über den Inhalt** des Textes verschaffst.

Arbeitsschritt 3
Nun solltest du die **Aufgabenstellungen genau lesen**, damit du weißt, unter welchen Aspekten du den Text bearbeiten sollst. Wenn du dann den Lesetext im Hinblick auf die jeweiligen Aufgabenstellungen liest, kannst du ganz gezielt wichtige **Schlüsselwörter** bzw. **Textpassagen markieren**, damit du sie bei der Bearbeitung der Aufgaben schnell wiederfindest.
Jetzt bist du für die Beantwortung der Aufgaben gut gerüstet!

Tipp
- Schau dir den Lesetext insgesamt an. Kannst du vom Layout auf die Textsorte schließen?
- Lies den Text genau durch und verschaffe dir so einen guten Überblick über den Inhalt.
- Lies die Aufgabenstellungen sorgfältig. Markiere beim nochmaligen Lesen des Textes wichtige Textaussagen im Hinblick auf die Aufgabenstellungen.

2.2 Häufige Aufgabenstellungen im Bereich „Leseverstehen"

In diesem Kapitel findest du viele verschiedene Aufgaben zur Bearbeitung eines Textes. Damit kannst du trainieren, wie man einen Text genau erschließt, und bist auf Aufgaben zum Leseverstehen gut vorbereitet. Im MSA kommen besonders häufig folgende Aufgabentypen vor: Multiple-Choice-Aufgaben (teilweise mit Textbeleg), *true/false* mit Textbeleg, Kurzantworten, Zuordnungsaufgaben sowie evtl. auch Sortieraufgaben.

Multiple choice (teilweise mit Textbeleg)

Bei diesem Aufgabentyp werden dir der Anfang eines Satzes und **drei mögliche Satzenden** vorgegeben. Aus diesen Möglichkeiten musst du diejenige auswählen, die am besten zum Inhalt des Textes passt, und **das richtige Kästchen abhaken**. Oft wird in der Aufgabe nicht genau dieselbe Formulierung verwendet wie im Text; du musst also nach Schlüsselwörtern mit einer ähnlichen Bedeutung suchen und den Text und die möglichen Satzenden genau vergleichen. Manchmal wird auch von dir verlangt, dass du deine Entscheidung für ein bestimmtes Satzende begründest, indem du die dazu passende Textstelle zitierst. Der Arbeitsauftrag lautet dann z. B. "Give one piece of evidence from the text." oder "Give evidence from the text by quoting short passages from the text."

Beispiel

Text:
A large number of young people in South Africa are HIV-positive. Women are much more likely to be infected than men, and they suffer not only from insufficient medical treatment but also from social stigmatisation.

Task (and solution):
Tick the correct box and give evidence from the text by quoting short passages from the text.

One problem of HIV-positive women in South Africa is …

☐ the lack of child care.

☐ the cost of medication.

☑ negative attitudes towards HIV in society.

▶ One piece of evidence from the text:
Women … suffer … from social stigmatisation.

True/false (mit Textbeleg)

Bei diesem Aufgabentyp musst du entscheiden, ob **Aussagen** zum Text **richtig** oder **falsch** sind, und das entsprechende Kästchen abhaken. Es ist wichtig, dass du genau liest, denn ein einziges Wort kann ausschlaggebend sein, ob ein Satz korrekt ist oder nicht. Auch hier musst du deine Entscheidung meist mit einem Textzitat belegen.

Beispiel

Text:
In the USA young criminals can be sent to boot camp instead of going to prison. The first American boot camp for teenagers was created in the 1980s to reduce the number of prisoners and to lower costs.

Task (and solution):
Tick the correct box and give evidence from the text by quoting short passages from the text.

Boot camps have existed in the USA for about 15 years.

This statement is …   ☐ true.   ☑ false.

▶ One piece of evidence from the text:
The first American boot camp … was created in the 1980s …

Leseverstehen | 57

Short answers

Manchmal musst du auch Fragen zum Text beantworten oder Beispiele für bestimmte Sachverhalte aus dem Text heraussuchen. Lies dir die Aufgabenstellung genau durch und markiere die entsprechenden Stellen im Text. Meistens reicht es, wenn du in Stichpunkten antwortest, gelegentlich musst du aber auch einen ganzen Satz formulieren. Es kann auch vorkommen, dass bereits ein Satz vorgegeben ist und du nur eine Lücke vervollständigen musst.

Text:
Many projects for volunteers in Australia focus on the protection of wildlife, for example looking after threatened animals like the tree kangaroo or the southern hairy-nosed wombat. By collecting rubbish or planting trees, volunteers can help to restore the typical living space of these species.

Task (and solution):
What can volunteers do to protect the living space of threatened species? Give two examples from the text:

▸ _collect rubbish_

▸ _plant trees_

Beispiel

Matching

Matching- bzw. Zuordnungsaufgaben können ganz unterschiedlich aufgebaut sein. Häufig werden dir Überschriften vorgegeben, die du bestimmten Abschnitten im Text zuordnen musst. Es kann auch vorkommen, dass du Informationen oder Aussagen verschiedenen Personen, Ländern, Organisationen o. Ä. zuordnen sollst. Gelegentlich sind in den Aufgaben mehr Auswahlmöglichkeiten vorgegeben als eigentlich nötig wären, sodass einige Elemente übrig bleiben – achte auf entsprechende Hinweise in der Aufgabenstellung.

Text:

A Australia has long been one of the top gap-year destinations for young people from around the globe who have just finished school and want to travel for a year before starting a job or continuing their education.

B Many of them feel they want to do "something useful" during this time and decide to do voluntary work for a few weeks. Apart from spending an adventurous time and making new friends, many volunteers also cherish the feeling of learning something about the environment and contributing to its protection.

Beispiel

Task (and solution):
Match the headlines (1–3) to the paragraphs (A and B). There is one more headline than you need.

	Headlines	Paragraphs
1	Teaching and learning	–
2	Learn, help and have fun	B
3	A land of dreams for many	A

Sequencing

Bei diesem Aufgabenformat musst du die verschiedenen Abschnitte eines Textes in die richtige Reihenfolge bringen. Du musst also überlegen, welche Abschnitte sprachlich und inhaltlich am besten hintereinander passen, damit ein schlüssiger Gesamttext entsteht.

Beispiel

Task (and solution):

The sentences in the following short text have been mixed up. Read the parts (A–D) and put them in the correct order (❶–❹). Write your answer in the grid.

A	You never have to think about what to wear – which saves lots of time.

B	At English schools pupils usually have to wear a school uniform.

C	There also aren't any arguments with your parents about whether or not a skirt is too short or the slogan on a T-shirt is suitable for school.

D	Although many pupils would prefer to be able to choose their clothes themselves, most of them also see the advantages of a uniform.

❶	❷	❸	❹
B	D	A	C

2.3 Übungsaufgaben zum Bereich „Leseverstehen"

Reading Test 1: The Kiwi – New Zealand's Iconic Bird

A The United States has the eagle as its proud national animal, the United Kingdom the "King of the Jungle", the lion, and India the strong and dangerous tiger. And New Zealand? Their national animal is slightly different.

B It is a small, shy, but smart creature living in the forests: the kiwi. This unusual animal is unique to New Zealand. Due to its very small wings the bird cannot fly. It does not have a tail either, but strong legs. The kiwi is almost as big as a domestic chicken. Its feathers rather look like fur.

Thanks to its good sense of smell, the kiwi can look for food at night and hides in self-dug small holes during the day. That is why you hardly ever see it in the wilderness. The kiwi eats worms, centipedes, but also fruits and insects. Kiwis are monogamous – they stay with the same partner their whole life.

C The Māori consider the kiwi to be sacred and only very occasionally hunted the bird. They wore "kahu kiwi", cloaks[1] made from its feathers. White settlers also sold kiwi feathers and skin, before hunting was eventually forbidden. However, the greatest threat to the kiwi came in the form of new species that settlers from other continents brought with them. Predators[2] such as cats, dogs, weasels and possums had not existed in New Zealand before and became a real danger to the flightless bird. In addition, as more and more forests were cut down to be turned into towns and farming land, the kiwi lost much of its living space.

D There are two different theories as to how the kiwi got its name: The first one is that the bird is named after the shrill call of the male kiwi, "kiwii-kiwiii", the second one is that it got its name from a bird that looks similar to the kiwi, the Polynesian kivi.

E Around the middle of the 19th century, pictures of the kiwi appeared on regimental badges of the New Zealand army. At the beginning of the 20th century the name "kiwi" was used in sports, for example to refer to the New Zealand rugby team. During the first world war an Australian boot polish called "Kiwi" was used by soldiers and sold in the US and the United Kingdom. Thus, the name and picture of the bird became famous worldwide and was more and more linked to people from New Zealand. Today the term "kiwi" is used as a nickname for all New Zealanders. They also use this expression themselves because they are proud of their unique country and often unconventional way of life.

F If you visit New Zealand you have got many opportunities to see a kiwi. Although it is difficult to encounter a bird in the wild, there are 13 national parks run by the Department of Conservation (DOC) of New Zealand. You find many different animals there, but the star is always the kiwi. One of the best places is the National Kiwi Centre in Hokitika on the southern island of New Zealand.

G These places are very important because the kiwi bird population is on the decline. According to the DOC there are less than 70,000 kiwis left and their number is falling continuously. However, there are a lot of projects in order to rescue the bird from extinction. Let us hope that these programmes are successful, so we can meet this very special creature during a trip to New Zealand in the future.

---
1 cloaks – coats
2 predator – an animal that hunts and eats other animals

1. **True/false mit Textbeleg:** Are the following sentences true or false? Tick (✓) the correct box and give evidence from the text by quoting short passages. To help you, an example has been given.

   The kiwi can be found in Australia and New Zealand.

   This statement is … ☐ true.   ☑ false.

   ▶ One piece of evidence from the text:
   <u>This unusual animal is unique to New Zealand.</u>

   a) It is quite likely to encounter a kiwi during a hiking tour.

   This statement is … ☐ true.   ☐ false.

   ▶ One piece of evidence from the text: _____

   b) Kiwi birds form lifelong couples.

   This statement is … ☐ true.   ☐ false.

   ▶ One piece of evidence from the text: _____

   c) Kiwi feathers were used for clothing.

   This statement is … ☐ true.   ☐ false.

   ▶ One piece of evidence from the text: _____

   d) Cats and kiwis have always existed in New Zealand.

   This statement is … ☐ true.   ☐ false.

   ▶ One piece of evidence from the text: _____

   e) New Zealanders would never refer to themselves as "kiwis".

   This statement is … ☐ true.   ☐ false.

   ▶ One piece of evidence from the text: _____

   f) The quirky bird is very popular.

   This statement is … ☐ true.   ☐ false.

   ▶ One piece of evidence from the text: _____

   g) The population of the kiwi bird is stable and secure.

   This statement is … ☐ true.   ☐ false.

   ▶ One piece of evidence from the text: _____

2. **Matching:** Match the headlines (1–7) to the paragraphs (A–G).
   One headline has already been matched correctly.

	Headlines	Paragraphs
1	Origin of the name "kiwi"	
2	Places to see kiwis	
3	An animal in danger	
4	Becoming a national icon	
5	A slightly different national animal	A
6	Efforts to save the kiwi	
7	Appearance and typical behaviour	

3. **Short answers:** Fill in the information.

   a) What are the greatest threats to the survival of the kiwi?
      Give two examples.

      ▶ _____

      ▶ _____

   b) What are two theories as to how the kiwi got its name?

      ▶ _____

      ▶ _____

   c) Where can you go to see a kiwi?

      _____
      _____

4. **Multiple choice (mit und ohne Textbeleg):**
   For task **a** tick (✓) the correct box. For tasks **b and c** tick the correct box and give evidence from the text by quoting short passages from the text.

   a) The national animal of the UK is the …
      ☐ tiger.
      ☐ lion.
      ☐ kiwi.

   b) The kiwi was first used as an emblem …
      ☐ in the 18th century.
      ☐ in the 19th century.
      ☐ in the 20th century.
      ▶ One piece of evidence from the text: _____
      _____

c) An Australian boot polish called "Kiwi" was sold …
- ☐ mainly in Europe.
- ☐ in Britain and America.
- ☐ in New Zealand and Australia only.
  ▶ One piece of evidence from the text: _____
  _____

Additional task

5. Complete the flyer about the kiwi with information from the text.

The Kiwi

Living space: _____

Size: _____

Food: _____

Sleeping place: _____

What is special about it: it can't _____,

but its _____ is very good

Reading Test 2: Young Refugees Learn about U.S. on the Soccer Field

Young refugees in the United States are learning about each other and their new country on the soccer field. One player is 13-year-old Win La Bar. His family is from Myanmar, also known as Burma. Win was born in Thailand after his family fled their Burmese homeland. Now he is one of about 200 refugee children who play at the North Phoenix Christian Soccer Club, in the western state of Arizona. The players in the club's twelve teams are between six and eighteen years old.

Win and his ten family members share two apartments. Win has his own bedroom, but his sister sleeps in a room with her three young children. Win's parents and three other children live in another apartment. He loves his new home: "I've got a better chance to get a better education, and I get to play more soccer without worrying about gunshots."

The soccer club has helped him make friends and learn about his new home. His coaches have taught his family about life in the United States. Win says it was "very different, very hard to adapt into this world", because he had never seen cars or planes.

Alondra Ruiz works for the soccer club. She brings the players to games and drives them home. Sometimes she drives for hours a day, and hundreds of kilometers a week. During the rides the students ask her many questions about the United States. Ruiz tells them "you're not different. You're here. And you can become anything you want."

"Being part of this club, and keeping kids busy is very rewarding to me because it's good for them, and it's good for the future," she says. "What I hear often is that they're being treated different at school, that they're not being accepted. I relate to that 100 percent. I wasn't accepted coming from Mexico."

Ruiz was an immigrant child who grew up in the United States. Whereas her husband has permission to work in the U.S., she is not here legally.

More than 70,000 refugees from many countries have been resettled in Arizona in the past ten years. The U.S. State Department says more than 33,000 refugees have begun new lives in Arizona since 2002. Only Texas, California, New York, Minnesota, Florida and Washington have accepted more refugees than Arizona. In the past year, refugees from thirteen countries have moved to Arizona. There are players from at least twelve countries in the soccer club this year.

Zara Doukoum knows what the other refugee students have dealt with, including when people did not understand what they were saying when they were just learning to speak English. "Every refugee in America went through that," she says. This year she will graduate from Central High School, the public school attended by most of her teammates. It will be four years since she arrived in Phoenix with her mother and three sisters. She wants to attend college, where she may play soccer or tennis.

Adapted from: Christopher Jones-Cruise, Anna Matteo, Voice of America Learning English, January 25, 2016.

1. **True/false und Multiple choice mit Textbeleg:** For tasks **a, b, d, f and g** tick the correct box and give evidence from the text by quoting short passages from the text.
   Short answers: For tasks **c, e and h** fill in the information.

   a) Win's place of birth is in …
      ☐ the USA.
      ☐ Thailand.
      ☐ Myanmar (Burma).
      ▶ One piece of evidence from the text: _____

   b) The La Bar family have little space in their new home as they have to share two bedrooms.
      This statement is …   ☐ true.   ☐ false.
      ▶ One piece of evidence from the text: _____

   c) What does Win like about his new life in America? Give two examples from the text:
      ▶ _____
      ▶ _____

   d) At the soccer club the refugee children …
      ☐ get additional lessons in English.
      ☐ can learn more than just soccer rules.
      ☐ also learn how to choose the right college.
      ▶ One piece of evidence from the text: _____

   e) Why does working for the soccer club feel good for Alondra Ruiz? Give two examples from the text:
      ▶ _____
      ▶ _____

   f) Alondra Ruiz and her husband are illegal immigrants.
      This statement is …   ☐ true.   ☐ false.
      ▶ One piece of evidence from the text: _____

   g) About one third of the refugees who come to the USA settle down in Arizona.
      This statement is …   ☐ true.   ☐ false.
      ▶ One piece of evidence from the text: _____

h) What problems do child refugees have to cope with when they arrive in America? Give two examples from the text:

   ▸ _____

   ▸ _____

2. Match the people and institutions from the text (❶–❹) to the statements (**A–F**). Write the correct letter in the table. Be careful, there are two statements that you do not need.

   ❶ Win La Bar
   ❷ North Phoenix Christian Soccer Club
   ❸ Alondra Ruiz
   ❹ Zara Doukoum

   A The most important thing for us is that the kids do well at school.

   B I'm really proud that I've made it this far. And believe me, school wasn't always easy, especially in the first few months.

   C I'm grateful for all the opportunities that are offered to me in the US.

   D I'd like to become a legal American citizen, too.

   E I can't imagine what it must feel like to start a new life in a new environment.

   F We offer an integration program for child refugees.

❶	❷	❸	❹

Reading Test 3: The History of Halloween

The origin of our modern holiday "Halloween" goes back to the old Gaelic festival of "Samhain", which for the Celts marked the end of the harvest period and the beginning of the "dark season" of winter. It was celebrated from sunset on October 31st to sunset on November 1st. This was the time when the cattle was brought back from its summer meadows and the preparation for the less fertile months began.

On Samhain, which was celebrated in what is now Ireland, the Isle of Man and parts of Scotland, the people lit bonfires and held special feasts and meals. There were also offerings for the old gods and the "aos sí", a mystical and supernatural race comparable to fairies or elves that the Celts commonly believed in. There was also the belief that on Samhain – as well as on Midsummer's Eve – the borders between this world and the world of the spirits could be crossed more easily, which made it possible for the dead to visit our world once again. However, this was not only a frightening event. The Celts believed that their ancestors wanted to join them on this date to make sure that they were well and protected. That is why people put empty chairs next to their own, which were meant for the dead members of the family.

Of course, not only the good and gentle spirits came to visit our world. Therefore, the Celts often wore special clothes and costumes to hide from the unpleasant and dangerous spirits. In those costumes they sometimes went from house to house and asked for blessings and small gifts. This tradition is still practised on Halloween by the many children that roam their neighbourhood playing "trick or treat". And just as the evil spirits that could do bad things to the people not welcoming the dead, the children play tricks on people who do not open the door or give them sweets.

1. For tasks **a**, **b**, **d and e** tick the correct box and give evidence from the text by quoting short passages from the text.
   For task **c** fill in the information.

   a) The tradition of Halloween has its roots in a Gaelic holiday.
      This statement is … ☐ true.   ☐ false.
      ▶ One piece of evidence from the text: _____
      _____

   b) The celebration of Samhain lasted …
      ☐ for about 24 hours.
      ☐ for two whole days.
      ☐ for the winter months.
      ▶ One piece of evidence from the text: _____
      _____

c) How did the Celts celebrate Samhain? Give two examples from the text:

▸ _____

▸ _____

d) The term "aos sí" refers to …

☐ supernatural beings.

☐ the Celts' dead ancestors.

☐ the Celts' gifts to the gods.

▸ One piece of evidence from the text: _____

_____

e) Something similar to "trick or treating" already existed in Celtic times.

This statement is … ☐ true. ☐ false.

▸ One piece of evidence from the text: _____

_____

2. This is the second part of the text about the history of Halloween. Unfortunately, the paragraphs have been mixed up. Put them back in the right order (❶–❹) by writing the correct letter in the table below. One paragraph has already been put in the correct place.

| A | Thus, the practice and celebration of "All Saints' Day", also called "All Hallows' Day", on which Christians should think about their dead saints, was shifted to the main date of Samhain (November 1st), turning the night before into "All Hallows' Evening". |

| B | Today, however, many people do not remember the origin of traditions like going "trick or treating" or the carving of the pumpkins to look like evil spirits. They believe that it is just childish behaviour and has no purpose at all because the meaning behind those rites has been lost over the centuries. |

| C | Between the 4th and the 10th centuries, the Roman Catholic Church took over many pagan and Jewish holidays and shifted their own special days to dates of existing festivals and around them. The day of the birth of Christ, for example, became connected to the Roman "Festival of the Sun" and the "Passion" and "Resurrection of Christ" – now known as "Easter" – was linked to the Jewish "Passover". |

| D | Over the years, decades and centuries, this phrase was shortened to become the word "Halloween", which was still connected to the traditions and the belief of the Gaelic Samhain, where the spirits of the dead came to visit the living – just as the deeds of the Christian saints were commemorated on the day of "All Saints". |

❶	❷	❸	❹
C			

Reading Test 4: Getting to Know Canada

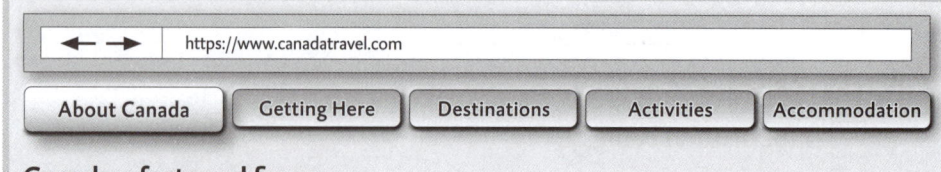

https://www.canadatravel.com

About Canada | **Getting Here** | **Destinations** | **Activities** | **Accommodation**

Canada – facts and figures

A Canada, whose name means "village" or "settlement", is the world's second-largest country after Russia. It consists of ten provinces and three territories. The country's smallest province is Prince Edward Island, named after Queen Victoria's father; the largest territory is Nunavut in the far north. There is the Pacific Ocean in the west, the Atlantic Ocean in the east and the Arctic Ocean in the north. In the south, Canada shares the world's longest land border with the USA. Four of the five Great Lakes are also part of the border between these two countries.

B Nunavut, which means "Our Land", is the coldest, largest and least populated territory. It is about the size of Western Europe, but only about 31,000 people live there, 85 % of whom are indigenous. It was created in 1999 and is therefore the youngest territory of Canada. Visitors can only fly into Nunavut as there are no roads that connect the 25 communities with each other or the rest of Canada. As rivers, lakes and the Arctic Ocean are frozen for three-quarters of the year, even very heavy vehicles can drive on the ice for more than six months. When the ice has melted, some communities can be visited by boat in July and August. In the summer months, the sun never sets, whereas in the winter, the sky is lit by the Northern Lights.

C There are two official languages in Canada – English and French – but that doesn't mean that every Canadian is bilingual. Quebec is the only Canadian province that uses French as its only official language. However, many people also speak English there, especially in Montreal and other popular tourist destinations.

D More than a century ago, in 1885, when people realised that it was necessary to protect plants and animals, the history of Canada's national parks started with the creation of Banff National Park in the province of Alberta in the Canadian Rockies. Today, Canada has got more than 40 national parks and park reserves, which vary from between 9 km² and 45,000 km² in size. Some of the most popular activities are wildlife viewing, hiking, mountain biking, horseback riding, climbing, kayaking or canoeing, cross-country skiing, ice skating, skiing and snowboarding.

E One of the most famous tourist attractions is the Niagara Falls, located in the Canadian province of Ontario and New York State. The term "Niagara Falls" comprises three waterfalls, namely the Horseshoe Falls, the American Falls and the Bridal Veil Falls. One way to experience the falls is to go on a breathtaking "Journey Behind the Falls", taking an elevator down to the bottom of the falls and watching the water fall down from behind. Thrill-seeking visitors, however, might want to go on a cruise that travels past the American and Bridal Veil Falls to get as close to the Horseshoe Falls as possible. Although a lot more visitors tend to look at the falls on the Canadian side of the border, the American side is also worth a visit.

About us | Contact us | Copyright | Press | En français

Leseverstehen

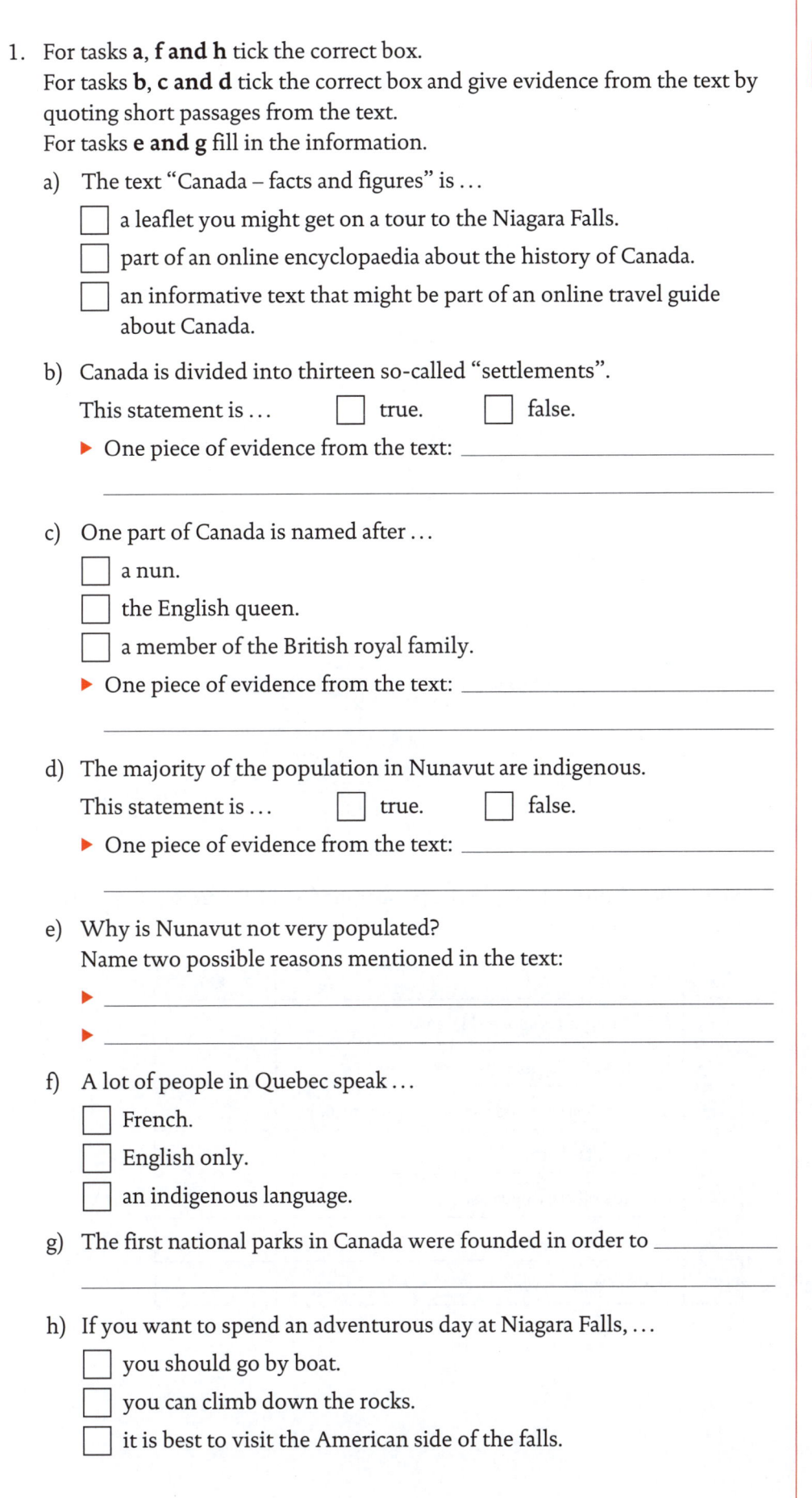

1. For tasks **a, f and h** tick the correct box.
   For tasks **b, c and d** tick the correct box and give evidence from the text by quoting short passages from the text.
   For tasks **e and g** fill in the information.

   a) The text "Canada – facts and figures" is …
      - ☐ a leaflet you might get on a tour to the Niagara Falls.
      - ☐ part of an online encyclopaedia about the history of Canada.
      - ☐ an informative text that might be part of an online travel guide about Canada.

   b) Canada is divided into thirteen so-called "settlements".
      This statement is …   ☐ true.   ☐ false.
      ▶ One piece of evidence from the text: _____
      _____

   c) One part of Canada is named after …
      - ☐ a nun.
      - ☐ the English queen.
      - ☐ a member of the British royal family.
      ▶ One piece of evidence from the text: _____
      _____

   d) The majority of the population in Nunavut are indigenous.
      This statement is …   ☐ true.   ☐ false.
      ▶ One piece of evidence from the text: _____
      _____

   e) Why is Nunavut not very populated?
      Name two possible reasons mentioned in the text:
      ▶ _____
      ▶ _____

   f) A lot of people in Quebec speak …
      - ☐ French.
      - ☐ English only.
      - ☐ an indigenous language.

   g) The first national parks in Canada were founded in order to _____
      _____

   h) If you want to spend an adventurous day at Niagara Falls, …
      - ☐ you should go by boat.
      - ☐ you can climb down the rocks.
      - ☐ it is best to visit the American side of the falls.

2. Use the information from the text to find the correct place on the map for these geographical names. Write the letters (a–e) in the correct box. Be careful, there is one more box than you need.

a) Niagara Falls
b) Quebec
c) Nunavut
d) Alberta
e) Arctic Ocean

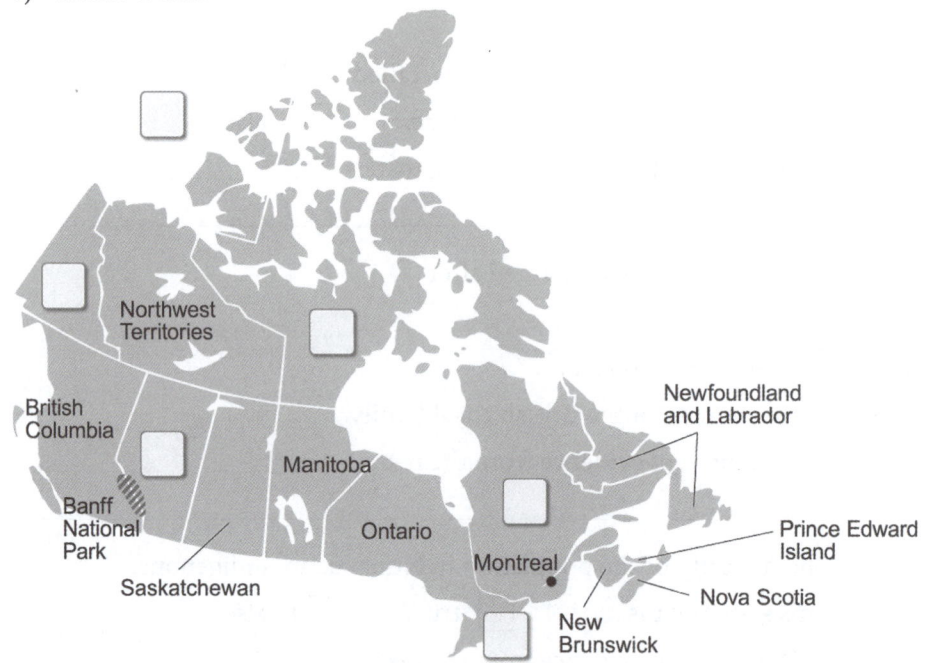

3. Match the headlines (1–7) to the paragraphs (A–E). Be careful, two of the headlines do not match.

	Headlines	Paragraphs
1	All the languages spoken in Canada	
2	How to visit Niagara Falls	
3	Geographical facts and background information	
4	Life in the far north	
5	Canada's official languages	
6	Winter in Nunavut	
7	National parks in Canada	

Reading Test 5: Volunteering in Australia

School's over? About time to learn something useful!

That's what 17-year-old Zachary Wilson thought after leaving Senior High School in Emerson, New Jersey – and he set out to the rain forest of the Southern Tablelands in Queensland, Australia, where he now helps to restore the living environment of tree kangaroos. At first his age was a problem as Conservation Volunteers Australia (CVA) – an organisation that coordinates volunteer projects across Australia – requires international volunteers to be over the age of 18. In the end he went together with his cousin Jacob, who is 28 and has just quit his job as a lawyer and is also looking for a new experience.

Australia has long been one of the top gap-year destinations for young people from around the globe who have just finished school and want to travel for a year before starting a job or continuing their education. Many of them feel they want to do "something useful" during this time and decide to do voluntary work for a few weeks. "Doing my bit towards helping with conservation in Australia made me feel I earned my right to travel in the country I was in," says Amy from Glasgow, UK.

There are all sorts of projects in Australia in need of volunteers who are willing to get their hands dirty for a while. Most of those projects focus on the protection of wildlife, for example looking after threatened animals like the tree kangaroo, the flatback sea turtle or the southern hairy-nosed wombat. By collecting rubbish, planting trees or removing plants that do not naturally belong to the Australian landscapes, volunteers can help to restore the typical living space of these species[1]. Constructing and maintaining walking trails or building fences in national parks are also very common activities. Sometimes volunteers also get the chance to assist in research programmes, for example they set up cameras to monitor endangered species. Last year CVA's over 7,000 volunteers planted 210,000 trees, performed 2,860 environmental surveys, and cleaned up 156 tonnes of rubbish.

Some of these volunteers are international travellers like Zach from New Jersey, but Australia is also known as a nation of volunteers with 38% of women and 34% of Australian men volunteering regularly. Imani, who volunteered at Townsville Conservation Park, is one of them and sums up her experience:

The best part was meeting six strangers and coming out of it with six new friends.

Apart from spending an adventurous time and making new friends, many volunteers also cherish the feeling of learning something about the environment and contributing to its protection. Amber, from Arizona, thinks: "This programme has taught me a great deal about conservation and what it takes to keep parts of a country safe for animals and plants. Life is too precious not to help the world and give something back." Especially young people who set out on a gap year feel that volunteering also makes a difference for themselves. "I've grown as a person and conquered so many fears," says Maggie from Canada. And of course it's not all about hard work. As Ben from South Africa puts it, he had "a blast[2]" and learned lots about himself, others, and the "great Aussie land".

1 species – type of plants or animals
2 to have a blast – to have lots of fun

Leseverstehen

For tasks **1, 2, 4, 6 and 7** tick the correct box and give evidence from the text by quoting short passages from the text.
For tasks **3 and 5** fill in the information.

1. Zachary Wilson went to Australia together with his cousin because …
   - [ ] he was afraid of travelling on his own.
   - [ ] his cousin had been offered a job as a lawyer there.
   - [ ] he was too young to take part in the volunteer programme alone.
   ▶ One piece of evidence from the text: _____
   _____

2. Many young people do voluntary work for one year after leaving school.
   This statement is …   [ ] true.   [ ] false.
   ▶ One piece of evidence from the text: _____
   _____

3. Why do young people decide to become volunteers in Australia?
   Give two examples from the text:
   ▶ _____
   ▶ _____

4. As a volunteer you shouldn't be afraid of physical work and getting dirty.
   This statement is …   [ ] true.   [ ] false.
   ▶ One piece of evidence from the text: _____
   _____

5. What are typical activities that volunteers can do?
   Give two examples from the text:
   ▶ _____
   ▶ _____

6. CVA's over 7,000 volunteers are from abroad.
   This statement is …   [ ] true.   [ ] false.
   ▶ One piece of evidence from the text: _____
   _____

7. Many young people feel that volunteering …
   - [ ] has changed them in a positive way.
   - [ ] has helped them decide which profession to choose.
   - [ ] has taught them how to travel safely in a foreign country.
   ▶ One piece of evidence from the text: _____
   _____

Reading Test 6: "We May Be 'Born Free', but …"

In South Africa, young people born after 1994 – the year when Nelson Mandela was elected the first black president – are often referred to as "born frees". They are the first generation to grow up in a free and democratic society, the first who no longer experienced the system of racial segregation that had characterised South Africa for almost half a century.

For "born frees" like Mbali Legodi, a black teenager from Cape Town, this period seems far away. "Of course, my parents and grandparents have often told me about it, but I can't really imagine what it must have been like. I think for most of our generation, it's normal to move around freely or be allowed to vote." Young South Africans nowadays take many of the hard-won privileges for granted, which has led some of the older generation to think of the "born frees" as spoiled or naive. Yet today's youngsters have to cope with problems of their own.

"Many of my friends are unemployed, there simply aren't enough jobs," Mbali says. According to recent statistics, about 50 per cent of South Africans between the ages of 15 and 24 are out of work. Black Africans seem to be particularly at risk of facing long-term joblessness. In addition, those who do find work also earn considerably less than the average white person. "I guess if you look at it from that perspective, not so much has changed. Even twenty years after the end of apartheid, the old inequalities are still in place."

Another problem is health: A large number of young people in South Africa are HIV-positive. Women are much more likely than men to be infected and suffer not only from insufficient medical treatment but also from social stigmatisation.

Like many of her generation, Mbali is frustrated with the government, who, she feels, is doing too little to fight HIV/AIDS, improve education or create new jobs. "If you ask me, our politicians are all corrupt. They only take our money to line their own pockets[1]."

Has she ever considered leaving South Africa and moving to another country? "I knew you would ask that. But no, never. I mean, just look around you: I live in the most beautiful country in the world. There are so many creative people, people who want to change things. We may be 'born free', but there's still a lot for us to do in this society."

What is Apartheid?

During the so-called "apartheid" era, the population was divided into four racial groups: "White", "Bantu" (black Africans), "Coloured" (of mixed ethnic origin) and "Asian". While people with British or Dutch roots enjoyed a lot of privileges, the non-white groups (especially black people) were systematically oppressed. For example, they were not allowed to vote and were forced to live in particular areas called "homelands". Public facilities were usually segregated into white and non-white zones so that white people did not have to share the same space with members of the other groups.

---

[1] to line one's own pockets – to take money for yourself that does not belong to you

For tasks **1** and **7** tick the correct box.
For tasks **2**, **3**, **4**, **5**, **8** and **9** tick the correct box and give evidence from the text by quoting short passages from the text.
For tasks **6** and **10** fill in the information.

1. The term "born frees" refers to …
   - [ ] the children of president Nelson Mandela.
   - [ ] black people who were released from prison.
   - [ ] young South Africans born after the end of apartheid.

2. A lot of young South Africans …
   - [ ] have never even heard of apartheid.
   - [ ] would like to have lived before 1994.
   - [ ] consider it normal to be living in a democratic society.
   ▸ One piece of evidence from the text: _____
   _____

3. Most young South Africans have a good chance of finding a job they like.
   This statement is … [ ] true.   [ ] false.
   ▸ One piece of evidence from the text: _____
   _____

4. Today, the inequalities of apartheid …
   - [ ] can still be felt.
   - [ ] have completely disappeared.
   - [ ] are laid down in the constitution.
   ▸ One piece of evidence from the text: _____
   _____

5. In South Africa, men have a higher risk of getting infected with HIV than women.
   This statement is … [ ] true.   [ ] false.
   ▸ One piece of evidence from the text: _____
   _____

6. What could the South African government do to improve the situation for the born frees? Give two examples from the text:
   ▸ _____
   ▸ _____

7. Mbali Legodi wants to …
   - [ ] study in Europe.
   - [ ] stay in her country.
   - [ ] start a new life abroad.

8. Like Mbali Legodi, a lot of young South Africans want to build a new society.
   This statement is … [ ] true.   [ ] false.
   ▶ One piece of evidence from the text: _____
   _____

9. During apartheid, people whose ancestors came from Great Britain or the Netherlands had many more rights than non-white people.
   This statement is … [ ] true.   [ ] false.
   ▶ One piece of evidence from the text: _____
   _____

10. What did racial segregation mean for black people?
    Give two examples from the text:
    ▶ _____
    ▶ _____

Reading Test 7: School Life Abroad

For this month's Teens Abroad *magazine, our reporter Joe Thompson met Tanja Huber, a girl from Germany, who has been staying with a host family and going to an English school for the past few months.*

A	"My host parents are really nice and I've become close friends with their two twin daughters, Amy and Megan." Together with her "sisters", Tanja leaves the house every morning at quarter to nine to go to St Thomas College in Bristol, which is only a five-minute bike ride away from the Millers' home.
B	"I'm also really glad that we're allowed to wear a polo shirt instead of a blouse, because it's much more comfortable." Registration is another thing that was new to her. As in all British schools, pupils at St Thomas College have to go to registration every morning and every afternoon after lunch to show that they are present.
C	When I met Tanja Huber for the first time, I was impressed by her English. "During the first month in which I did a language course in London and my four months here in Bristol I've learned a lot," Tanja says.
D	What she likes about it is that she does not have to think about what to wear to school every morning. "It saves a lot of time," she says. "I have to wear a blue skirt and blazer or pullover with the school's coat of arms[1] and a white polo shirt."
E	There is a quick registration in every lesson, too. "At first, I found it quite funny when teachers called out the pupils' names, and the pupils shouted out, 'Yes, sir' or 'Yes, ma'am', like in the military … But actually, it's a good thing: if a pupil is not there, everyone knows immediately, and it's very hard to miss a class on purpose."
F	Although school is very different in England, Tanja has got used to it, and she says that she enjoys it a lot. Wearing a school uniform is one of the things she did not like at first, but that has changed.
G	"But when I first came here, I had a lot of problems … My English was rubbish," she adds with a laugh and explains that this was one of the reasons why she decided to spend an entire school year in an English-speaking country. During this time, Tanja is staying with a host family, the Millers.

[1] coat of arms – *Wappen*

The text has been mixed up. Put the parts back in the correct order (❶–❼) by writing the correct letters in the table.

❶	❷	❸	❹	❺	❻	❼

Reading Test 8: The Double Life of Cassiel Roadnight

I was in a hostel[1], a stop-off for impossible kids in east London somewhere. I'd been there a couple of days, walked in off the streets half-starved, because I had to. […]

They gave me old clothes, washed thin and mended and almost the right size. They asked me lots of questions in return for two meals and a dry place to sleep. […]

"I'm Gordon," [the man] said. "And the lady's name is Ginny."

"Well done," I said. "Good for you."

"And you are?" he said.

I looked at my shoes, somebody else's shoes, black and lumpy and scuffed. […]

"I'm nobody," I said. […]

The Ginny woman came with something in her hand, a piece of paper. "Can I have a word?" she said.

Gordon got up and they left me in the room on my own again. I could hear them on the other side of the door. They were whispering, but I could still hear.

She said, "I only saw it this morning. Pure coincidence."

"Bloody hell."

"He's been gone nearly two years."

"Well. I. Never."

"Do you think it's him?"

"Look at it. It's got to be."

The door handle moved. […] When they came back in they were altered, careful, like I was a bomb that might go off, a sleeping tiger, a priceless vase about to fall. […]

"Cassiel?" [Ginny] said.

I looked straight at her. I didn't know what was going on. "What?"

"Cassiel Roadnight?" she asked.

My name is not Cassiel Roadnight. It never has been. […]

"Who, *me*?" I said. Gordon gave me the piece of paper. It was a printout, a picture of a boy with the word MISSING across his forehead. […]

"Oh my God," I said, and took in a breath and I held it. […]

My face exactly – my nose, my mouth, my chin. […] I kept my eyes on the picture. There was something wrong with it.

Here are some things I know for sure about my face. I see them every time I look in the mirror.

One. I have two scars. […]

Two. I have three piercings in my left ear and two in my right. […]

Three. My teeth are bad. […]

In the picture there were no scars on my face, no piercings. I had perfect teeth. I was happy and well fed and wholesome.

In other words, it wasn't me.

I tried to tell them. I looked up from the picture and I said, "No."

"Cassiel," Gordon said. He crossed his legs. His trousers and his mouth made a shushing noise.

I shook my head. "Not me." […]

"What are the odds," Gordon said to Ginny, like I wasn't there, "of there being two *identical* missing boys?"

"*Billions* to one," Ginny said, like that settled it.

"I don't care what the odds are," I said. "It's not me." […]

They didn't believe me. They wanted it to be right, I could tell that. They were going to insist on it. It doesn't matter what you say to people like that. When they have made up their minds they stop listening.

I breathed in hard and I tried not to think. I looked at the boy in the picture. I thought how incredible it was to have a double like that, somewhere out there in the world, to look exactly like a total stranger. I looked at Cassiel Roadnight's happy, flawless, fearless face. And the thought occurred to me then, that I could be him, if I wanted. […]

There were people looking for Cassiel Roadnight, but they were people who cared. He had a family and friends. He had loved ones. He had a life I could step right into. And what did I have?

Nobody. Nothing […].

I always wanted to be someone else. Doesn't everyone?

"OK," I said to the thought, so quietly I almost didn't say it at all.

"What?" Gordon said.

They looked at each other and then back at me. It was like they'd been holding everything in. Suddenly there was this noise in the room of them breathing.

"OK," I said.

"Good," said Ginny, and Gordon said, "Your name is Cassiel Roadnight?"

"Yes," I told him. "My name is Cassiel Roadnight," and I watched the smile spread and stick to his face.

1 hostel – here: shelter for homeless people

Adapted from: Valentine, Jenny. 2010. The Double Life of Cassiel Roadnight. London: HarperCollins, pp. 7–17.

For tasks **1**, **5 and 6** tick the correct box and give evidence from the text by quoting short passages from the text.
For tasks **2**, **3 and 7** tick the correct box.
For task **4** fill in the information.

1. The narrator comes to the hostel …
   - [ ] while he is on holiday in London.
   - [ ] to buy some second-hand clothes.
   - [ ] because he desperately needs something to eat.

   ▶ One piece of evidence from the text: _____

2. The narrator's real name is …
   - [ ] Gordon.
   - [ ] not mentioned.
   - [ ] Cassiel Roadnight.

3. The man and woman suddenly treat the narrator differently because they …
   - [ ] think he might be dangerous.
   - [ ] want him to identify another boy.
   - [ ] think he might be a missing person.

4. What do we know about the narrator's looks?
   Give two examples from the text:
   - ▸ _____
   - ▸ _____

5. The narrator is sure that the picture shows …
   - [ ] him.
   - [ ] someone he knows.
   - [ ] a person he does not know.
   - ▸ One piece of evidence from the text: _____

6. The narrator is quite satisfied with his life as it is.
   This statement is … [ ] true.   [ ] false.
   ▸ One piece of evidence from the text: _____

7. Eventually, the narrator decides to …
   - [ ] return to his family.
   - [ ] take on a new identity.
   - [ ] stay at the hostel for a longer time.

Reading Test 9: Boot Camps for Teenagers

Teenagers doing military-style drill practices and being shouted at by their supervisors for the smallest mistake? – You might think this is just a TV invention, but they exist for real: boot camps were introduced in the U.S. in the early 1980s as one idea to reduce youth crime and to re-educate young criminals. The name was first used by the U.S. military for camps in which new soldiers were trained under extreme conditions. Soldiers had to learn to obey at all times and cope with enormous stress. After the non-stop, all-day training in boot camps they knew how to use military equipment in their sleep. Officers did not praise them, but any mistake or weakness was immediately punished. The idea was to break a person down and then rebuild them with the "correct" behaviour. While these methods might be acceptable for soldiers, can you do the same to young criminals?

Boot camps are seen as a punishment that is worse than probation[1], and not as bad as prison. The central ideas behind boot camps are the following: deterrence – the idea that they could go to boot camp should scare youths. More practical ideas are that this system will reduce the number of prisoners and lower costs. Another aim is that young people who have been to boot camp will not return to crime.

The methods can be called "shock treatment": military-style training and marching. Teenagers have to stay at boot camp for 90 to 180 days. Some youths choose boot camp instead of a prison sentence, or a judge can send them to boot camp as their punishment. It is also possible for parents to send their children to boot camp if they feel they can no longer handle them at home.

The harsh methods in boot camps received a lot of criticism, especially after 14-year-old Martin Lee Anderson was beaten to death by his instructors in a camp in Florida. After this incident boot camps were closed down in Florida in 2006, but they still exist in other U.S. states. Since 1980 there have been at least 30 deaths in boot camps.

As a reaction to the criticism, many boot camps now also offer other activities: educational courses, therapy, and special programmes for drug addicts. However, critics think these measures are still not enough to balance the strict system.

The goals of the boot camp system – deterrence and the reduction of recidivism[2] – have so far not been achieved. The rate of recidivism for boot camps and prisons is about the same; youths coming out of a boot camp are just as likely to return to crime as those coming out of prison. And boot camps as a deterrence? Very hard to say. How can anyone calculate how many youths have not committed crimes because they are scared of boot camp?

The most common criticism of the system is this: Is it possible to force children to submit[3] to a system of exhausting physical and psychological stress, in an unfamiliar and aggressive environment, and expect them to develop respect for themselves and other people? Or is it more likely that such a system fixated on obedience and strict rules will develop frustration, a feeling of inferiority and, of course, aggression? These seem to be exactly the factors that lead young people to commit crime in the first place.

Canadians have been studying their neighbours' system, too. Like most European countries, Canada is against military influences in civil society. Canadians have chosen something else – "wilderness camps", which count on

"adventure therapy" and "outdoor education". They try to work on the youths'
95 behaviour by using more positive methods. The Canadian approach has a far lower rate of recidivism.

1 probation – the young person does not have to go to prison, but is under regular supervision
2 recidivism – criminals who are involved in crime again after having been punished for a crime already (Rückfallkriminalität)
3 (to) submit to sth – (to) accept sth, (to) give in to sth

For tasks **1**, **6 and 11** tick the correct box.
For tasks **2**, **4**, **7**, **8**, **9 and 10** tick the correct box and give evidence from the text by quoting short passages from the text.
For tasks **3 and 5** fill in the information.

1. Boot camps were originally developed …
   - [ ] for the army.
   - [ ] for a TV show.
   - [ ] by the owner of a fitness studio.

2. The extreme training methods used in boot camps were meant to …
   - [ ] break people's will.
   - [ ] increase people's physical fitness.
   - [ ] strengthen people's self-confidence.
   ▶ One piece of evidence from the text: _____
   _____

3. Which goals did the government have in mind when they introduced boot camps for teenagers? Give two examples from the text:
   ▶ _____
   ▶ _____

4. Youths can be sent to boot camp for as long as six months.
   This statement is …   [ ] true.   [ ] false.
   ▶ One piece of evidence from the text: _____
   _____

5. What are the reasons for teenagers being sent to boot camp?
   Give two examples from the text:
   ▶ _____
   ▶ _____

6. After a teenager's death in boot camp, …
   - [ ] there have been attempts to reform the system.
   - [ ] the instructors were sent on educational courses.
   - [ ] this kind of punishment was forbidden in the USA.

7. The number of teenagers who return to crime …
   - [ ] is lower with boot camps than with prisons.
   - [ ] is higher with boot camps than with prisons.
   - [ ] is more or less equal with boot camps and prisons.
   - ▶ One piece of evidence from the text: _____
   _____

8. It is not quite clear whether boot camps have an effect as a deterrent.
   This statement is …   [ ] true.   [ ] false.
   - ▶ One piece of evidence from the text: _____
   _____

9. Critics of the boot camp system …
   - [ ] say that there is too little state regulation of the camps.
   - [ ] worry that the camps might increase problematic feelings.
   - [ ] admit that it can teach young criminals to respect other people.
   - ▶ One piece of evidence from the text: _____
   _____

10. Canada's approach to fighting youth crime is almost the same as in the USA.
    This statement is …   [ ] true.   [ ] false.
    - ▶ One piece of evidence from the text: _____
    _____

11. Look at the text as a whole again. The overall aim of the text is to …
    - [ ] compare military boot camps to wilderness camps.
    - [ ] inform the reader about boot camps for young criminals.
    - [ ] give an overview of different boot camp systems in Europe and North America.

Reading Test 10: Bog Child

The novel Bog Child *by Siobhan Dowd is set in the early 1980s in the border region between Northern Ireland and the Irish Republic. Joey McCann has joined the Provisional IRA ("Provos") and is in Long Kesh prison on a hunger strike. His younger brother Fergus secretly smuggles packages for the Provisional IRA over the border, while pretending to simply go running in the hills. During some of his tours across the border, Fergus chatted with the British border guard Owain and even became something of a friend with him, but of course told him nothing about his secret mission. One day, their encounter is different from the ones before.*

Read the following extract, then do the tasks.

1 Fergus stood up, checked his packages and began his final run.
He didn't loop the long way round, but headed straight to the sentry hut[1]. [...]
Perhaps nobody would be there. Perhaps if nobody was there, that would be a sign. A sign that he should just take the packets and post them through the door of the police
5 station in Roscillin and wash his hands of it.
Perhaps ...
He drew up to the hut, and in the doorway was a slender silhouette: half a rifle, half a cigarette, half a torso. For a moment the figure looked taller than Owain. Fergus froze. He'd never once considered the possibility that somebody other than Owain might
10 be on duty.
The figure turned and peered, shading its eyes. "Fergus. I'm glad it's you. It's a good cool day for running."
Fergus's heart leaped, then fell again. He swallowed and walked forward. "Owain."
He walked into Owain's sights and raised his hands.
15 Owain raised two eyes to heaven. "Hello, Mr Terrorist." He rattled the rifle on his shoulder. "How's the rebellion going?"
Fergus scrunched up his eyes. "I'm serious. I'm handing myself in."
"Great. So what am I supposed to do? Frog-march you all the way to Roscillin?"
"Owain. Honest. I've two packages here." Fergus slowly drew a brown bag from his
20 waistband. Owain made no move. He looked on with a wondering smile. Fergus put the packet on the ground at Owain's feet. He placed the second packet alongside it.
"There. All yours."
Owain's cigarette burned down to the stub. He flicked it away. "What's in them?"
"Dunno.[2]"
25 "You're pulling my leg[3], Fergus. [...]" [...]
They both stood still, watching each other. Owain grinned. "OK. So tell me more about these packets."
Beads of sweat trickled down Fergus's back. "Can I sit on that rock?"
"Feel free."
30 [...] "You know the brother I told you about last time? The one I said was in Rome?"
"Yeah. The lucky bugger. What about him?"
"He's not in Rome."
"No?"
"He's in Long Kesh." The words were like a door slamming shut, the end of the
35 chatting and the camaraderie.
Owain frowned as if puzzled. "You mean the Maze[4]?"
"Yes. Our Joey's in there and he's on hunger strike. Day fifty."
"Day fifty?" Owain echoed.

Fergus nodded.
[…] "I'm sorry, Fergus."
"Yeah. Me too."
"Is he –?"
"Conscious? Kind of. We expect to hear he's gone into a coma any day."
They said nothing. Fergus pressed his palm into a crack in the rock, hard.
"So what's that got to do with these?" Owain tipped the rifle nozzle towards the packets on the ground. […]
"The Provos approached me. Don't ask me who. I can't say."
"The Provos?"
Fergus nodded. "They asked me to smuggle these back and forth over the border. And that's what I've been doing. All summer long."
"So you haven't exactly been training for the Olympics?"
"No. I did run before the packets. But the Provos caught on to me. They saw their chance." Fergus wrung his hands. "Believe me, Owain, I didn't mean to get involved. But they said if I did this for them, they'd send in the word to Joey to order him off his strike."
"And you believed them?"
Fergus's cheeks were on fire. "Yes. At first." He wiped the sweat off his forehead. "Then nothing happened. Joe said the Provos were right behind him. So I stopped believing."
"But you kept going with the packets."
"Yes."
"Why?" […]
Fergus was silent.
"Why, Fergus? Did they threaten you?"
"No."
"Your family?"
"No." He looked up.
Owain stared at him, his face pinched.
Fergus gulped. "You. They threatened you."
"Me?"
Fergus nodded. […]
"But why pick on me?"
Fergus sighed, sick to his stomach. "I told them about you. How we'd got talking. And your being from Wales. He said you'd have been better off staying down a mine."
[…]
"So what d'you want me to do, Fergus?"
"Shoot me. Arrest me. I don't care. I just want out. […] Those packets, Owain. Somebody out there's received the ones I've already delivered. They're putting together a bomb, I know it. You have to turn me in. I can't stand the guilt. It's killing me. I'd rather go to prison. Serve time. Like I said, I want out."
Owain picked up the packets from the ground and placed them on the rock where Fergus had been sitting. Together they stared at them. "Tell you what, Fergus. We'll open them." Owain got a Swiss army knife out of a pocket and opened up a narrow silver blade.

Abridged and adapted from: Dowd, Siobhan. 2010 (2008). Bog Child. Oxford: David Flickling Books. pp. 244–249.

1 sentry hut – *Wachhäuschen*
2 Dunno. [colloquial] – I don't know.
3 You're pulling my leg – You're kidding me / You're making that up
4 the Maze – another name for Long Kesh prison

Leseverstehen | 85

Tick the correct box and give evidence from the text by quoting short passages from the text.

1. Fergus is trying his best to avoid the border station.

   This statement is ... ☐ true. ☐ false.

   ▶ One piece of evidence from the text: _____
   _____

2. Fergus is sure that a border guard different from Owain will be there.

   This statement is ... ☐ true. ☐ false.

   ▶ One piece of evidence from the text: _____
   _____

3. At first, Owain thinks that Fergus ...

   ☐ is only joking.
   ☐ is bringing a present.
   ☐ wants to threaten him.

   ▶ One piece of evidence from the text: _____
   _____

4. Fergus's brother Joey is ...

   ☐ in Rome to recover.
   ☐ getting better day by day.
   ☐ in a very critical condition.

   ▶ One piece of evidence from the text: _____
   _____

5. Fergus agreed to smuggle the packets for the Provisional IRA because ...

   ☐ he was convinced of their political agenda.
   ☐ they promised to send him to the Olympics.
   ☐ he was hoping they might make Joey stop his hunger strike.

   ▶ One piece of evidence from the text: _____
   _____

6. Fergus kept holding his smuggle tours ...

   ☐ in order to protect Owain.
   ☐ because his family was in danger.
   ☐ because he had to finish a mission for the IRA.

   ▶ One piece of evidence from the text: _____
   _____

7. Fergus is turning himself in because …
   ☐ he has a bad conscience.
   ☐ Owain is threatening to shoot him.
   ☐ he wants to join his brother Joey in the hunger strike.
   ▶ One piece of evidence from the text: _____
   _____

8. In the end, Owain decides to …
   ☐ arrest Fergus.
   ☐ destroy the packets.
   ☐ find out what is inside the packets.
   ▶ One piece of evidence from the text: _____
   _____

3 Wortschatz – Verfügbarkeit sprachlicher Mittel

Die Aufgabenstellungen, die dir im Unterricht, in Klassenarbeiten und in Prüfungen zum Kompetenzbereich Wortschatz begegnen, sind sehr vielfältig. Ziel dieser Aufgaben ist es, deinen persönlichen Wortschatz zu testen. Um dich mit möglichst vielen Aufgabenformaten vertraut zu machen, enthält der Übungsteil auch Aufgaben, denen du in der MSA-Prüfung vermutlich nicht begegnen wirst, die aber in anderen Prüfungen verlangt sein können.

3.1 Strategien zum Bereich „Wortschatz"

Strategien zum Vokabellernen

Um im Bereich Wortschatz gut abzuschneiden, ist es wichtig, dass du langfristig und nachhaltig übst. Vokabeln zu lernen klingt nicht gerade aufregend, ist für den Erwerb einer Fremdsprache aber unerlässlich. Und es liegt an dir, kreativ zu sein und eine Methode zu finden, die dir vielleicht sogar ein bisschen Spaß macht. Je größer dein aktiver Wortschatz ist, je mehr Wörter du also in der Fremdsprache kennst und selbst in Gesprächen oder beim Schreiben anwenden kannst, desto treffender und abwechslungsreicher kannst du dich in der Fremdsprache ausdrücken. Um den aktiven Wortschatz zu vergrößern, gibt es verschiedene Methoden. Sieh dir am besten das Lernvideo ▶ zum effektiven Vokabellernen an und lies dir die folgenden Seiten gut durch.

Natürlich ist zunächst einmal das **Vokabelheft** zu erwähnen. Du weißt, wie es funktioniert: Richte dir auf jeder Doppelseite **drei Spalten** ein, eine für den englischen Begriff, eine für die deutsche Bedeutung und eine, in der du den Ausdruck in einem Beispielsatz verwendest. Zum Lernen deckst du dann jeweils eine Spalte ab.

Methode **1**

Noch effektiver ist es, die Vokabeln mit einem **Karteisystem** zu lernen.
Falls du gerne am Computer oder mit dem Smartphone arbeitest, findest du viele Programme/Apps, die dich dabei unterstützen. Du kannst die Vokabeln aber natürlich auch auf Papierkärtchen notieren. Schreibe den englischen Begriff auf die Vorderseite der Karte. Notiere dazu auch einen englischen Satz, in dem die Vokabel vorkommt. So lernst du gleich die Verwendung des Wortes mit. Notiere auch sonst alles, was zu dem Begriff gehört. Bei Verben solltest du z. B. nicht nur den Infinitiv, sondern ggf. auch unregelmäßige Formen oder die Präposition, die das Verb nach sich zieht, ergänzen. Auf der Rückseite der Karteikarte schreibst du die deutsche Bedeutung der Vokabel auf.
Die Karteikartenmethode hat im Vergleich zum Vokabelheft **Vorteile**:

Methode **2**

▶ Du kannst die Karteikarten drei Stapeln zuordnen.
Stapel 1: **Wörter, die neu für dich sind.** Diese Wörter solltest du mindestens jeden zweiten Tag durchgehen. Lies dabei auch immer den englischen Satz durch, den du auf der Karteikarte notiert hast. Manchmal ist es leichter, sich ein Wort im Satzzusammenhang zu merken als als einzelne Vokabel. Sobald du die neue Vokabel kennst, legst du sie auf Stapel 2 ab.

Stapel 2: **Wörter, die du noch nicht so sicher im Kopf hast.** Diesen Stapel solltest du regelmäßig durchgehen und dabei die Vokabeln üben. Wenn du eine Vokabel sicher weißt, legst du sie auf Stapel 3 ab.

Stapel 3: **Wörter, die du schon sehr gut beherrschst.** Diesen Stapel solltest du hin und wieder einmal durchblättern, um zu sehen, ob du alle Vokabeln noch richtig beherrschst.

Eine App erkennt in der Regel selbst, welche Wörter du schon gut beherrschst und welche du noch üben musst. Sie unterstützt dich dabei, die schwierigen Wörter in regelmäßigen Abständen zu wiederholen.

▶ Bei einem System aus Papier bist du dafür etwas freier bei der Zusammenstellung der Wörter. Du kannst die Karteikarten je nach augenblicklicher Lernsituation nach **Wortfeldern** (z. B. *weather: wind, to snow, sun*) oder nach **Wortfamilien** (z. B. *business, businessman, businesswoman, busy*) ordnen. Dabei bist du sehr flexibel und kannst die Wortfelder bzw. Wortfamilien jederzeit erweitern bzw. umbauen.

Egal ob mit dem Smartphone oder auf Papierkärtchen, ein paar Vokabeln kannst du bestimmt auch einfach zwischendurch – z. B. auf dem Weg zur Schule oder ins Kino – wiederholen.

Bei beiden Methoden, Vokabelheft oder Karteisystem, solltest du dir auch sinnvolle Ergänzungen zu den Vokabeln überlegen. Manchmal kann dir ein **Bild** dabei helfen, dir ein Wort oder eine Wendung besser zu merken. Füge also Zeichnungen oder Fotos hinzu. Denke auch an die **Aussprache** und sage die Wörter beim Lernen am besten laut vor dich hin. Wenn du dir unsicher bist, kannst du dir in einem Online-Wörterbuch (z. B. „LEO") die richtige Aussprache anhören.

Methode 3

Du kannst natürlich auch kreativ sein und dir deine eigene Methode zum Vokabellernen ausdenken. Das macht viel Spaß und bringt langfristig gesehen sicherlich den besten Lernerfolg. Je intensiver du dich mit dem Wortschatz beschäftigst, desto besser kannst du ihn dir einprägen und desto schneller hast du auch die passenden Wendungen parat, wenn du etwas sagen oder schreiben möchtest.

▶ Zeichne dir **Mindmaps** zu gelernten Vokabeln. Du kannst sie – auch hier wieder abhängig von deiner augenblicklichen Lernsituation – nach Wortfeldern oder Wortfamilien zusammenstellen. Diese Mindmaps kannst du an zentralen Stellen in deinem Zimmer aufhängen. Jedes Mal, wenn du daran vorbeikommst, gehst du die entsprechenden Vokabeln im Kopf durch.

Beispiel

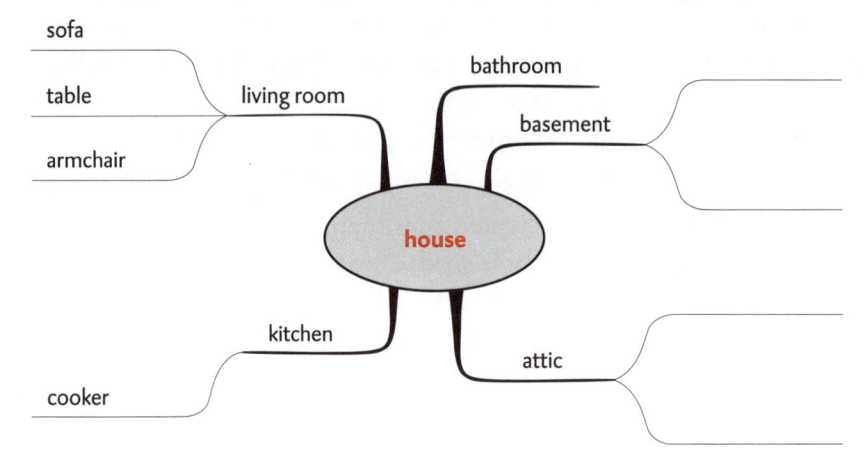

```
sofa
table        living room      bathroom
armchair                      basement
                    house
             kitchen           attic
cooker
```

▶ Immer, wenn du eine neue Vokabel gelernt hast, schreibst du den Begriff auf einen Zettel und befestigst ihn am entsprechenden Gegenstand bei dir zu Hause. So klebst du beispielsweise einen Zettel mit dem Begriff „cupboard" an euren Küchenschrank. Das funktioniert zum Teil auch mit abstrakten Begriffen: Die Vokabel „proud" könntest du z. B. an das Regalfach heften, in dem deine Schulsachen sind. Denn sicherlich bist du „stolz" darauf, dass du in der Schule schon so weit gekommen bist, oder? Mit dieser Zettelmethode kannst du neue Vokabeln jedenfalls ganz einfach nebenbei, quasi „im Vorbeigehen", trainieren.

▶ Du kannst auch deiner Fantasie freien Lauf lassen und dir eine Methode überlegen, die dir gefällt, selbst wenn sie ein bisschen verrückt ist – z. B. Smartphone-Videos für verschiedene „feelings" zu drehen oder eine Collage mit Ausschnitten aus Filmplakaten zu erstellen, zu denen du Verben schreibst, die die „Action" beschreiben ... Es liegt ganz bei dir.

Versuche grundsätzlich immer wieder, die neuen Vokabeln anzuwenden, am besten in einem vollständigen englischen Satz. Wenn du dich mit Klassenkameraden unterhältst, könnt ihr daraus vielleicht ein richtiges Spiel machen.

Welche Methode du auch anwendest oder mit anderen Strategien kombinierst, lerne nie zu viele Vokabeln auf einmal! Am besten ist es, wenn du neue Vokabeln immer in kleinen Gruppen von sechs bis sieben Wörtern lernst. Lies sie dir zunächst ein paar Mal durch, wiederhole sie auch laut und lege sie dann für etwa 20 Minuten zur Seite. Dann fängst du von vorne an. Diese Pausen sind wichtig, damit sich das gerade Gelernte „setzen" kann. So wird es dir ein Leichtes sein, bald einen großen englischen Wortschatz anzusammeln.

Tipp

- Lerne langfristig. In der Fremdsprache einen großen aktiven Wortschatz zu haben, ist sehr wichtig.
- Lege ein Vokabelheft an oder arbeite mit einem Karteisystem. Lerne die Vokabeln im Satzzusammenhang.
- Lerne deine Vokabeln immer in Gruppen von sechs bis sieben Wörtern. Mache zwischen deinen Lerneinheiten regelmäßig kleine Pausen, damit sich das Gelernte „setzen" kann.
- Trainiere beim Lernen auch die Aussprache.
- Sei kreativ beim Vokabellernen: Zeichne Mindmaps, beschrifte die Gegenstände in deinem Zimmer, drehe ein Video ...

3.2 Häufige Aufgabenstellungen im Bereich „Wortschatz"

Im Wortschatz-Teil der MSA-Prüfung wird dir meist ein Text über ein bestimmtes Thema vorgelegt (beispielsweise „Tipps on how to deal with social media"). Um dein Vokabular zu testen, ist der Text in einzelne Sätze oder Abschnitte unterteilt, in denen du jeweils einen passenden Begriff einsetzen *(filling in gaps)* oder das richtige Wort aus einer vorgegebenen Auswahl abhaken musst *(multiple choice)*. Diese beiden Aufgabentypen kommen in der Prüfung am häufigsten vor.

Multiple choice

Bei den Multiple-Choice-Aufgaben musst du auswählen, welches der vorgegebenen Wörter am besten in den Satz passt. Du musst dich also z. B. für das passende Verb oder die richtige Präposition entscheiden und die richtige Lösung abhaken.

Beispiel

Task (and solution):
Tick (✓) the correct box.

You can find information about the British school system …

☐ at   ✓ on   ☐ over   ☐ in

the internet.

Filling in gaps

Bei diesem Aufgabenformat wird dein Vokabular anhand von Lückensätzen geprüft. Du musst also einen Begriff finden, der inhaltlich und grammatikalisch in den vorgegebenen Satzzusammenhang passt.

Beispiel

Task (and solution):
Fill in suitable words.

Unemployment is an enormous challenge – many people nowadays have __problems / difficulties__ finding a job.

Neben Multiple-Choice-Aufgaben und Lückensätzen sind in der MSA-Prüfung prinzipiell auch andere Aufgabenformate denkbar, z. B. *Matching*-Aufgaben oder Mindmaps:

Matching

Matching- bzw. Zuordnungsaufgaben können unterschiedlich aufgebaut sein. Es kann z. B. sein, dass dir einzelne Begriffe aus einem Text vorgegeben werden. Du sollst diesen Begriffen die passende Umschreibung zuordnen und die richtige Lösung in eine Tabelle eintragen. Manchmal stehen dabei mehr Umschreibungen zur Auswahl als es Begriffe gibt – du darfst dich also nicht durch falsche Auswahlmöglichkeiten in die Irre führen lassen.

Text:
One environmental problem that particularly affects countries in northern Africa is desertification. Huge areas of land which were once used for farming or as pasture for cattle or sheep are now deserts.

Task (and solution):
Look at the text. What do the following words mean? Match the expressions (A–C) with their corresponding definitions (1–4). Write the correct numbers in the grid. Be careful: there is one more definition than you need.

A pasture
B cattle
C desert

1 an area of land that has very little water and very few plants in it
2 a type of plant with sharp spines that grows in dry areas
3 land on which animals can graze
4 a group of cows, bulls and calves

A	B	C
3	4	1

Beispiel

Creating a mind map

Dein Wortschatz kann z. B. auch mithilfe von Mindmaps oder anderen „offenen" Aufgabenformaten überprüft werden. Dabei musst du Begriffe, die zu einem vorgegebenen Thema oder Überbegriff passen, ergänzen.

Task (and solution):
Complete the mind map with words relating to means of transport.

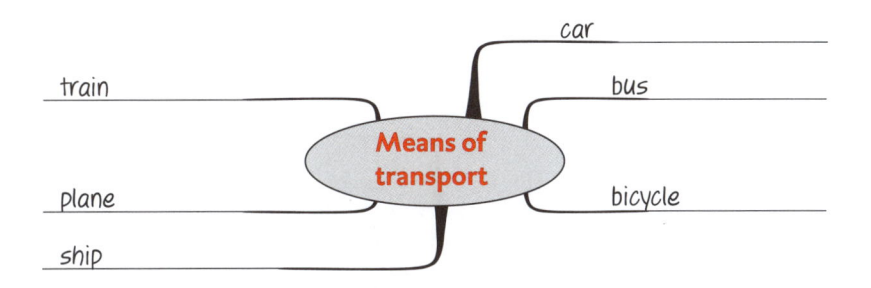

Beispiel

Mind map: **Means of transport** — car, bus, bicycle, ship, plane, train

In Klassenarbeiten und Tests kann darüber hinaus eine Vielzahl weiterer Aufgabenformate zum Einsatz kommen, die hier nicht alle thematisiert werden können. Einige davon (z. B. *synonyms and opposites*, Wortfamilien) sind aber im folgenden Kapitel mit Übungsaufgaben enthalten (Kapitel 3.3). Bei den Aufgaben 1 bis 13 handelt es sich um **Übungen zum Grundwissen**, mit denen du ganz allgemein deinen Wortschatz wiederholen kannst. Wenn du gerne testen möchtest, ob du schon für den MSA gerüstet bist, findest du am Ende des Kapitels drei **prüfungsähnliche Aufgaben** (Aufgaben 14 bis 16).

3.3 Übungsaufgaben zum Bereich „Wortschatz"

Aufgaben zum Grundwissen

1. **Word fields** – Complete the mind maps below.

   a) Use the words from the box to complete the three mind maps. You can use each word only once.

   > ~~window~~ – pencil – rain – pupil – hot – living room – teacher – storm – exercise book – kitchen – subject – snow – floor – lesson – sun – bath tub – cold – bedroom

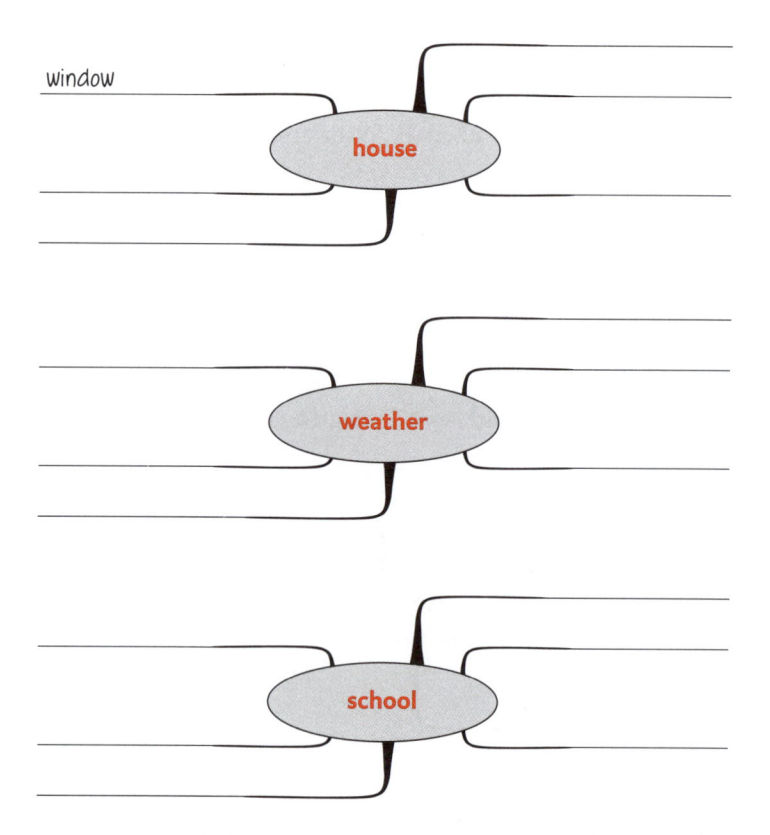

   (mind map: house, with "window" filled in)

   (mind map: weather)

   (mind map: school)

   b) Make a mind map for "furniture". This time you do not have any help.

   (mind map: furniture)

Wortschatz | 93

2. **Word fields** – Find the missing nationalities, countries and languages. Complete the table.

the people	the country	the language
(the) Australians	Australia	English
	England	
(the) French		
(the) Spanish		
		Italian
(the) Americans		
	Germany	
		Dutch
		Turkish
(the) Canadians		

3. **Word fields** – Fill in the missing words.

Peter moved to Poland two months ago. As he doesn't speak any Polish yet, he started a language course last week. The other students in his course are from many different countries. Jenny, for example, is from Manchester in the North of _____. She's _____. Jan comes from Amsterdam in _____. He's _____. Ismael is _____. He's from Istanbul. Istanbul is in _____. Then there's Pietro. He comes from Rome, the capital of _____. Pietro only speaks _____. Louise used to live in Paris. She's _____. Many people in _____ only speak _____, but Louise speaks Portuguese and English, too. José is from Madrid, the capital of _____. He isn't _____, because he was born in Mexico, where people also speak _____. The girl Peter likes the most is called Sophia. She's _____. She was born in Quebec. That is why her native language isn't English, but _____.

4. **Word fields** – Each job has something to do with an object, people or animals. Join them together.

   ❶ doctor   A restaurant
   ❷ vet   B boat
   ❸ pilot   C pupils
   ❹ builder   D plants
   ❺ mechanic   E plane
   ❻ teacher   F house
   ❼ sailor   G cars
   ❽ gardener   H hospital
   ❾ chef   I animals

❶	❷	❸	❹	❺	❻	❼	❽	❾

5. **Words in context** – Read the following story carefully and fill in the missing words. You are only given the first letter.

   London is the c_____ of England. It's a very l_____ city with m_____ interesting s_____. It's also a city with a great nightlife. There are lots of c_____, theatres, and, of course, clubs, r_____ and pubs. There is a_____ lots to do and see. You can v_____ Buckingham Palace or see Downing Street where the prime minister l_____. There is also a big wheel called the "London Eye". From the t_____ of it there is a f_____ view over London, but it is very h_____! The b_____ way to see London, though, is on f_____ or by a city tour on a r_____ double-decker b_____. London is a w_____ city – everyone should visit it s_____.

6. **Words in context** – Fill in the missing words and phrases. Add the preposition "of" where necessary.

   On _____ (date: 5/8) last year I went to Paris for the day. The flight was only 75 minutes long. In Paris, I bought a lot of things. They had lovely biscuits, so I got six _____ (Packungen) very nice ones. Paris was very hot, so I had to carry a _____ (Flasche) water around with me all the time. I drank so many _____ (Flaschen) water I didn't count them all. I bought my mum a _____ (Glas) French marmalade and my dad a _____ (Liter) French wine. I had a great time!

7. **Crossword puzzle** – Find out the name of a famous American singer.
   1. Native Americans are the original ??? of America.
   2. During the so-called "??? rush" in the nineteenth century many people came to California looking for the precious metal.
   3. The American bison, or ??? (as it is called by some people), nearly died out.
   4. The idea that everyone can make it if he or she tries hard enough is called the American ???.
   5. The Declaration of Independence from 1776 promises the right to life, ??? (= freedom) and the pursuit of happiness.
   6. ??? was not abolished until 1865 – before that time, most black people were "owned" by white people and forced to work for them.
   7. The Civil Rights Movement fought for ??? (= the same) rights for African Americans.
   8. President Kennedy called the United States a nation of ??? because many people came from other countries to live there.

   The famous American singer who won the Nobel Prize for Literature in 2016 is _____.

8. **Opposites** – Make the opposite of each sentence. The word that you have to change is underlined.
   a) The train is late.

   b) I have just caught the last bus home.

   c) I've lost my watch.

   d) He's bought a car.

   e) Julie's water bottle is full.

9. **Synonyms** – Find words or expressions which mean more or less the same as the underlined words.

   a) The frontier between the USA and Mexico is 1,954 miles long.

   b) The entire world was shocked when the popular actor died so young.

   c) Last year he at last got the academy award he had been hoping for for so long.

   d) Huge skyscrapers shape the skyline of Manhattan.

   e) Do you have any plans to spend some time abroad after your GCSEs?

   f) If you live in an English-speaking country for a few months, your English will improve significantly.

   g) Just a few more miles. We're almost there!

   h) When I saw her face, I knew at once what had happened.

10. **Definitions** – Write in complete sentences to explain the meanings of the following words.

    a) century

    b) to shake hands

    c) a first aid kit

    d) rubbish

    e) school subject

    f) to explore

11. **Word families** – Complete the following table of word families.

verb	noun(s)	adjective(s)	verb + preposition
to believe	belief	believable	to believe in (sb/sth)
to know			
		educational, educated	
to mean			
	success		
to differ			
		various, varied	
to act			
		spoken	
		inviting	

12. **Word forms** – Read the text. Write down the suitable form of the words or find a word or expression yourself where there is a "?".

I really like music. I have never played a _____ (music) instrument in my life but I have always found _____ (sing) fascinating. For me they are _____ (interest) in two ways. First, I find that as time goes _____ (?) they remind me of things that have happened in my _____ (live). I remember my first girlfriend, _____ (?) example, by a song that was always on the radio at that time. Secondly, I'm fascinated with what the lyrics really _____ (meaning). It was only _____ (recent), for example, that I discovered what Bob Marley was singing about in his song "Buffalo Soldier". Buffalo soldiers were _____ (Africa) who fought for the Americans against the Native Americans. June is also a _____ (create) but maybe not very _____ (fame) singer-songwriter. Although I _____ (probable) won't remember many of her songs in the future, I can relate to the _____ (express) of _____ (feel) in her lyrics and enjoy her live _____ (perform). If you ever find the time, listen to a song carefully and try to find _____ (?) what it is about and why it was written – you'll probably find it interesting, too.

13. Underline the correct word to use for each sentence.

    a) Tim gave his *meaning / opinion / think* about the film to his friends.

    b) On the *back side / backside / back* of the letter there was a small picture.

    c) I'm going to *drive / go / run* to London by train.

    d) We need to talk *on / about / to* the problems we have got.

    e) It was *happily / warmly / terribly* wet in Scotland when we went there.

    f) Can I *see / look at / watch* television, please?

    g) Chloe isn't home yet but you can call her on her *mobile / handy / telly*.

    h) I'm really looking *about / forward to / for* our holiday in Canada – I'm sure it'll be great!

    i) Could you turn *off / out / in* the computer before you go to bed, please?

14. *Teen-e-news* is an online magazine for young people. Their latest article deals with the possible dangers of the internet.
    Fill in suitable words or tick (✓) the correct box.

    a) Most of us _____ the internet several times a day.

    b) But are there some things that one should be careful …

    ☐ off ☐ about
    ☐ over ☐ to

    when being online?

    c) The _____, of course, is a very big "Yes".

    d) Firstly, you should always …

    ☐ stick ☐ bury
    ☐ keep ☐ stay

    in mind that not all the information on websites is correct.

    e) So try to find things out from …

    ☐ costly ☐ dependent
    ☐ confident ☐ reliable

    sources.

    f) Also, _____ attention to what you tell people on social networking sites.

    g) "Hi, my parents are away – I'm having a party on Saturday," isn't a very _____ thing to write.

h) It is always advisable not to …

☐ give ☐ do
☐ write ☐ tell

away too many personal details, especially ones that can put you in a bad light.

i) Yesterday, it might have been cool to write "I'm a lazy guy", but some _____ use websites to find out more about the people who want to work for them.

j) So these kind of messages or posts could turn into a real problem when you are applying …

☐ on ☐ at
☐ for ☐ about

a job.

15. Noah is a blogger from London. In his latest blog entry, he writes about proms in the USA and Britain.
Fill in suitable words or tick (✓) the correct box.

a) What _____ at your school when you have finished your final exams and are going to leave for good?

b) In America the students have a prom, which is a formal end-of-school dance. You'll …

☐ eventually ☐ probably
☐ extremely ☐ factually

know this from films.

c) Usually, the students …

☐ buy ☐ borrow
☐ lend ☐ hire

big limousines to take them to the dance.

d) There are also very strict _____ on how to dress for the occasion.

e) In the UK, most schools now have proms, too, and British pupils like to think …

☐ for ☐ on
☐ to ☐ of

particularly original ways to get to their prom and celebrate it.

f) In the school I was at, for example, some pupils _____ in a helicopter.

g) "How did the students …
- [ ] get
- [ ] become
- [ ] drive
- [ ] come

a helicopter?" you might ask.

h) Well, they …
- [ ] evenly
- [ ] easily
- [ ] simply
- [ ] fully

asked the owner of the helicopter if he would fly them to school.

i) He said OK, and because it was such an original idea, he did not want any …
- [ ] amount
- [ ] payment
- [ ] bill
- [ ] honour

for it.

j) How would you …
- [ ] mind
- [ ] succeed
- [ ] prefer
- [ ] admire

to get to your prom – in a stretch limo or a helicopter?

k) Or do you find all that exaggerated? I'd be interested to hear your _____ on school proms.

16. The website *Good@School* offers advice for pupils. Read their advice on how to give oral presentations.
Tick (✓) the correct box or fill in suitable words.

a) First of all, preparation is everything. Start …
- [ ] collecting
- [ ] achieving
- [ ] winning
- [ ] bearing

information on your topic early enough – do not wait until the very last minute.

b) Write down the keywords of your presentation on a flashcard or a _____ of paper.

c) You should use these notes as a memory aid during your talk, to make sure that you don't …
- [ ] tell
- [ ] forget
- [ ] miss
- [ ] remember

anything.

d) Practise the presentation at home …
☐ before ☐ behind
☐ in front of ☐ during
a mirror, a friend or family member.

e) Don't worry if you are nervous on the day of the presentation – that is …
☐ hardly ☐ perfectly
☐ possibly ☐ ideally
normal!

f) Try to turn your excitement into positive energy. _____
in yourself – you are well-prepared, you have got interesting things to say, and your audience will enjoy listening to you!

g) Smile at your listeners – it will put them in a good _____
and it will also help you to relax.

h) Look …
☐ at ☐ for
☐ on ☐ about
your audience – making eye contact will help you keep people's attention.

i) Speak _____ – this will make it easier for your listeners to follow what you are saying.

j) So you see – giving an oral presentation is not that difficult after all!
You just need to …
☐ hold ☐ contain
☐ follow ☐ cover
some basic rules, and everything will work out just fine.

Good luck for your presentation!

Das ActiveBook enthält zusätzlich einige gemischte Aufgaben zu Wortschatz und Grammatik *(Mixed Language Tests)*.

Du möchtest deinen Wortschatz noch weiter ausbauen?
Im Band „**Englisch-KOMPAKT – Prüfungswortschatz Realschule**" (Bestell-Nr. 914503D) findest du Vokabeln und Beispielsätze zu den wichtigsten Themengebieten der Lehrpläne. Zusätzlich zum gedruckten Buch stehen dir alle Vokabeln auch als digitale Lernkarten zur Verfügung, sodass du die Wörter bequem am Smartphone wiederholen und dir auch gleich die richtige Aussprache anhören kannst.

4 Grammatik – Sprachliche Korrektheit

4.1 Strategien zum Bereich „Grammatik"

Der Bereich „Grammatik – Sprachliche Korrektheit" ist zwar kein eigenständiger Prüfungsteil im MSA, dennoch ist ein Beherrschen der wichtigsten Grammatikregeln für ein erfolgreiches Bestehen der Prüfung unerlässlich: Ganz gleich, ob du (wie im Fall der Hör- und Lesetexte) die Sprache passiv verstehen oder sie (wie beim Schreiben) aktiv einsetzen musst – es ist immer wichtig, dass du bestimmte Satzkonstruktionen kennst und selbst anwenden kannst.

Zu Beginn dieses Buches findest du eine **Kurzgrammatik** mit einer Übersicht über die wichtigsten Strukturen der englischen Grammatik. Du kannst auf unterschiedliche Weise damit arbeiten:

Methode 1 Wenn du das Gefühl hast, dass du dich schon ganz gut in der englischen Grammatik auskennst, kannst du die Regeln und Beispiele erst einmal überspringen. Sollten dir dann beim Lösen der Übungsaufgaben zur Grammatik (Kapitel 4.2) Fragen einfallen, kannst du gezielt in der Kurzgrammatik Erklärungen und Beispiele zu einzelnen Strukturen nachschlagen. Damit du dich leicht zurechtfindest, sind die Bezeichnungen der grammatischen Strukturen in den Aufgabenstellungen **fett** gedruckt. Zu einigen Grammatikthemen kannst du dir auch ein **Lernvideo** ansehen.

Methode 2 Vielleicht weißt du aber schon, dass du noch den einen oder anderen Schwachpunkt im Bereich Grammatik hast. Dann liest du dir am besten alle Erklärungen und Beispiele in der Kurzgrammatik sorgfältig durch. Überlege dir zu jedem Beispiel ein eigenes Beispiel. Präge dir auch das Beispiel zu den Regeln ein. Wenn du eine Regel mit einem Beispiel verknüpfen kannst, fällt es dir bestimmt leichter, dir die Regel zu merken. Markiere gleich beim Lesen der Grammatik die Bereiche, die du noch intensiver üben möchtest.

Methode 3 Sieh dir Texte, die du in Klassenarbeiten oder als Hausaufgabe geschrieben hast und die dein Lehrer oder deine Lehrerin korrigiert hat, einmal nur im Hinblick auf Grammatik an. Oft sind Grammatikfehler z. B. mit der Abkürzung „Gr" markiert. Erkennst du Bereiche, in denen du noch Probleme hast? Frage deinen Lehrer bzw. deine Lehrerin, wenn du dir nicht sicher bist, bei welchen Strukturen du Fehler gemacht hast. Schlage diese Strukturen in der Kurzgrammatik nach und mache Übungen dazu.

Vielleicht findest du, dass Grammatik lernen und üben nicht sehr spannend ist. Hast du schon einmal ausprobiert, selbst eine Grammatikübung zu erstellen? Suche dir einen englischen Text zu einem Thema aus, das du besonders interessant findest (z. B. aus dem Bereich Leseverstehen in diesem Buch). Mache dir eine Kopie und lösche alle Verben. Zu den Lücken schreibst du nur die Grundform auf (z. B. „did" → „to do"). Schon hast du eine Übung, mit der du Verbformen in allen Zeiten üben kannst. Und nebenbei beschäftigst du dich mit einem Thema, das du spannend findest.

Grammatik

4.2 Übungsaufgaben zum Bereich „Grammatik"

1. **Prepositions** – Look at the picture and choose the right prepositions to complete the sentences. You can use each preposition only once.

   > inside – in front of – beside – between – at – under – outside – behind – on

   a) The family is sitting _____ their tent, _____ their car.

   b) Everybody is _____, there is no one _____ the tent.

   c) There is a tree _____ the car.

   d) The little girl is sitting _____ her sister and brother.

   e) There's lots of food _____ the table and a bowl of water _____ the table.

   f) The father is looking _____ the dog.

2. **Prepositions** – Fill in the prepositions in the following short texts.

   a) I got a letter _____ my brother today. He put the wrong stamps _____ the letter. As no one was _____ home when the postman came, he left a note _____ the front door. I had to go _____ the post office and pick _____ the letter myself. I had to pay 50 p _____ the extra postage.

   b) It happened _____ 31st October, _____ about nine o'clock _____ the evening. Amy had been waiting _____ her boyfriend _____ what seemed like hours. He had said he'd be there _____ six at the latest. She was just about to go _____ home, when he suddenly appeared right _____ her. Of course she was scared – but what else should you be _____ Halloween?

3. **Conjunctions** – Complete the following texts using the conjunctions from the box. There are two conjunctions you do not need.

> after – although – as – as long as – as soon as – before (2×) –
> but – both – because – or – and (2×) – while

a) _____ James McAlister has finished school, he is _____ going to apply for an internship with the American company Open Access Music Library, _____ take a job with the Scottish firm UnlimitedAccess.co.uk. _____ he is in Scotland, he will be able to work with the American company online, _____ he will have to fly to the States to present himself _____ he can start to work for them.

b) _____ Caroline's mother is a journalist, that is the last thing Caroline wants to become! _____ finishing school Caroline is going to study medicine in London, _____ then she hopes she will be able to get some practical experience working in America _____ Canada. _____ still at school she has been doing some voluntary work at a hospital near her home. _____ she can study medicine, though, she really needs to study hard.

4. **Modal auxiliaries** – A school trip to London

a) Mrs Smith is talking about a visit to London as a final trip before everyone leaves school.
Complete what she says with a modal auxiliary from the box. You can use each item only once.

> must – have to – can – can't – needn't

We _____ fly or go by train, but we _____ go during your exams – that's clear – so we'll go on 26th July for a week. If you want to go to London, you _____ return the form to me by Monday. You _____ bring any money until next week – I'm not collecting it before then. But don't forget, I _____ _____ have the forms on Monday.

b) The class representative has sent Mrs Smith an e-mail about the London visit. Choose the correct modal auxiliary to complete the sentences.

I _1_ find my form. _2_ I have a new one, please? I think most people _3_ come. Jenny _4_ have a problem, though. Her parents say that she _5_ pass her exams if she wants them to pay. She _6_ afford the trip if her parents don't pay. Thomas says he _7_ ask his parents' permission because he _8_ go on every school trip. When we go to London, _9_ we visit Madame Tussauds? Everyone _10_ like to go there. Another suggestion is that we _11_ have a party in Regent's Park on our last night. We _12_ do that, won't we? I know that we _13_ drink alcohol on a school trip, but we _14_ have a barbecue and then we _15_ have lots of fun together for the last time.

#			
1	☐ had to	☐ can't	☐ won't
2	☐ May	☐ Need	☐ Am allowed to
3	☐ needn't	☐ have to	☐ will be able to
4	☐ was allowed to	☐ must	☐ might
5	☐ has to	☐ will	☐ might
6	☐ shouldn't	☐ can't	☐ can
7	☐ mustn't	☐ needn't	☐ should
8	☐ is allowed to	☐ couldn't	☐ doesn't have to
9	☐ must	☐ could	☐ needn't
10	☐ will	☐ would	☐ has to
11	☐ may	☐ are able to	☐ should
12	☐ are able to	☐ will be allowed to	☐ could
13	☐ needn't	☐ shouldn't have	☐ mustn't
14	☐ could	☐ need	☐ mustn't
15	☐ may	☐ would	☐ have to

5. **Tenses** – Look at the photograph. Then complete the sentences using the "**present progressive**".

a) The man in the van _____ (verkaufen) ice creams.

b) The ice-cream man _____ (schauen) out of the side window.

c) Another man _____ (stehen) behind the ice-cream van.

d) The man behind the ice-cream van _____ (anrufen) a friend.

e) No one _____ (kaufen) an ice cream.

f) The ice-cream man _____ (warten) for customers.

6. **Tenses: "simple present" or "present progressive"** – First underline any signal words you can find in the sentences. Then fill in the correct verb form.

a) Karen always _____ (zu Fuß gehen) to school.

b) She _____ (tragen) her large school bag now.

c) Karen and her family _____ (fliegen) to England this year. Normally, they _____ (fahren) there.

d) Karen's dad _____ (arbeiten) on his computer at the moment. When he is busy he never _____ (sprechen) to anybody.

7. **Tenses (irregular verbs)** – There are many irregular verbs to learn. Here are some you use often. Give the "**simple past**" and the "**present perfect**" forms.

		simple past	present perfect
a)	be	_____	_____
b)	have	_____	_____
c)	say	_____	_____
d)	go	_____	_____
e)	take	_____	_____
f)	write	_____	_____
g)	buy	_____	_____

8. **Tenses (signal words)** – Below are signal words for the "**simple past**" and the "**present perfect**". Put the signal words with the correct tense.

already – ever – five years ago – for three weeks – in 2010 – how long – just – last month – last week – not … yet – since May – yesterday

simple past	present perfect

9. **Tenses (signal words)** – Which words or expressions take "since" and which ones take "for"?

_____	2012	_____	my birthday
_____	six days	_____	Easter
_____	last weekend	_____	a long time
_____	three hours	_____	many years
_____	last summer	_____	seven days

10. **Tenses** – "**simple past**" or "**present perfect**", "**progressive**" or "**simple**"? Fill in the correct verb form.
    a) Yesterday, I _____ (go) to the cinema.
    b) She _____ (write) since 3 o'clock.
    c) He _____ just _____ (finish) his homework.
    d) It was many years ago that I _____ (visit) America.
    e) How long _____ you _____ (wait)?
    f) In 1999 we _____ (drive) to Italy. Then two years ago we _____ (fly). We _____ not _____ (be) there since then.
    g) Last week we _____ (have) our last English lesson before our exams.

11. **Tenses** – "**simple past**" or "**past perfect**"? Put the verbs into the correct tenses.
    a) After Ellis Island _____ (serve) as a fort and execution site it _____ (become) an immigration center in 1892.
    b) It was there that doctors and officials _____ (decide) the futures of all those who _____ (leave) Europe in the hope of a new life in America.
    c) After they _____ (pass) through the baggage room, the newcomers _____ (climb) the long stairs up to the Great Hall.
    d) Once the doctors _____ (examine) everybody, officials _____ (come) and _____ (question) them.
    e) When they _____ (give) the right answers, they _____ (start) to explore the New World.

12. **Mixed tenses** – Ruby is keeping a blog about her first journey abroad. Fill in each gap with the correct tense – do not use the future.

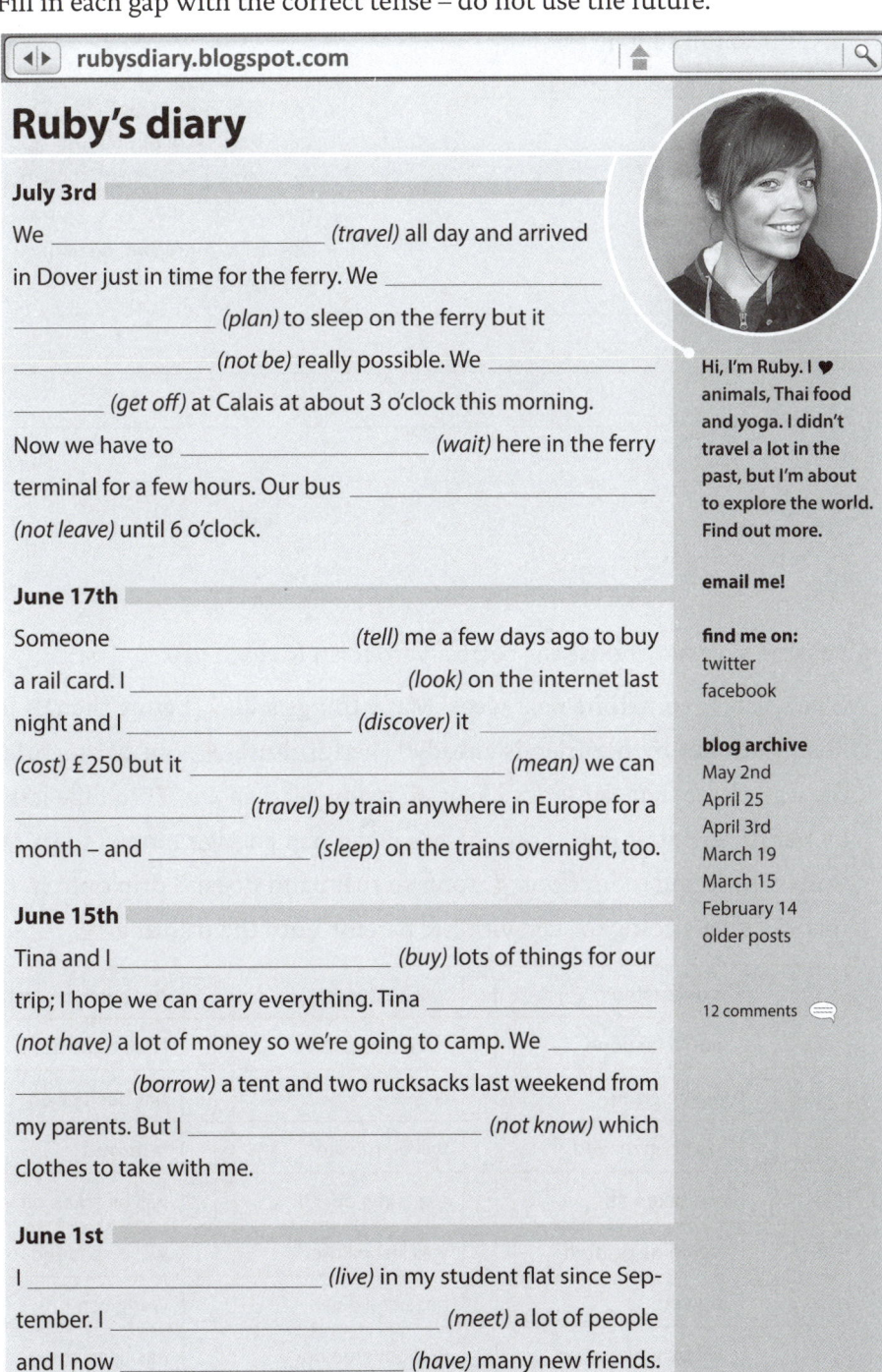

Ruby's diary

July 3rd

We _____ (travel) all day and arrived in Dover just in time for the ferry. We _____ (plan) to sleep on the ferry but it _____ (not be) really possible. We _____ (get off) at Calais at about 3 o'clock this morning. Now we have to _____ (wait) here in the ferry terminal for a few hours. Our bus _____ (not leave) until 6 o'clock.

June 17th

Someone _____ (tell) me a few days ago to buy a rail card. I _____ (look) on the internet last night and I _____ (discover) it _____ (cost) £250 but it _____ (mean) we can _____ (travel) by train anywhere in Europe for a month – and _____ (sleep) on the trains overnight, too.

June 15th

Tina and I _____ (buy) lots of things for our trip; I hope we can carry everything. Tina _____ (not have) a lot of money so we're going to camp. We _____ (borrow) a tent and two rucksacks last weekend from my parents. But I _____ (not know) which clothes to take with me.

June 1st

I _____ (live) in my student flat since September. I _____ (meet) a lot of people and I now _____ (have) many new friends. I _____ (ask) Tina yesterday if she wanted to come with me to the Continent in the summer holidays. She _____ (say) she'd love to come.

subscribe   home   © All rights reserved.

Hi, I'm Ruby. I ♥ animals, Thai food and yoga. I didn't travel a lot in the past, but I'm about to explore the world. Find out more.

email me!

find me on:
twitter
facebook

blog archive
May 2nd
April 25
April 3rd
March 19
March 15
February 14
older posts

12 comments

Grammatik

Talking about the Future

13. **Future tenses** – Use the "**will-future**" or the "**going to-future**" to make the notes into full sentences.

- send Karen an e-mail (spontaneous)
- 27th Dec. – Venice
- cinema with friends
- dentist – tomorrow 4.30 p.m.
- next week: school holidays start
- Grandma is 70 – next month
- meet Luke – 11.00
- buy Julie a present: sometime next week

a) I'll send Karen an e-mail.

b) _____

c) _____

d) _____

e) _____

f) _____

g) _____

h) _____

Active and Passive voice

14. **Passive voice** – Choose the correct verb form for each gap.

Ellie's flat __1__ sometime next week. Many things still __2__ before then. A lot of help __3__ to her by her friends already. The furniture __4__, but her pictures __5__ the walls later. The flat looks like it __6__ many years ago. It __7__ to Ellie last year by her parents, but until now she has never had enough money to paint the walls. The living room floor __8__ soon so that paint doesn't drip onto it. Once that __9__, Ellie's going to stay with her parents until the painting __10__.

1	☐ is decorated	☐ will be decorated	☐ has been decorated
2	☐ would be done	☐ have been done	☐ have to be done
3	☐ will be given	☐ is given	☐ has been given
4	☐ has been moved	☐ will be moved	☐ is moved
5	☐ was taken off	☐ are taken off	☐ will be taken off
6	☐ would be painted	☐ was last painted	☐ will be painted
7	☐ is given	☐ has been given	☐ was given
8	☐ will be covered up	☐ was covered up	☐ has been covered up
9	☐ has been done	☐ will be done	☐ had been done
10	☐ had been completed	☐ has been completed	☐ was completed

15. **Passive voice** – Put the verbs into the passive.
    a) English _____ (speak) all over the world.
    b) Last week a new crew _____ (send) up to the ISS.
    c) Up to now Atlantis _____ (not discover).
    d) The door should always _____ (lock).

16. **Infinitive or gerund?** – Read the information about three courses that are on offer at an activity centre. Fill in the gaps with either the *-ing*-form or the infinitive. Add a preposition where necessary.

    1 _____ (climb) is a good sport, but you have _____ (be) fit. If you want to learn _____ (climb), it's probably best to start _____ (do) it on a climbing wall. There is no chance _____ (fall) very far because you'll have a rope _____ (stop) you from _____ (do) that. After _____ (learn, climb) on our wall we'll take you to a real mountain. We look forward _____ (see) you on our course.

    2 _____ (windsurf) is fun. On our courses we'll show you how to windsurf from the very beginning – you just shouldn't be afraid _____ (get) wet. Before _____ (go) onto the lake you'll learn how _____ (control) the windsurfer on the land. In this way, you'll avoid _____ (spend) many hours in the lake trying to pull yourself back onto the windsurfer.

    3 Have you ever been on a horse? _____ (ride – horse) is a very nice way _____ (see) the countryside. Our horses are friendly and there's very little danger _____ (have) an accident with one. You'll never forget _____ (get) onto a horse for the first time.

17. **Question words** – Read the advert and the answers to the questions carefully. Then write the questions.

   a) _____?
   The advert is for a party night.

   b) _____?
   There are three bands playing.

   c) _____?
   The party is in the Old Factory.

   d) _____?
   It starts at half past seven.

   e) _____?
   It costs £ 7.50.

   f) _____?
   Because the last bus leaves at 3.00 a.m.

PARTY NIGHT
Bands:
Level Two, Big Feet, Loud 26

Area 1: HipHop – RnB
Area 2: Electro – House

**The Old Factory
Queen Street
Birmingham**

7.30 p.m. – 3.00 a.m.
Tickets: £ 7.50

Tel: 0876 /78465
e-mail: partynight@birmingham.co.uk
Buses to city centre every 30 mins.
Last bus 3.00 a.m.

18. **Negation** – Make the following sentences negative.

   a) They are learning English.

   b) Mary drives a fast car.

   c) We can take the next train to Manchester.

   d) My homework is very hard today.

   e) Noah plays football every weekend.

   f) I am going to go to the theatre.

   g) We have got your telephone number.

   h) Jenny will make the cakes.

i) I read my new book for hours last night.

j) Lucy arrived late for her doctor's appointment.

19. **Conditional sentences** – Complete the gaps in the conditional sentences.

To... amelia16@meyers.co.uk
Cc...
Subject: theatre visit

Hi Amelia,
If I had more time, I _____ (write) a much longer e-mail to you. But I haven't, so this will be a short message. If you want a longer one, you _____ (have) to wait until next week!
I was in London last week, as you know. If you _____ (be) there, we could have gone to the theatre together. But that's why I'm writing. If you have time, _____ _____ (you – want) to come to the theatre with me next weekend? I noticed two or three more shows that I would love to see. Would you be interested in going if I _____ (get) tickets? If you _____ (be), phone me tomorrow evening – I can book them online.
Oh, I almost forgot. Maxime _____ (come) with me last week if he hadn't had to fly to Paris to meet his mum … but he wants to come with us next time if you _____ (not mind).
I _____ (send) you the theatre details if you would like to see what's on.
Love, Sam

20. **Reported speech** – Write the following sentences in reported speech.

a) He says, "I want to listen to the radio because my favourite group are in concert today."
   He says that …

b) She told us, "I think the book was better than the film."

c) He said, "Yesterday we lost the football match. We played badly."

d) The man explained, "I was here when the accident happened. It was no one's fault."

Grammatik

21. **Reported speech** – Two people tell you about one of their favourite objects. Write what they say in reported speech. In the first part of the exercise the words you need to change are underlined to help you.
Underline the words in the second part that need changing before you start.

a) George said, "This is the only trophy I have ever won.
I don't need another reason to keep it, do I?
It sits on a shelf and sometimes I show people my greatest sporting award."

George said that ...

b) Katy asked, "Why do I keep the teddy bear?" She answered, "I don't really know. I bought it during our holiday last year because it looks so happy. It sits here above my sofa, smiles across the room and makes me think of the nice holiday we had in Sweden. There is no other reason for keeping it. It's just a souvenir."

Das ActiveBook enthält zusätzlich einige gemischte Aufgaben zu Wortschatz und Grammatik *(Mixed Language Tests)*.

5 Schreiben

Viele Schülerinnen und Schüler sind der Meinung, dass sie sich auf den Bereich „Schreiben" nicht vorbereiten können, da die Aufgabenformen stark variieren und die Note – wie im Deutschunterricht – ohnehin stark von der individuellen Einschätzung der Lehrkraft abhänge. Erschwerend kommt im Fach Englisch noch die Fremdsprache und die damit verbundene Fehleranfälligkeit hinzu. Aus diesen Gründen beschäftigen sich manche Schüler*innen erst gar nicht mit dem Thema „Schreiben", was umso schlimmer ist, wenn man bedenkt, dass dieser Bereich etwa 60 % der Note in der schriftlichen Prüfung ausmacht. Mache nicht den gleichen Fehler! Lies die folgenden Seiten gut durch. Du wirst sehen: Eine sinnvolle Vorbereitung auf das Schreiben englischer Texte ist möglich.

5.1 Strategien zum Bereich „Schreiben"

Langfristige Vorbereitung

Auf den Bereich „Schreiben" kannst du dich nur langfristig gut vorbereiten. Wenn du dir erst zwei Tage vor der Prüfung überlegst, dass du in diesem Bereich noch Schwächen hast, dann ist es für eine sinnvolle Beschäftigung mit diesem Thema definitiv zu spät.

Schaue bzw. höre dir englischsprachige Interviews mit deinen Lieblingsstars im Internet (z. B. bei YouTube) oder im Fernsehen an. Sieh dir Filme im Original an, entweder im Kino – falls sie in deiner Stadt im Original vorgeführt werden – oder auf DVD bzw. über einen Streaming-Dienst im Internet (z. B. Netflix). Als Hilfe kannst du dir – falls möglich – auch die englischen Untertitel einblenden lassen und die Dialoge mitlesen. *Methode 1*

Versuche, möglichst viel in englischer Sprache zu lesen; auch hier wirst du im Internet fündig. Du kannst dich z. B. über Themen, die dich interessieren, im Online-Lexikon Wikipedia informieren. Hier gibt es übrigens auch den Bereich „Simple English", falls dir die Texte zu schwierig sind. Oder probiere, Romane und Geschichten auf Englisch zu lesen. Deine Lehrerin oder dein Lehrer können dir sicher Tipps für geeignete Bücher geben. Du wirst sehen: Mit der Zeit verstehst du mehr und mehr, und viele Ausdrücke und Redewendungen kommen dir immer vertrauter vor, sodass du sie für deine eigenen Texte verwenden kannst. *Methode 2*

Eine gute Übung ist es auch, sich viel in der Fremdsprache zu unterhalten. Sprich doch hin und wieder mit deinen Freunden oder deinen Geschwistern englisch. So wird dir das eigenständige Formulieren von Mal zu Mal leichter fallen.
Wichtig ist also, dass du dich mit der englischen Sprache auch in deiner Freizeit beschäftigst. Dabei geht es nicht nur darum, das Schreiben englischer Texte zu üben, sondern ganz generell sollst du möglichst viel mit dem Englischen in Kontakt kommen. So kannst du deinen Wortschatz erweitern und Sicherheit im Gebrauch der Fremdsprache erwerben, die du zum Verfassen eigener Texte brauchst. *Methode 3*

Das Schreiben eines Textes

Ganz gleich, welche Art von Text (*Summary*, persönliche Stellungnahme etc.) du schreiben musst, die Vorgehensweise ist dabei immer dieselbe.

Arbeitsschritt 1 Lies die Aufgabenstellung gut durch und überlege genau, was darin von dir verlangt wird. Enthält die Aufgabenstellung bestimmte Vorgaben (z. B. ein Zitat, zu dem du Stellung beziehen musst)? Oder sollst du einen „freien" Text schreiben?

Arbeitsschritt 2 Wenn du mehrere Themen zur Auswahl hast, dann suche dir dasjenige aus, das dir besser liegt. In der MSA-Prüfung musst du dich z. B. oft zwischen einer kreativen und einer sachlich-erörternden Aufgabe entscheiden. Überlege, zu welcher Aufgabenstellung dir spontan mehr einfällt und welche Art zu schreiben dir generell leichter fällt.

Arbeitsschritt 3 Hast du dich für ein Thema entschieden, dann solltest du dir genau überlegen, was du dazu schreiben könntest. Achte darauf, wie der Arbeitsauftrag formuliert ist: Sollst du einen Text als Ganzes zusammenfassen, nur auf einen bestimmten Teilaspekt eingehen oder z. B. eine Fortsetzung schreiben?
Wenn sich die Aufgabe auf eine Geschichte o. Ä. bezieht, so lies dir den Text noch einmal im Hinblick auf die Aufgabenstellung durch und markiere alle relevanten Stellen. Mache dir zu den wichtigsten Aspekten Notizen.

Arbeitsschritt 4 Versuche als Nächstes, deine Notizen in eine sinnvolle Reihenfolge zu bringen – so erhältst du bereits eine grobe Gliederung für deinen Text. Kontrolliere anschließend noch einmal, dass du alle in der Aufgabenstellung geforderten Aspekte berücksichtigt hast.

Arbeitsschritt 5 Nun musst du den Text formulieren. Orientiere dich an deinen Notizen und formuliere Schritt für Schritt die einzelnen Sätze aus. Achte darauf, dass du Abhängigkeiten, Folgen etc. durch entsprechende Konjunktionen (Bindewörter) deutlich machst. Greife auf Redewendungen zurück, die du gelernt hast. Schreibe kurze, überschaubare Sätze; so kannst du Grammatikfehlern leichter vorbeugen. Bemühe dich dennoch, deine Sätze abwechslungsreich zu gestalten. Beginne z. B. nicht jeden Satz gleich. Wenn du etwas nicht ausdrücken kannst oder dir der Wortschatz fehlt, dann versuche einen anderen Aspekt zu finden. Enthält die Aufgabenstellung Angaben zur Textlänge (z. B. *Write about 80 words. / Write at least 100 words.*), so solltest du versuchen, dich daran zu halten. Wo es keine konkreten Vorgaben gibt, kannst du oft anhand der zu vergebenden Punkte abschätzen, wie viel du zu einer Aufgabe schreiben musst.
In Kapitel 5.3 haben wir einige Redewendungen und Ausdrücke zusammengestellt, die dir beim Aufsatzschreiben helfen werden. Lerne sie auswendig. Du wirst sie immer wieder einsetzen können.

Arbeitsschritt 6 Nimm dir auf jeden Fall die Zeit, am Ende alles noch einmal in Ruhe durchzulesen. Achte dabei auf die inhaltliche Geschlossenheit deines Textes. Ist alles logisch aufgebaut oder gibt es Gedankensprünge? Wichtig ist aber auch, dass du noch einmal gezielt nach Rechtschreib- und Grammatikfehlern suchst und sie verbesserst.

Dieses Verfahren kommt dir vielleicht ein bisschen zeitaufwändig und umständlich vor. Versuche dennoch einmal, genau danach vorzugehen: Du wirst merken, dass es dir bei den Hausaufgaben, in Klassenarbeiten und natürlich erst recht in der Prüfung wertvolle Zeit spart. So wird es kaum passieren, dass du die falsche Aufgabe auswählst und das erst merkst, wenn du schon mitten im Schreiben bist. Klar sollte dir allerdings auch sein, dass du dieses Verfahren – das sich auch für kürzere Texte im Deutschunterricht eignet – üben musst.

> **Tipp**
> - Lies die Aufgabenstellung genau und analysiere sie.
> - Wenn du mehrere Themen zur Auswahl hast, entscheide dich für dasjenige, das dir besser liegt.
> - Notiere dir einige Stichpunkte. Wenn sich die Aufgabe auf einen Text bezieht, so markiere die für die Aufgabenstellung relevanten Passagen.
> - Bringe deine Notizen in eine sinnvolle Reihenfolge und überprüfe noch einmal, ob du alle Aspekte der Aufgabenstellung berücksichtigt hast.
> - Formuliere den Text anhand der Aufgabenstellung und deiner Notizen Schritt für Schritt aus.
> - Lies deinen Text abschließend noch einmal genau durch und überprüfe dabei, ob alles logisch aufgebaut und verständlich geschrieben ist. Verbessere Rechtschreib- und Grammatikfehler.

5.2 Häufige Aufgabenstellungen im Bereich „Schreiben"

Textgebundene Aufgaben

Der Bereich „Schreiben" wird in der MSA-Prüfung meist mit einem Lesetext verknüpft. Du bekommst eine kurze Erzählung oder einen Sachtext vorgelegt und musst in der Regel drei verschiedene Aufgaben dazu bearbeiten:

Im ersten Teil musst du zeigen, dass du den Text auch wirklich verstanden hast. Häufig sollst du bestimmte Aspekte des Texts in deinen eigenen Worten beschreiben oder zusammenfassen – die Arbeitsanweisungen dazu lauten z. B. „**Describe …**" oder „**Sum up …**". — Teil **1**

Der zweite Teil geht meist über eine reine Textwiedergabe hinaus. Statt den Text nur zusammenzufassen, musst du ihn genauer analysieren und ein Stück weit interpretieren, d. h., du musst dich etwas tiefer mit dem Text auseinandersetzen und bestimmte Zusammenhänge erklären. Außerdem musst du deine Untersuchungsergebnisse durch konkrete Textbelege untermauern. — Teil **2**

Der Arbeitsauftrag in Teil 2 lautet „**Explain …**" oder „**Analyse …**"; es kann aber auch sein, dass du Vergleiche anstellen musst („**Compare …**"). Am besten gehst du den Text noch einmal genau durch und hebst die für die Aufgabe relevanten Informationen mit einem Textmarker hervor. So vermeidest du, dass du wichtige Aspekte in deiner Antwort vergisst.

Tipp

> Für das **Einbinden von Textbelegen in Teil 2 (analytisch-interpretierende Aufgabe)** gibt es verschiedene Möglichkeiten:
> - **Direktes Zitat:** Du kannst ein wörtliches Zitat aus dem Text in deine Lösung einfügen. Verwende dazu englische Anführungszeichen, kennzeichne durch eckige Klammern, wenn du etwas ausgelassen oder angepasst hast, und gib am Ende die Zeile(n) an.
>   Beispiel 1: The protagonist is happy and thankful when she finally gets her exam results: "Zoe felt a wave of joy and gratitude, when she saw an 'A' written on her exam paper. All the hard work […] had finally paid off." (ll. 8/9).
>   Beispiel 2: The protagonist is happy and thankful when she finally gets her exam results. She feels "a wave of joy and gratitude" (l. 8) and is relieved that "[a]ll the hard work […] had finally paid off." (l. 9).
> - **Indirekter Textverweis:** Hierbei gibst du den Inhalt der Textpassage in deinen eigenen Worten wieder und verweist lediglich in Klammern mit „cf." (*confer* = vergleiche) auf die entsprechende(n) Zeile(n).
>   Beispiel: The protagonist is happy and thankful when she gets her exam results and feels relieved that the effort has been worth it after all (cf. ll. 8/9).

Teil 3

Im dritten Teil schließlich musst du dich noch stärker von der Textgrundlage lösen und **eigene Ideen einbringen**. Meist werden dir hier zwei Themen zur Auswahl gestellt – eine Aufgabe, bei der du dich persönlich-wertend mit dem Text auseinandersetzen musst, und eine eher kreative Aufgabenstellung. Konkret können dich in Teil 3 z. B. folgende Aufgabenformen erwarten:

▶ **Persönliche Stellungnahme:** Oft wird von dir erwartet, zu einem im Ausgangstext genannten Thema oder Zitat Stellung zu beziehen. Du wirst dann z. B. aufgefordert, die Vor- und Nachteile bestimmter Aspekte abzuwägen oder deine persönliche Meinung zu einem Thema zu formulieren. Gerade bei diesem Aufgabentyp ist es wichtig, dass du dir vorher kurz Notizen machst und überlegst, in welcher Reihenfolge du deine Argumente anbringen möchtest. So vermeidest du, dass dein Text chaotisch wird oder du wichtige Punkte übersiehst.

▶ **Fortsetzung einer Erzählung:** Handelt es sich beim Ausgangstext um einen literarischen Text (z. B. eine kurze Erzählung), kann es auch sein, dass du die Geschichte weiterspinnen sollst. Deine Fortsetzung sollte sich (sofern nicht anders verlangt) möglichst nahtlos an den vorangegangenen Text anschließen. Wenn also der Ausgangstext in der 1. Person geschrieben ist (Ich-Erzählung), solltest du nicht plötzlich in die 3. Person wechseln. Wenn der Ausgangstext viele Dialogpassagen enthält, solltest du ebenfalls Dialoge einbauen. Auch die Charakterzüge der einzelnen Figuren und der weitere Verlauf der Handlung sollten mit der Ausgangserzählung zusammenpassen.

▶ **E-Mail / Brief:** Manchmal musst du auch eine E-Mail oder einen Brief schreiben, z. B. an eine im Text genannte Figur, Person oder Institution. Überlege dir vorher, in welche „Rolle" du in deinem Schreiben schlüpfen sollst und an wen es sich richtet. Bei formellen E-Mails oder Briefen sollte deine Ausdrucksweise sachlich und nüchtern sein. Versuche also, umgangssprachliche Ausdrücke und Formulierungen zu vermeiden. Bei persönlichen E-Mails oder Briefen hingegen kann der Tonfall auch lockerer sein.

- **Dialog:** Es ist auch denkbar, dass du einen Dialog zwischen zwei Figuren oder Personen aus dem Text schreiben musst. Auch hier solltest du darauf achten, dass die Sprache zu den jeweiligen Figuren bzw. Personen passt. Wenn beispielsweise zwei Schüler miteinander sprechen, werden sie vermutlich Umgangssprache oder Jugendsprache verwenden. Außerdem sind dann eher Kurzformen statt Langformen einzusetzen (z. B. „I'd …" statt „I would …").
- **Erfahrungsbericht/Tagebucheintrag:** Manchmal wird auch von dir verlangt, über bestimmte Erfahrungen oder Erlebnisse zu berichten, z. B. in Form eines Tagebuch- oder Blogeintrags. Auch hier kann es sein, dass du aus der Sicht einer Person oder Figur aus dem Ausgangstext schreiben musst – achte also darauf, dass Sprache und Inhalt deines Berichts zu der entsprechenden Rolle passen.

Offene Aufgabenformate

Im MSA wird dir meist ein Text vorgelegt, an dem sich die Schreibaufgaben orientieren. In Klassenarbeiten und Hausaufgaben musst du teilweise auch ohne eine solche Textgrundlage eine **Stellungnahme**, einen **Bericht**, eine **E-Mail**/einen **Brief** o. Ä. verfassen. Darüber hinaus sind auch noch andere Aufgabenstellungen denkbar, beispielsweise dass du ein **Bewerbungsschreiben** oder einen **Lebenslauf** schreiben musst oder auf **Bildimpulse**, **Diagramme** oder **Grafiken** reagieren sollst.

5.3 Hilfreiche Wendungen für den Bereich „Schreiben"

Folgende Formulierungen sind eine gute Basis für das Verfassen der Textsorten, die typischerweise in der Prüfung von dir verlangt werden. Alle Ausdrücke sind übrigens auch als digitale „MindCards" verfügbar: Mit diesen Lernkarten kannst du bequem am Smartphone üben.

Formulierungshilfen für *Summaries* und Textanalysen

ein „Summary" einleiten	The story "(title)" by (author) is about …
	The excerpt from the novel *(title)*, written by (author), deals with …
	In the story "(title)", the author aims to present … by focusing on …
	In his/her article "(title)", the author argues that …
	The text was published in (year) in (*Teen Magazine*).
bestimmte Textaspekte beschreiben	The text focuses on …
	The narrative is set in …
	The story is told by (a first-person/third-person narrator).

	The story is told from (Jane)'s point of view.
	The protagonist/main character of the story is …
	(Life in the city) is presented in a positive/negative light.
	(The characters' relationship) is characterised by …
	This can be seen in the fact that …, for example.
einen Text analysieren	The author wants to show/point out that …
	The author criticises …
	The author uses (stylistic devices/repetitions) in order to …
	This allows the reader to (identify with the protagonist).

**Formulierungshilfen zur Strukturierung von Texten
(z. B. für eine persönliche Stellungnahme)**

einen Text einleiten	To begin with, … First of all, …
einen Text abschließen	To sum up, … / In summary, … All in all, … To conclude, … / In conclusion, …
Argumente aufzählen	Firstly, … Secondly, … Thirdly, … Finally, …
Argumente gegeneinander abwägen	On the one hand … On the other hand …
auf Widersprüche hinweisen / etwas einräumen	but however yet although despite … / in spite of … in contrast to … otherwise nevertheless
zusätzliche Aspekte anführen	In addition, … Moreover, … Furthermore, … Another important point/aspect (to mention) is …

Beispiele geben	for example / e.g.
	for instance
	like
	such as
Gründe anführen	Due to …
	Thanks to …
	The reason for this is that …
	because (of)
	as
	since
	therefore
auf die Folgen von etwas hinweisen	As a result, …
	Consequently, …
die eigene Meinung ausdrücken	In my opinion/view, …
	Personally, I think/believe that …
	To my mind, …
	As far as I am concerned, …
	As for me, …

Verben des Sagens (z. B. für Erzählungen oder Dialoge)

sagen	to say something / to tell someone
fragen	to ask
	to enquire
sich fragen	to ask oneself
	to wonder
antworten/erwidern	to answer
	to reply
	to retort
flüstern	to whisper
murmeln	to murmur
	to mutter
	to mumble
schreien	to call (out)
	to yell
	to scream
	to shout
erwähnen	to mention

Formulierungshilfen für E-Mails und Briefe

Anrede und Schlussformeln in formellen E-Mails und Briefen (z. B. Geschäftsbrief / Anfrage / Beschwerde)

wenn du den <u>Namen</u> der Ansprechperson <u>nicht kennst</u>:

Sehr geehrte Damen und Herren,	Dear Sir or Madam,
	Dear Sir / Madam,
Mit freundlichen Grüßen,	Yours faithfully,

wenn du den <u>Namen</u> der Ansprechperson <u>kennst</u>:

Sehr geehrte Frau Roberts,	Dear Mrs Roberts,
Sehr geehrter Herr James,	Dear Mr James,
wenn du nicht weißt, ob die Frau verheiratet ist oder nicht	Dear Ms Bell,
Mit freundlichen Grüßen,	Yours sincerely,

Layout eines Geschäftsbriefes

```
                                      24 Castle Street      ⎫
                                           Blackburn        ⎬ Absender
                                         Lancashire         ⎪ (ohne Namen)[1]
                                           LK6 5TQ          ⎭

                                       6th March 20…        Datum[2]

  Mrs J. Fox                                                ⎫
  Dane Cleaners                                             ⎪ Name + Adresse
  3 Arthur Road                                             ⎬ des Empfängers
  Doddington                                                ⎪ (bei Geschäfts-
  NE3 6LD                                                   ⎭ briefen)



  Dear Mrs Fox,                                             Anrede

  Thank you for your letter …




  Yours sincerely,                                          Schlussformel
  Adam Smith                                                Unterschrift
  Adam Smith                                                Name
```

[1] Die Adresse des Absenders kann auch auf der linken Seite stehen.
[2] Das Datum kann auch links stehen. Die Schreibungen 6 March 20… und March 6(th) 20… sind alternativ möglich.

Anrede und Schlussformeln in persönlichen E-Mails und Briefen

Liebe Jane,	Dear Jane,
Viele Grüße / Liebe Grüße	Best wishes,
	Love, (nur bei sehr guten Freunden; von Frauen häufiger verwendet als von Männern)

Mögliche Einleitungs- und Schlusssätze

Wie geht es dir?	How are you?
Danke für …	Thank you for …
Ich habe … erhalten.	I received …
Ich hoffe, dass …	I hope that …
Ich hoffe, dir hat … gefallen.	I hope you liked/enjoyed …
Im letzten Brief hast du mir erzählt, dass …	In your last letter you told me that …
Entschuldige, dass ich … vergessen habe, aber …	Sorry that I forgot to …, but …
Es wäre schön, wenn wir uns treffen könnten.	It would be nice if we could meet.
Ich muss jetzt …	I have to … now.
Ich denke, es ist besser …	I think it's better to …
Sage bitte … / Richte … bitte aus …	Please tell …
Bitte richte … (schöne) Grüße aus.	Best wishes to …
	Please give my (best) regards to …
	Please say hi/hello to … from me.
Bitte schreibe mir bald zurück.	Please write soon.
Ich freue mich darauf, bald von dir zu hören.	I'm looking forward to hearing from you soon.
	I hope to hear from you soon.
Ich freue mich auf deinen Brief.	I'm looking forward to your letter.
Ich werde dich anrufen.	I'll call/ring you.

Weitere häufig vorkommende Redewendungen/Ausdrücke

sich entschuldigen	I'm sorry …
etwas bedauern/Enttäuschung ausdrücken	It's a pity that …
	I'm disappointed that …
	I was deeply disappointed by …
an etwas erinnern	Please remember to …
Überraschung äußern	I was surprised that …
eine Bitte äußern	Could you/Would you …, please?
einen Wunsch äußern	I'd like to … / I'd love to …

einen Entschluss mitteilen	I've decided to …
	I've made up my mind to …
	I'm going to …
eine Absicht mitteilen	I intend to
	I will …
	I want to …
	I'm planning to …
Freude ausdrücken	I'm happy/glad about …
Überzeugung ausdrücken	I'm convinced that …
	I'm sure that …

Auskunft über sich geben

Ich wohne in …	I live in …
Ich wurde am … in … geboren.	I was born in … on (17th August 20…).
Ich interessiere mich für …	I'm interested in …
Ich war schon in …	I've (already) been in …/to …
Ich möchte gerne … werden.	I'd like to be a/an …
Mir geht es gut.	I'm fine.
Mir geht es nicht gut.	I'm not well./I don't feel well.
Ich mag …	I like …/I enjoy …
Ich mag … lieber (als …)	I prefer … (to …)
	I like … better (than …)
Ich weiß … noch nicht genau.	I still don't know exactly …
Ich plane, … zu tun.	I plan to …
Ich freue mich (sehr) auf …	I'm (very much) looking forward to …
	I'm (very) excited about …
Ich konnte nicht …	I wasn't able to …/I couldn't …
In meiner Freizeit …	In my free time/spare time …
Ich nehme regelmäßig an … teil.	I take part in … regularly.

5.4 Allgemeine Übungsaufgaben zum Bereich „Schreiben"

1. Improve the following sentences. Choose the best word from the box for each sentence.

   > dark – horror – long – loud – narrow – old – sandy –
   > seafood – small – so – summer – terrible – quickly – young

   a) The _____ house was at the end of the _____ street.

   b) Jane likes listening to _____ music in her _____ bedroom.

   c) The _____ boy ran away _____.

   d) We had a _____ meal in the _____ restaurant.

   e) I didn't like the _____ film because it was _____ boring.

   f) My _____ holiday was great.

   g) There was a _____, _____ beach with no one on it.

   h) The sky was very _____ before the storm.

2. Look at the photograph. What can you say about it? Take some notes.

3. Look at the photo again. Answer the following questions in complete sentences.

   a) Where does the scene take place?
      It takes place in front of a building.

   b) Describe who you can see …
      ▶ in the foreground: _____
      _____
      ▶ in the background: _____
      _____

   c) Describe …
      ▶ the boy's face: _____
      ▶ what he is holding: _____
      ▶ where he is in relation to the others: _____
      _____

   d) Describe …
      ▶ the other people's clothes: _____
      _____
      ▶ what they are doing: _____
      _____

4. Look at your answers to task 3. Improve each answer by adding more information – an adjective, an adverb or an additional phrase.

   a) Where does the scene take place?
      It takes place in front of **a big white/grey building – probably outside** **a school building.**

   b) Describe who you can see …
      ▶ in the foreground: _____
      _____
      ▶ in the background: _____
      _____

   c) Describe …
      ▶ the boy's face: _____
      ▶ what he is holding: _____
      ▶ where he is in relation to the others: _____
      _____

d) Describe …
   - ▶ the other people's clothes: _____
   _____
   - ▶ what they are doing: _____
   _____

5. What is the story behind the picture? Think of four questions you could ask about the picture.

   ▶ _____
   _____
   _____

   ▶ _____
   _____
   _____

   ▶ _____
   _____
   _____

   ▶ _____
   _____
   _____

6. Imagine what is going on between the boy in the foreground and the other teenagers. Think of answers to the questions you asked in task 5 and write a short story in about 120 words.

   _____
   _____
   _____
   _____
   _____
   _____
   _____
   _____
   _____
   _____
   _____
   _____

7. Imagine you have spent a fantastic holiday with other young people in an English-speaking country. After returning home you write a message to your American friend about your holiday.

   a) To collect some ideas make a mind map before you start to write your message. Some questions have been included to help you.

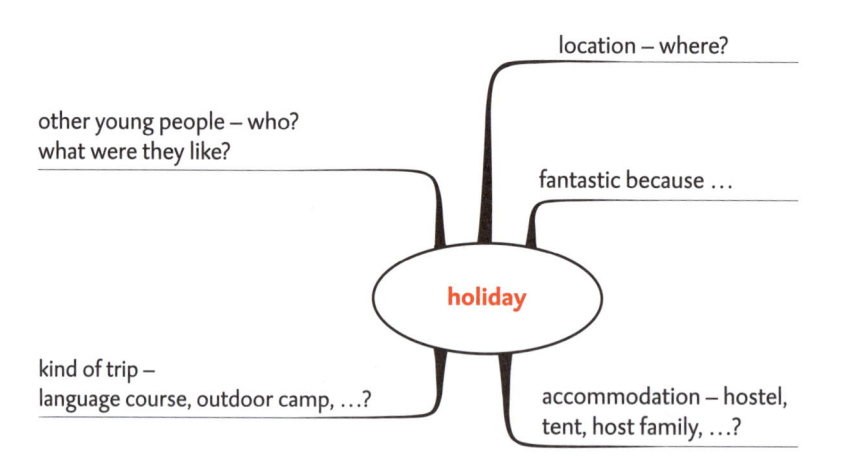

   - location – where?
   - other young people – who? what were they like?
   - fantastic because …
   - **holiday**
   - kind of trip – language course, outdoor camp, …?
   - accommodation – hostel, tent, host family, …?

   b) Choose your best ideas and write a chat message to your friend in about 120 words.

8. Write a story.

   a) Look at the beginning of a story. Then collect ideas for the rest of the story. The following questions are there to help you.

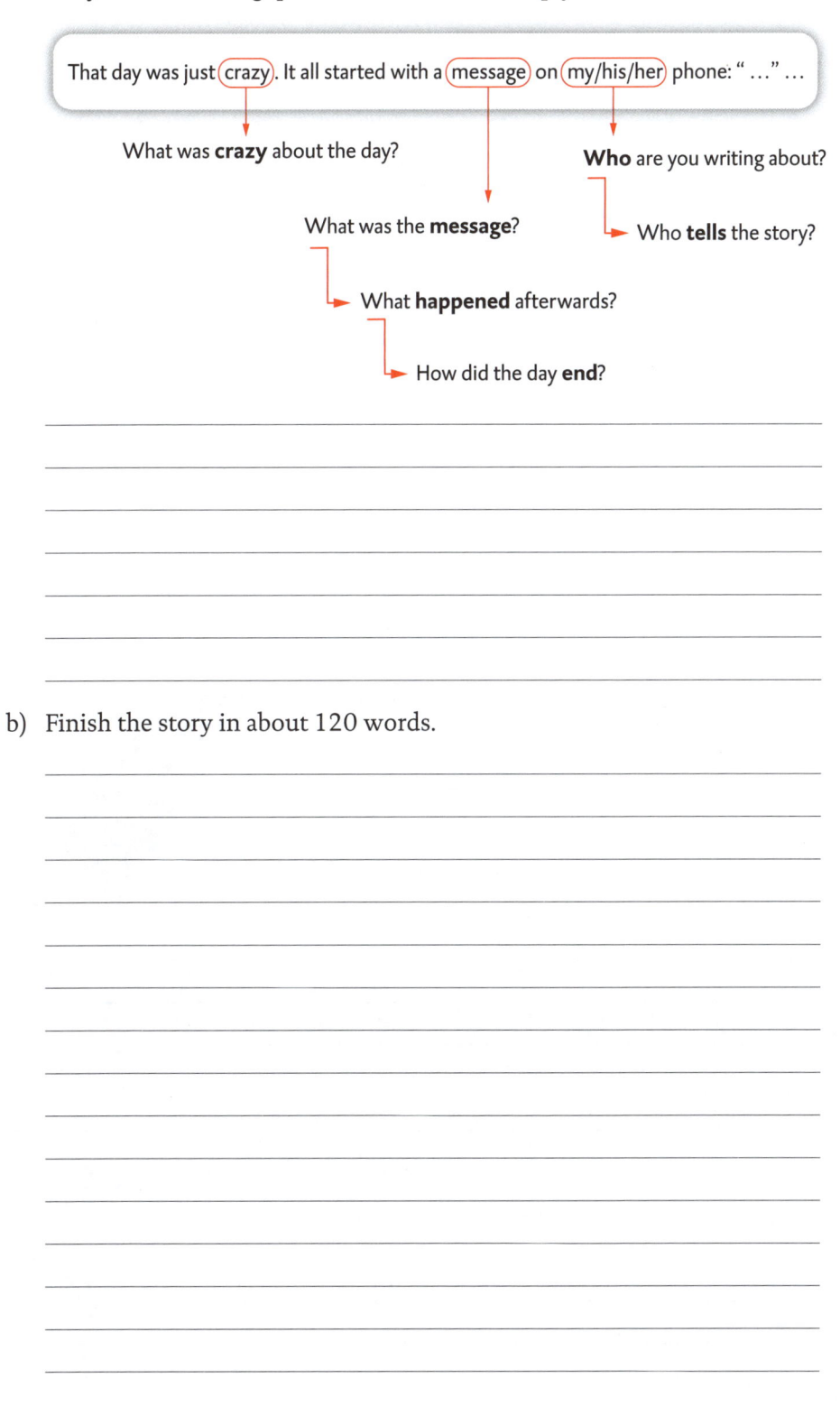

   > That day was just (crazy). It all started with a (message) on (my/his/her) phone: " …" …

   What was **crazy** about the day?

   What was the **message**?

   Who are you writing about?

   Who **tells** the story?

   What **happened** afterwards?

   How did the day **end**?

   _____
   _____
   _____
   _____
   _____
   _____
   _____

   b) Finish the story in about 120 words.
   _____
   _____
   _____
   _____
   _____
   _____
   _____
   _____
   _____
   _____
   _____
   _____
   _____
   _____
   _____

9. Finish the following story. Write about 120 words.

   Hi, I'm X23 and it's my first day on planet Earth. ...

10. Write a diary entry with the following ending. Write about 120 words.

    ... And those red lights were the last I ever saw of him/her.

11. Read the following statements and imagine they are from your contacts on a social networking site. Do you like them or not? Collect ideas for possible answers and fill in this grid:

Statements	Arguments for 👍	Arguments against 👎
❶ Action films are only for boys.		
❷ In times of climate change flying should be at least twice as expensive as it is today.		
❸ People who eat meat are killers.		
❹ Living in a small village is the most boring thing I can imagine.		
❺ Pupils should be allowed to choose whatever subjects they want.		

12. Choose at least two of the topics in task 11 and give your opinion. Write at least 60 words.

Topic	

_____
_____
_____
_____
_____

Topic	

_____

_____

_____

_____

_____

_____

13. Choose the correct address for each situation.

    a) In a letter to Carlos Fernandez, your pen friend in South America:
        ☐ Dear Mr Fernandez,
        ☐ Sir,
        ☐ Hi Carlos,

    b) In an e-mail to Diana Watson, the manager of a hotel you stayed at (you only know her name and have never met her in person):
        ☐ Dear Ms Watson,
        ☐ Dear Mrs Watson,
        ☐ Dear Sir/Madam,

    c) In a letter of application to the personnel manager of a company:
        ☐ Dear lady or gentleman,
        ☐ Dear Sir or Madam,
        ☐ Dear everyone,

    d) In an e-mail to Linda Evans, your grandmother:
        ☐ Dear Granny,
        ☐ Hi Evans,
        ☐ Dear Mrs Evans,

14. Choose the correct ending for each situation.

    a) In a letter to Carlos Fernandez, Mike's new pen friend in South America:
        ☐ Love, Mike
        ☐ Best wishes, Mike
        ☐ Yours sincerely, Mike

    b) In an e-mail to Diana Watson, the manager of a hotel you stayed at (you only know her name and have never met her in person):
        ☐ Yours sincerely,
        ☐ Love,
        ☐ Best wishes,

c) In a letter of application to the personnel manager of a company:
  ☐ Regards,
  ☐ Yours faithfully,
  ☐ All the best,

d) In an e-mail to Linda Evans, your grandmother:
  ☐ Yours sincerely,
  ☐ Yours faithfully,
  ☐ Love,

15. In the summer holidays you are going to attend a language course in San Francisco. You are travelling together with an Italian friend you met in your last holidays. Here's your friend's e-mail:

> Hi there,
>
> So cool – only a few more weeks and we'll be in San Francisco together!
> OK, we've got English lessons in the morning, but we'll have plenty of time to explore the city, too. Have you got any special plans? I've attached two nice pictures to give you some ideas ☺.
> Did you also get an e-mail from the language school today? They want to know whether we would like to stay with a host family or share an apartment with other students from the language course.
> What do you think? I think it would be fun if we could stay at the same place.
>
> Best wishes,
> Fabio

Write an answer to Fabio. In your e-mail, include the following aspects:
▶ one or two activities you would like to do in San Francisco
▶ what you would like about sharing an apartment with other students
▶ what you would like about staying in a host family
▶ which of the two options you would prefer

Find a suitable beginning and ending. Write about 200 words.

a) Make a table and collect ideas for your e-mail.

b) Write the e-mail to Fabio.

To: fabio-fantastico@yahoo.it
Cc:
Bcc:
Subject: Re: San Francisco, here we come!

5.5 Spezielle Übungen zu textgebundenen Schreibaufgaben

1. In each of the mind maps below, there are several examples of a certain topic. Find a suitable phrase that could serve as a headline or general term *(Überbegriff)* and write it in the middle.

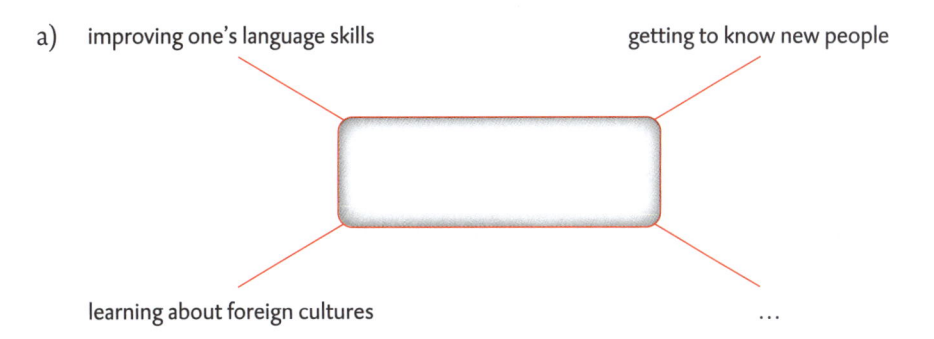

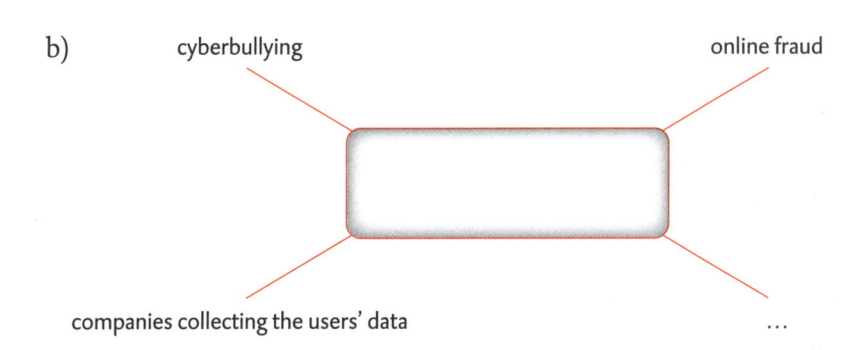

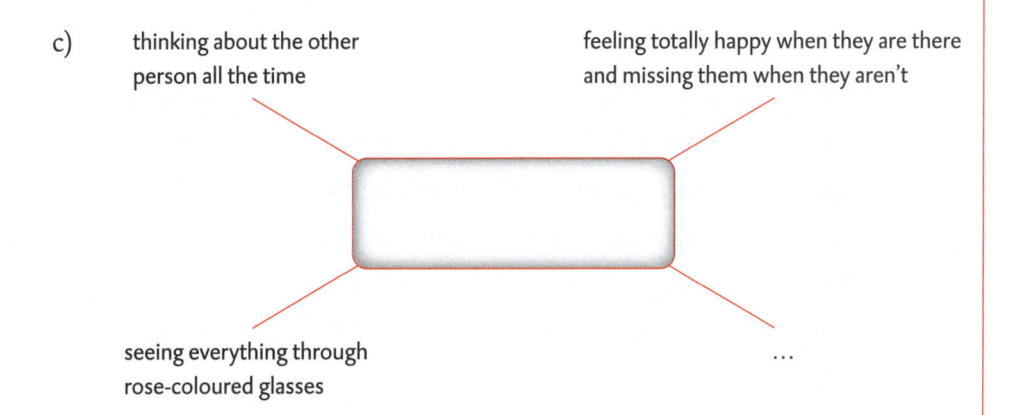

a)
- improving one's language skills
- getting to know new people
- learning about foreign cultures
- …

b)
- cyberbullying
- online fraud
- companies collecting the users' data
- …

c)
- thinking about the other person all the time
- feeling totally happy when they are there and missing them when they aren't
- seeing everything through rose-coloured glasses
- …

2. Which elements should a good summary include? Tick (✓) the correct box(es). More than one answer can be correct.

☐ the title and author of the text
☐ an exact re-telling of the story/text in chronological order
☐ who the main character(s) is/are (if it is a literary text)
☐ your personal opinion on the text
☐ interesting dialogues
☐ the main topic
☐ lots of details and examples
☐ the most important aspects of the text "in a nutshell"
☐ phrases or sentences copied from the text

3. Below, there are two summaries of the text *Inventing Elliot* (see chapter 6, Listening Test 9) – a bad one and a good one.

   a) First look at the negative example. The text contains some of the typical mistakes one can make when writing a summary. Identify the mistakes and write them in the margin next to the text.

> Elliot was already in bed when his mother knocked on the door. "You've got to be patient with him, Elliot. He's ill. And we're going to have to accept that," said his mother. Elliot and his mother talked about his father. I think Elliot should be more understanding because it was not his father's fault that he was attacked.
>
> The night that his father didn't come home, Elliot had already gone to bed. Half-asleep he heard the front door bell, unfamiliar voices, the door closing again, chairs scraping across the kitchen floor under his bedroom. Two policemen came into the room. The woman went back into the kitchen, and the man told the boy: "Can you go and get dressed?" Elliot and his mother visited his father in hospital. Elliot prayed, although he didn't believe in God. That was three years ago. The bones had healed, his dad had come home, but it didn't get better. Finally, Elliot said to his mother: "I know it takes time, like the hospital said. I just wish – I just wish it had never happened, that's all."

b) Now look at the positive example. Write what is positive about it next to the text.

> The excerpt from the novel *Inventing Elliot* by Graham Gardner is about a boy, Elliot, and the relationship to his father, who was seriously injured in an attack and needs a long time to recover.
>
> A conversation with his mother one night leads Elliot to play over in his mind what happened. He thinks back to the time long before the accident, when he, his mum and dad had spent lots of time together and were a happy family. He remembers how all that changed when his dad became increasingly busy with his work, and the shock he felt on the night of the attack: He almost couldn't believe it when the police told him that his dad had been attacked out of the blue and was lying seriously injured in hospital. Although Elliot's father's was finally able to leave the hospital, he still suffers from depression and is not the same as before, a fact that seems hard for Elliot to accept.

Text 1: The Double Life of Cassiel Roadnight

1. Read the excerpt from *The Double Life of Cassiel Roadnight* (see chapter 2, Reading Test 8).

2. **Summarise** what the text is about. Use at least 80 words.

3. **Explain** why the protagonist pretends to be Cassiel Roadnight in the end.
   a) Before you start writing: Tick (✓) the correct boxes.
   In this task, you have to …
   ☐ sum up the story as a whole.
   ☐ give possible reasons for the protagonist's decision.
   ☐ give your personal opinion on the protagonist's decision.
   ☐ write about how the story might continue.
   ☐ support your findings with evidence from the text.

   b) Now write your text. Use at least 100 words.

Text 2: The Art of Being Normal

1. Read the extract from *The Art of Being Normal* (see chapter 6, Listening Test 5).

2. **Explain** why Leo and Alicia seem to get along with each other so well. Write at least 100 words.

Text 3: The OMG Blog

The pupils Jessie, Shanice, Rose and Zarah have become friends because they all think their mums are a bit crazy. When the school launches a blogging competition, the four decide to write about their mothers in a blog called "OMG!" (short for "Our Mums – Grrrr!"). In the scene below, they are presenting their idea to their teacher, Miss Singh.

1 "Sorry I'm late," [Jessie] gasped.
 Miss Singh and Jessie's blog-buddies were already huddled around a computer.
 "No worries," said Miss Singh. "I was just saying that the site's looking great, Jessie. I'm impressed by the design, as well as the idea. Well done to all of you!"
5 Jessie, Zarah, Rose and Shanice beamed with pride.
 "And I like the fact that you're being positive too," said their teacher. "The way you finish your posts with *'I love you, but grrrrrrr!!'* It's sweet and kind, so the blog is not just a big fat moan about mothers." […]
 "And when other students read the blog and make comments, they'll say they love
10 their mums too. Hopefully!" said Jessie.
 "OK …" Miss Sing said slowly. "But other students – they are your problem now, aren't they?"
 Jessie wondered what Miss Singh meant. So did the other girls – she could tell by their confused silence.
15 Miss Singh began to explain herself. She held her fingers up one by one as she made each point.
 "This blog competition will be won by the group that has the best idea, the best design AND is the most popular blog with students here at Newton Academy."
 Right, thought Jessie. So, Miss Singh had just said she really liked the OMG! design
20 and idea. Only one thing was missing.
 "We need lots of people to view our blog, don't we?" Jessie asked. "And respond to it …"
 "Today's Thursday. The competition closes on Monday," said Zarah. "So we need *lots* of views over the weekend."
25 "Exactly," Miss Singh said. "You need to think about how to let other students know the blog exists – and fast."
 "We could make posters today," Jessie suggested. […]
 "[Or] we could set up an Instagram account to advertise the site," said Zarah, holding up her phone.
30 "Hmm. It might take you a while to get people signed up that way," Miss Singh reminded them.
 "I guess so," said Zarah, looking at her screen. "Still, lots of people at school *have* Instagram and – *NOOO!*"
 Miss Singh looked alarmed – but Jessie, Rose and Shanice knew what was wrong.
35 "What? What's your mum written *this* time?" asked Shanice.

She grabbed Zarah's wrist and pulled her close to see the phone better. Jessie and Rose leaned forward too.

OK, so it seemed that Zarah had posted an old clip of Blondie singing the original, much cooler version of 'One Way or Another'. Fine. And, underneath, there were LOTS of comments.

The first was –

| mama2z | Hey, that's got a great beat! |

which Jessie and her blog-buddies all knew was Mrs Bashir.

Then Jessie began to read the comments that followed – and felt *so* bad for Zarah. It was awful to have your mum leave a corny comment like that. But it was even WORSE when a whole stack of people had written stuff like …

| bizzie_lizzie | Is that your mum?! Hahahaha!! |

| ash_boy007 | Aw, Mummy likes your music … so sweet! NOT! |

"I am SO deleting my Instagram account," Zarah said, and began tip-tapping at her phone, her face a picture of pure frustration.

But suddenly Shanice grabbed Zarah's mobile from her and plonked the computer keyboard in front of her instead.

"Think it's *your* turn to blog, Zarah," she said with a grin. "Let all your *grrrrs* out!"

Adapted from: McCombie, Karen. 2016. The OMG Blog. Edinburgh: Barrington Stoke Ltd. pp. 89–95.

1. Read the extract from the novel *The OMG Blog* by Karen McCombie.

2. *"Parents should be in control of what their children are doing online."*
   Comment on the statement from your point of view.

   a) Before you start writing: Think of arguments for and against the statement and write them in the table.

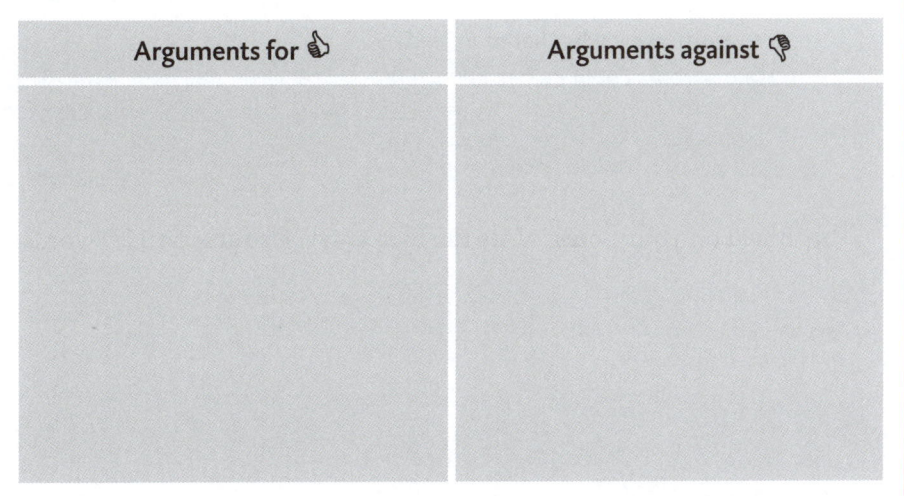

Arguments for 👍	Arguments against 👎

   b) Use your notes from a) to write the comment (in at least 120 words).
      Do not forget to give a short introduction to the topic and to end your comment with a personal conclusion.

3. *"Think it's your turn to blog, Zarah,"* she said with a grin. *"Let all your grrrrs out!"*

   Write Zarah's **entry** for the *Our Mothers – Grrrr!*-**Blog**.
   Include the following aspects:
   ▸ a direct address to Zarah's mum,
   ▸ a short summary of what happened and why Zarah is now angry with her mum,
   ▸ why she nevertheless loves her mum,
   ▸ a suggestion for what her mum and other parents could do better.

   a) Before you start writing: The aspects given in the task can serve as a basic structure for your text. Complete the table with further ideas, examples or useful phrases that come to your mind and which you could use in your text.

Aspects	Ideas/examples/useful phrases
a direct address to Zarah's mum:	
a short summary of what happened and why Zarah is now angry with her mum:	
why she nevertheless loves her mum:	
a suggestion for what her mum and other parents could do better:	

   b) Based on your notes, write the blog entry. Use at least 120 words.

Text 4: The Mystery of the Stolen FA Cup Medal

1 […] David always listened to football in the evenings. […] United had drawn at Liverpool. 2-2. So he was neither happy nor sad. This was one of his favourite bits of the day. He closed his eyes and pretended he had been at the United game, chanting with the crowd, celebrating the goals. […]

5 Although he lived less than a mile from United's stadium, David had never been to see them play. That cost £50 a ticket. Too much. Sometimes noises interrupted David's football fantasies. The kids on the street outside. Police cars going past with their sirens blasting. And, sometimes, noises from next door. David had never met his next door neighbour. In fact, he barely knew anyone in the street where he lived. But
10 he knew some things about the old man next door. He knew he went to bed at 10 pm. […] He also knew that every Saturday – and sometimes Sunday – a posh car would arrive and the old man would get into it and be away for a few hours. That that was the only time the man went out in a week. […]

   […] The day after the Liverpool-United game, David was playing [football in] the
15 back garden, trying to do keepy-uppies with his feet and his head. That's when it happened for the first time. He kicked the ball high, then headed it, then kicked it again and then – losing control – it flew over the high fence and into the next garden. […] He was just about to start [cursing] when, like a miracle, the ball came back, perfectly weighted to his feet. David was startled. How had that happened? He was so amazed
20 – and so puzzled – that he kicked the ball back over the fence. Just to see what would happen next? The answer came quickly. The ball was lofted back to him. So he headed it over the fence again. And it came back. Again. This went on until it was dark, when David had to go inside. He shouted thank you to whoever had been kicking the ball to him. But no-one replied. That night, as he went to sleep, David did not think about
25 playing for United. His mind was too busy wondering who was on the other side of the fence. […]

   [The next day, David was looking out of the window lost in thoughts, he saw s]omeone coming over the fence at the back of the houses. A young man wearing a baseball cap and scarf around his face. David watched the man walk swiftly across the garden
30 next door, then disappear from view. He waited and then heard something coming from the house next door. Bumps. Noises of someone opening and closing drawers. Someone was burgling the old man's house! David wasn't sure what to do. Should he phone the police? […] After a few more minutes he saw the man in the baseball cap leaving the house, climbing the fence, but struggling this time, because of something
35 he had in his hand. Then he heard a police siren. The man in the baseball cap reacted by running in one direction, putting his hands against a wall, then quickly running the other way. […]

   [… Two days later,] David sat in the kitchen […], looking at the newspaper. A photo on the front page shocked him. It was a picture of an old man. But not any old
40 man. It was the old man who lived next door. And underneath he read the headline UNITED HERO'S CUP FINAL MEDAL STOLEN. David read on: 'Arthur Stevens, the last surviving player from United's Cup winning team of 1952, returned from watching United's 3-0 home victory against Chelsea, to find his cup winning medal had been stolen from his house. […]' David couldn't believe that the old man next door
45 was a former United player. […]

   That night, [… David] lay in the dark wondering how the old man would be feeling. That medal must be one of his prize possessions. Maybe his favourite thing in the

world. And someone had just stolen it. [...Then, suddenly, he remembered] something. The man with the baseball cap. He'd run one way, then the other, when he heard the
50 police car coming. That had seemed strange to David at the time. The way he'd run to the wall, then come back running the other way. But he'd not given it any more thought. Now he was. Because what if ... what if the man had hidden the medal there? [...]

Adapted from: http://learnenglishteens.britishcouncil.org/uk-now/literature-uk/mystery-stolen-fa-cup-medal

1. Read the extract from "The Mystery of the Stolen FA Cup Medal".

2. **Describe** David's relationship to football.
   a) Before you start writing: Tick (✓) the correct box.

   In this task, you have to ...
   - ☐ write down everything you know about David.
   - ☐ sum up certain aspects of the story.
   - ☐ give your opinion on football.

   b) Now write the solution to the task. Use at least 80 words.

3. **Explain** why the person kicking the ball back over the fence does not say anything to David. Write at least 100 words.

4. **Analyse** how suspense is created in the story.
   a) Before you start writing: Tick (✓) the correct box.

   In this task, you have to ...
   - ☐ retell the whole plot.
   - ☐ also describe <u>how</u> the story is told.
   - ☐ say what you like or do not like about the story.

   b) Now write the solution to the task. Use at least 100 words.

5. **Write a suitable ending** in the way the story is told.
   Include the following aspects:
   ▶ what David does next,
   ▶ whether the medal is still there,
   ▶ what happens the next time David sees the old man.

   a) Before you start writing: Take a closer look at the style in which the novel is written. Then tick (✓) the correct box(es).

The story is told by ...	
☐ a first-person narrator.	☐ a third-person narrator.
It is written in the ...	
☐ simple present.	☐ simple past.
It includes ...	
☐ both dialogues and narrated passages.	☐ hardly any dialogues.

b) Collect ideas how the story might continue and write them in the grid.

Aspects	Ideas/examples/useful phrases
what David does next:	
whether the medal is still there:	
what happens the next time David sees the old man:	

c) Use the answers from a) and b) to write the ending.
Write at least 120 words.

Text: 5: Boot Camps for Teenagers

1. Read the text "Boot Camps for Teenagers" (see chapter 2, Reading Test 9).

2. **Summarise** what the text is about.

3. **Explain** why boot camps for teenagers are often criticised.

4. Write a **diary entry** from the point of view of a young criminal in a boot camp. Include the following aspects:
   - how long you have already been there,
   - what you had to do during the day,
   - what the instructors are like,
   - your feelings about being in the boot camp.

Text 6: Sundae Girl

1. Read the extract from the novel *Sundae Girl* (see chapter 6, Listening Test 12). Then do tasks 2 to 4. Try to complete the tasks in no more than 60 minutes.

2. **Describe** the narrator's family.

3. **Explain** why Jude lies to Kevin Carter.

4. You have a choice here. Choose **one** of the following tasks.
   a) *"One Cannot Choose One's Family."*
      Comment on this statement from your point of view.
   b) Jude is still standing next to Kevin Carter during Parents' Night. Suddenly her parents come over and begin talking to her.
      Write a suitable ending, in the way the story is told.

6 Anhang: Hörverstehenstexte

Listening Test 1: Robben Island

Theresa: Good morning listeners. I'm Theresa Miller and you're listening to WorldRadio. During the week we've been talking about South Africa and what visitors can do there. Today we'll be looking at Robben Island. In the studio with me is Mike James from the Robben Island Information Centre. Hi Mike!

Mike: Hi there.

Theresa: Mike, can you first of all tell our listeners where Robben Island is and how visitors can get there?

Mike: Sure. Robben Island is a small island about seven kilometres off the coast of Cape Town. It takes about 30 minutes to get there by boat.

Theresa: Most people have heard about the prison on Robben Island. Is it still there and is it possible to visit it?

Mike: Yes, of course. The prison is now a museum but you can only visit it with a guided tour where former prisoners show you around and tell you stories about the conditions there. Interestingly enough, most of the ex-prisoners still live on Robben Island and some of their ex-guards do, too.

Theresa: How strange – aren't there any problems between them?

Mike: No, not at all.

Theresa: Can you tell us what kind of people were imprisoned on Robben Island?

Mike: Well, the maximum-security prison was not for bank robbers or anyone like that, but for political prisoners. Many of them were locked up because they had fought against the system of racial segregation in South Africa.

Theresa: What was daily life like for them in the prison?

Mike: Well, at first, prisoners slept on mats on the floor but later they had bunk beds. From about 8 a.m. until 4 p.m. they had to work, then they ate and after that they were locked up in dormitories – large rooms, which had about 40 people in each one. These were for "normal" political prisoners – the leaders, like Nelson Mandela, had single cells and were separated from the others.

Theresa: What did they do in the evenings?

Mike: Many prisoners couldn't read or write when they arrived on Robben Island, so those people who could taught the others. They also formed small groups to discuss political issues and one person in each group – the group head – brought messages from the leaders, like Mandela.

Theresa: But you said leaders were kept in separate cells, so how could they pass on messages?

Mike: In many different ways. The doctor, for example, came every Wednesday – leaders and group heads often pretended to be ill on those days, and while waiting for the doctor they came into contact with each other.

Sometimes, the messages were also put into tennis balls and "accidentally" hit over the separating wall.

Theresa: Tell me something about the most famous prisoner on Robben Island – Nelson Mandela.

Mike: He was there for 18 years. His cell was about four square metres, with a mat on the floor as a bed. If he was offered a privilege, he wouldn't accept it unless all the other prisoners got it, too. He had hard outside work to do but that meant he could talk to the other leaders during the breaks.

Theresa: Why didn't anyone try to escape? Seven kilometres is a long swim but not impossible.

Mike: The easy answer is that you would probably have died trying to swim to the mainland. The sea is very cold, and there are strong currents and many sharks.

Theresa: Thanks Mike, I've learnt a lot today.

Mike: Thanks for having me.

Theresa: Now, over to the news room ... *(fade out)*

Listening Test 2: The News

News Item 1: The Pardoning of the Thanksgiving Turkey

Thanksgiving is one of the major holidays in the USA. Its origins can be traced back to the time of the Pilgrim Fathers, the first settlers to the newly founded colonies, who celebrated their first successful harvest. Today, it is a nationwide holiday, which is always celebrated on the fourth Thursday in November.

One rather peculiar tradition is the so-called pardoning of the turkey, when the US president saves one or more turkeys from being killed and eaten. There are different theories as to who started that custom. Harry Truman was the first president to be presented with a turkey as a gift to his family, but there are no records that he spared the bird. Some years later, John F. Kennedy freed one of the turkeys given to his family, but it was not an official pardon; it was rather a spontaneous action due to the massive size of the bird. Kennedy seemed to think that a turkey of 55 pounds was too big for his family to eat. The first time an official pardon was issued took place in 1987, when Ronald Reagan was asked whether he would pardon Oliver North, a man who was engaged in the so-called "Iran-Contra Affair", a political scandal during Reagan's presidency. As he did not want to answer the question, he preferred to pardon the turkey instead, in order to avoid further questions. Since George Bush senior's presidency two years later, the pardoning has been a permanent tradition.

News Item 2: What about a Batmobile?

Have you ever imagined being a superhero? What would driving a fantastic car like Batman feel like? This might be the line of thoughts that crossed 29-year-old Australian Zac Mihajlovic's mind a few years ago. And he didn't just stop at thinking. He spent two years of his life building an exact copy of the

Batmobile shown in the first movie from 1989 in his backyard. It took Zac another year to work in all the details needed for a registered car licence. Now the car is not just a life-sized model – it is actually driving with licence plates,
30 papers and all. The whole thing started with his grandfather, who told him that "any fantasy can become a reality", and he tried to prove that. But there is also a big problem he has with the car: Whenever he drives around, people regularly try to stop him to ask questions about the Batmobile or to take pictures of it. Once he even needed a police escort to get out of a place when he
35 was in Sydney with the car. By the way, Zac doesn't fight criminals. He actually uses the car for charity work.

Listening Test 3: Apple and Rain

1 [*Sound of a school bell ringing.*] "Good work today, folks. See you tomorrow," Mr. Gaydon says, giving us permission to pile out of the classroom into the heaving corridor.
Pilar and I are by the lockers when Donna, Hazel, and Mariah stop next to us.
5 Donna whispers something to Pilar, and they laugh.
"What's funny?" I ask.
"Oh, nothing. You had to be there," Donna says.
"Where did you have to be?" I ask.
Pilar fiddles with her gold stud earring.
10 "We went swimming on Sunday and there were these guys there who …," Donna begins, but she can't continue because she is laughing again. Uncontrollably.
"You went swimming together?" I ask. Pilar didn't tell me. She certainly didn't invite me.
15 "We all did," Mariah says.
"And then for kebabs," Hazel adds.
"I didn't ask you because I knew your nan would've said you couldn't come," Pilar says. She examines the floor.
"And it's always awkward with odd numbers," Donna says.
20 "I was busy on Sunday anyway," I tell them.
"Church?" Pilar asks. She's forgotten I told her I was meeting Mum. She's forgotten how important it was to me. […]
"Yeah, church," I say.
"Shall we get lunch, Pilar?" Donna asks. She doesn't look at me, so I know
25 I'm not invited, and I expect Pilar to tell Donna that she always eats with me – that it's the two of us at school and no one else.
"You hungry, Apple?" Pilar asks uncomfortably.
Donna sighs. Hazel rolls her eyes. Mariah walks away.
"No," I say. "I'm not sure what's happened to my appetite lately."
30 Donna's eyes rest on my belly. "Well, it's never a bad thing to lose a few pounds," she says.

I swallow hard and open my locker door to hide my face.

"I'll see you later then," Pilar says.

"Yeah, see you," I say.

And she is gone. […]

I know that Pilar isn't my wife or anything. She's allowed to have other friends. But I can't help feeling jittery with jealousy. I spend all lunch period pacing the corridors and wondering how I'll win her back from Donna. Pilar's my only friend. If I lose her, I'll have no one.

So I come up with a speech; when I get to drama [lesson], I'll be honest and tell her how I fell. We're performing a sketch together; she'll have to partner up with me and listen.

But when I get into the theater, Pilar is already sitting with Donna, Hazel, and Mariah. There's no way I'll get a chance to tell her how I feel now. I'll be alone all lesson. Everyone will stare and wonder why Pilar and I have fallen out. I don't want anyone knowing I've got no friends.

Without waiting another second, I scan the theater to make sure Ms. Court isn't hiding somewhere and make a run for it. I can hide out in some toilets until school finishes, then meet Nana in the playground as usual – no one needs to know I skipped a couple of lessons.

[… Or m]aybe I could go to the office and say I'm sick. But the nurse would probably call Nana, who would take one look at me and know I was lying. They might even send me back to class.

Only one person would understand. I reach into my bag for my phone.

© *Sarah Crossan: Apple and Rain. London 2014, Bloomsbury Publishing Plc, pp. 84–89.*

Listening Test 4: Grey Owl

Cameron: Gina, you write and draw comic books and your next one is about a man called Grey Owl. First of all, where does that name come from and what was so special about the man?

Gina: Well, "Grey Owl" is an Indian name. Grey Owl claimed that he was half-Apache but actually he was English. He was probably Canada's first conservationist and saved the beaver from extinction.

Cameron: An interesting guy.

Gina: He was. He was born in England in 1888 to English parents. His real name was Archibald Belaney. As a boy, Archie was fascinated with Native Americans and life in the wilderness. At 17, he left home to be a trapper in Canada, catching beavers for their fur. He married a woman from one of the First Nations and learnt her language. He started wearing indigenous clothes and also darkened his hair and skin. Unlike most indigenous people, however, Archie had blue eyes. But when the other trappers asked him about his identity, he always told them that his father was Scottish and that his mother was an Apache.

Cameron: Did he stay with his wife's people?

Gina: No – after some time, Archie left his wife and child to move to a small woodcutting community where he had a relationship and a child with an-
20　other woman, whom he soon abandoned as well …

Cameron: A restless guy …

Gina: Definitely. In the First World War, he fought with the Canadian army but was injured and sent to his aunt's house in England. There he married again, but eventually left his wife to return to Canada. During his travels in
25　Canada, he was rescued from snow blindness by a tribal chief who then taught him more about how to survive in the wilderness. Archie took the name "Grey Owl" and finally married another indigenous woman.

Cameron: You said at the beginning that he had been a trapper – why did he stop?

30 **Gina:** His new wife hated trapping. One day he'd killed a beaver but left its young behind alone, which would have meant certain death for them. His wife thought this was cruel so she made him bring the two beaver babies home where they raised them by hand. From that moment, his whole life changed.

35 **Cameron:** In what way?

Gina: He quit trapping and began writing books about protecting wildlife. He made films for the National Parks, and worked for them, too. He started touring North America and England telling people about the need to protect wildlife and the Canadian forests. The cost of his success, however,
40　was his marriage.

Cameron: I guess his wife left him.

Gina: She sure did! But he married again. By that time, he'd become so famous as a conservationist, he even gave a talk to the Royal Family in Buckingham Palace.

45 **Cameron:** And everyone still thought he was a Native North American.

Gina: Yes … but soon after he died in 1938, the press found out that Grey Owl, the supposed half-Apache, was really an Englishman named Archie Belaney.

Cameron: Did that matter? He'd achieved great things for conservation – he'd
50　saved the Canadian beavers from dying out; he'd made people see that nature had to be protected …

Gina: … but people were angry because of the lie. Some bookshops stopped selling his books, and others only sold ones with his real name on. Many indigenous people are still very angry that he pretended to be one of them.
55　But perhaps, if he hadn't claimed to be this, no one would have listened. So it's really hard to judge him …

Cameron: Well, let's hear what our listeners think about the story of Grey Owl. You can call our studio on … *(fade out)*

Listening Test 5: The Art of Being Normal

1 The next day I get to English to discover Matt, the kid I usually sit next to, is off school with glandular fever.
"We're going to be working in pairs today, discussing the symbolism in [Shakespeare's] *Twelfth Night*" Miss Jennings announces. She puts me in a
5 three with Alicia and Ruby, the girl who sits next to Alicia. Ruby's OK; a bit annoying, but OK.
I keep my cool, nodding casually as Alicia and Ruby turn their chairs round so they're facing me. Alicia's knee touches mine for a second.
[…]
10 "Are you going to Becky's party?" [Alicia] asks slowly.
"I didn't know she was having one," I reply.
This isn't quite true. Becky Somerville is in my form and has such a big mouth you'd have to be living on Mars not to have heard her go on about it.
"Yeah, next Saturday," Alicia says […].
15 "Oh, right. Cool."
"So, now you do know about it, do you think you might go?" Alicia asks […].
I clear my throat and shrug. "I dunno. Parties aren't really my scene."
"What do you mean, parties aren't your scene?" Alicia squeaks. "That's like saying food isn't your scene, or breathing isn't your scene. I mean, who doesn't
20 like parties?"
I look down, cursing myself for saying something so weird. Alicia's right – normal people *do* like parties.
"I'm just not great at crowds," I add. I regret my words straight away because I know I'm making it worse, blowing it big-time with my weirdness.
25 "That's too bad," Alicia says.
"Anyway, I'm not invited," I add. "I don't think Becky is my biggest fan."
Becky treats me like most of my other classmates seem to, with this mixture of fear and fascination, like I'm an exotic animal escaped from the zoo that may or may not be dangerous. Everyone apart from Alicia. Alicia doesn't act
30 like she's scared of me one bit.
"Becky just hasn't taken the chance to get to know you yet, that's all," Alicia says. "Cos if she did, she'd think totally differently, I know it."
I shrug and look at my hands. There's a long pause.
"You know, I was the new kid once."
35 "Yeah?" I say, looking up.
"Yep. Back in Year 8. My parents moved up here from London halfway through the year."
"And how was it?"
"Hideous."
40 "Really?" […]
"Uh-huh. In case you haven't noticed, Eden Park isn't the most diverse of schools. You can count the number of black kids here on two hands. […] Plus, everyone had friends already; I was a year and a half too late. […]"
"So what changed?" I ask.

⁴⁵ "Well, I forced myself to eat in the canteen for a start. Then I joined drama club and choir, smiled inanely at everyone I encountered, etcetera. And eventually I discovered there were lots of nice people, I just had to put myself out there in order to find them. […]" […]

Alicia clears her throat.

⁵⁰ "Look, Becky says I can bring someone," she says. "To her party I mean."

Heat creeps up my neck.

"Oh yeah? Who you bringing then?"

She takes a deep breath before looking me straight in the eyes.

"Well, no one at the moment."

⁵⁵ "Oh, right," I say, swallowing hard.

Ruby (who I'd forgotten was even there) raises her head […].

"For God's sake, you two are making me die. Leo, Alicia is trying to ask you out, you utter dickhead. Just say you'll go with her to Becky's party, please? Before I bang your stupid heads together." […]

⁶⁰ I look at Alicia who is hiding behind her hands. When she lowers them, her cheeks are all flushed. […]

"So, what do you think?" Alicia asks, biting her lower lip. "Do you want to?"

"Er, yeah, OK then." I find myself saying, my steady voice fighting my motoring heartbeat and sweaty palms.

⁶⁵ "Cool." she says.

There's a pause before she bursts into giggles. And suddenly I'm doing something I haven't done in forever, and it's like I'm having this weird, out-of-body experience – because I'm laughing too.

Adapted from: Williamson, Lisa. 2015. The Art of Being Normal. Oxford: David Fickling Books. S. 114–119.

Listening Test 6: The California Gold Rush

¹ **Speaker:** In 1847, California became a US territory. Most Americans at the time lived on the East Coast. But thousands traveled west to California after a settler reported finding gold there.

James Marshall found the gold nugget in January 1848. Mr. Marshall was
⁵ building a sawmill near the American River in central California. When he looked in the water, he saw shiny pieces of metal. One of them was about the size of a fingernail. Mr. Marshall took the piece and put it in his mouth. Paul Johnston is curator of Maritime History at the Smithsonian's Museum of American History here in Washington, D.C. The museum displays the
¹⁰ gold nugget Mr. Marshall found.

Paul Johnston: And you can see Mr. Marshall actually bit down on it. You can see the molar marks, his bite mark on it as well as a little chip taken out of the upper left hand corner for assaying, or testing the purity of the gold.

Speaker: Mr. Marshall knew he found gold because the metal was soft. He and
¹⁵ his boss gave the nugget to the US government to prove they found gold on the land.

News of James Marshall's discovery traveled to the East Coast. But communication was slow in the middle of the 19th century. People in the big eastern cities of New York and Boston heard only rumors about gold in California. It was not until December 1848, almost a year after Mr. Marshall's discovery, that President James Polk told Congress the rumors were true. During the next weeks and months, thousands of young men from the Northeast left their homes and families to seek great riches in California.

Paul Johnston: You didn't really have to work for it, as far as they knew. You just had to lean over and pick it up and you were rich.

Speaker: One of those young men was Benjamin Buckley. His records suggest he found thousands of dollars' worth of gold. Buckley put some money in banks and sent some to family members. Alexander Van Valen, however, was not as successful. The Smithsonian's Museum of American History has letters he wrote to his wife and daughters in New York.

Paul Johnston: His wife tried to make a living by sewing and by borrowing money from the financiers against her husband's future profits. But it was not any easier for her than it was for her husband 3,000 miles away in California.

Speaker: In two years, Alexander Van Valen earned only $500. Most people who traveled to California to find gold were like Van Valen – they did not get rich. But Paul Johnston says the California Gold Rush was important for other reasons.

Paul Johnston: The Gold Rush really put California on the map. It made it desirable. It made the East Coast want California to become part of the United States. So, it was huge.

Speaker: In 1850, California became the country's 31st state.

Adapted from: https://learningenglish.voanews.com/a/california-gold-rush-1849/1969067.html

Listening Test 7: The Stolen Generations

Greg: This is TopFM, my name is Greg and I'd like to welcome you to our special programme on the history of Australia. Jenny Green has come into the studio today to talk about the so-called Stolen Generations. Jenny, could you explain to our listeners what happened to these people?

Jenny: Sure. From the late nineteenth century to about 1970, various Australian governments took Aboriginal children – or children who had at least one Aboriginal parent – away from their families. Their aim was to make them adopt white culture.

Greg: What was the idea behind that?

Jenny: Well, basically, the governments were trying to get rid of Aboriginal peoples and their traditions. They thought that if Aboriginal children were forced to adopt white culture, the Aboriginal way of life would soon die out.

Greg: But Aboriginal peoples had been there long before the first Europeans arrived.

Jenny: That's true, of course, but many whites thought their culture was better than that of the Aboriginal peoples.

Greg: What happened to the children?

Jenny: The children were separated from their parents – their families – and often taken thousands of miles away, so they would never see each other again. You can imagine how awful this was for them. Many children were also told that their parents had died or just left them. These children were then put into homes run by the church or the state. Some were also adopted from the homes by white families. Most were given "white" names and the only language they were allowed to use was English, not their own – that was forbidden. They were taught to reject their Aboriginal past.

Greg: Sounds like something out of a bad film …

Jenny: But, sadly, it was for real. In some areas, one in three children were taken away – nearly every Aboriginal family lost children in this way. In the homes, children were badly treated and often left cold and hungry. They were given an education, but usually a rather poor one – one just enough to allow them to do basic work, for example as household servants or shepherds.

Greg: Things must have got better since then, though.

Jenny: Yes, but it's taken a long time. In 1997, there was a critical report of what happened to the Stolen Generations. One of its suggestions was to have an annual National Sorry Day for all Australians to remember this part of their country's history – it was later renamed the National Day of Healing. In 2000, during the Olympic Games in Sydney, an Aboriginal runner was chosen to light the Olympic fire. After winning a gold medal, she ran around the track carrying both the Aboriginal flag and the Australian one – a powerful symbol of reconciliation. But it wasn't until 2008 that an Australian prime minister officially apologised to the Stolen Generations.

Greg: So has the sad history of the Stolen Generations finally come to an end?

Jenny: Unfortunately, not completely. Many Aboriginal people still suffer from how they were treated by the whites. And apparently, the number of children who are taken away from their parents is still much higher for Aboriginal people than for white people. Even today, governments seem to spend a lot more money on putting Aboriginal children into state-run homes than on helping them to stay with their parents.

Greg: These aren't very happy facts, are they? Well thanks for now, Jenny, and we'll talk some more after the break …

Listening Test 8: Couchsurfing or Wilderness?

Reporter: I'm Marc White from CBC Radio 1. We're doing a short survey on how people in Vancouver like to spend their holidays. Could you tell me your first name and say what you usually do when you're on holiday?

John: I'm in a bit of a hurry, but that's an easy question to answer. My name's John and I'm 35. I've got a very stressful job, and I hardly ever go on holiday, but when I find the time, I only want to relax, so my wife and I usually go to a luxurious boutique hotel on Vancouver Island that doesn't allow small children. We go for long walks in the woods, get massages, go to the sauna and enjoy the fantastic food there.

Olivia: Hi, I'm Olivia and I'm a student at the University of British Columbia. I'm 21 and I love travelling, but I don't want to be seen as a tourist. Since I don't have much money, I usually go couchsurfing when I'm abroad. It's a great and cheap way to meet locals, make new friends and explore places far away from the typical tourist paths.

Hailey: I'm Hailey and I'm 25 years old. I wouldn't like to go couchsurfing. I think it's dangerous to stay at the house of someone you don't know. I love travelling, but I don't earn much money, so I always stay at youth hostels. I always choose a small hostel so that there's a cosy atmosphere and travellers get in touch with each other easily.

Carter: Hello, my name's Carter and I'm 16. In my summer vacation I usually go camping with my friends. I love hiking and fishing and being outside 24/7, so I wouldn't like to spend my holidays in any other way. My parents, in contrast, usually go on city trips together with their friends from the golf club.

Josh: Camping is great, isn't it? I'm Josh and I'm 15. My parents bought a large mobile home five years ago, so we always go camping. I like sleeping in the comfy bed of the mobile home, whereas my younger brother always sleeps in a tent. We always go to the same campsite, which is great, because we meet the same people every year.

Sara: Hi, I'm Sara and I'm a mum. When we go on holiday, we usually rent an apartment at the coast. Staying at a hotel's just too expensive for a family of six and a dog, although I'd really love to not have to cook. We tried camping once, but it rained for a week, so that wasn't much fun.

Reporter: Thanks everyone for sharing all this with me and our listeners. I hope you have a great time on your next holiday.

Listening Test 9: Inventing Elliot

1 He had just got into bed when there was a knock on the door and his mum came in. She sat on the edge of the bed – she hadn't done that since they'd moved house.
"You've got to be patient with him, Elliot. He's ill. Depression's an illness. And
5 he's still physically damaged too. It's not his fault, you've got to understand that. We've both got to try to understand."
"I just wish –" He stopped. He couldn't say what he wished.
She continued for him. "You just wish it was like it was before. I know. So do I. But it's never going to be. And we're going to have to accept that."
10 He looked away from her, remembering the night his dad didn't come home. Once the business had got properly started, his dad had begun to work late almost every night. That hadn't been so great: it meant he often skipped meals at home. Elliot missed the three of them eating together, talking about nothing in particular – just being a family. [...]
15 One night it had got very late, and his dad still hadn't arrived home. Elliot had been in bed waiting for him, half-asleep, when the front door bell had sounded. He heard the door open, unfamiliar voices, the door close again, chairs scraping across the kitchen floor under his bedroom.
He crept downstairs in his pyjamas. The kitchen door was closed.
20 He listened.
He couldn't hear clearly; he could just make out isolated words and phrases: "... assault ... multiple injuries ... hospital ... operating now ..."
Elliot had felt a growing sense of dread – the gnawing in his stomach which was soon to become so familiar. He willed the voices to continue; while they
25 did, everything was still OK, nothing was going to change.
Keep talking. Keep talking.
Then the noise of chairs pushed back, heavy footsteps, the kitchen door opening. Two police uniforms: a man and a woman. They saw Elliot, stopped, looked at one another, nodded. The woman went back into the kitchen. The
30 man smiled at Elliot, but it was a strained smile, as if he was having to remind himself to put it on.
"Hello there. You been listening?"
Elliot had said nothing.
"Can you go and get dressed? Your mum will be along soon."
35 Elliot had carried on saying nothing, thinking *Not real. Not real. Not real.* It was something that happened only on TV: the police car outside the house, the knock on the door, the figures in uniform, the calm words and sympathetic expressions. It wasn't real life. It would only be real if he became part of it. So he wouldn't become part of it.
40 "Your dad's been hurt. We're taking you with your mum to the hospital, because there's no one here to look after you. OK? Your mum's just getting ready."
Not real. Not real. Not real. Not real.
His dad had been attacked walking back to his car. Whoever it was – his dad
45 didn't remember anything and there had been no witnesses – had taken his

wallet and car keys and mobile. And fractured his skull, broken his ribs, ruptured his spleen. Left him lying on the pavement bleeding to death. Dying. *Not real.* But the words didn't hold back the world anymore.

"Elliot? Are you listening to me? I said, he will get better. It's going to take
50 time, that's all."

Visiting his dad in hospital; seeing his face swollen up like a puffball, tubes coming out of his nose, wrists and chest; watching him unable to move, hardly able to speak. Smashed.

Elliot had cried for him then. And prayed, although he didn't believe in God.
55 But that was three years ago. The bones had mended. His dad had come home. Only he hadn't got better.

"You do understand, don't you?" His mum was pleading.

Elliot forced himself to look at her. "Of course I do. I know it takes time, like the hospital said. I just wish – I just wish it had never happened, that's all."

Adapted from: Gardner, Graham. Inventing Elliot. London: Orion Children's Books 2003.

Listening Test 10: Sandringham

1 Hi, my name is John and I'd like to tell you a bit about my favourite place in Britain, Sandringham House in Norfolk. Sandringham belongs to the Queen – it's her private house in the country where she can relax.

Sandringham is about 100 miles north-east of London and quite near the
5 coast. The nearest big town is King's Lynn. The Royal Family have owned the house since 1862, when Queen Victoria bought it for her son.

People can visit the house and its gardens when the Royal Family are not there but that wasn't always the case: At the beginning, the house and its gardens were totally private. In 1908 King Edward VII then decided to allow
10 visitors to walk around the grounds. However, it wasn't until 1977 that people were allowed into a small part of the house.

So what can you see at Sandringham? There is the house and its gardens, of course, plus a beautiful small church and a museum. And there is Sandringham Estate, the land surrounding the house, which is also owned by the
15 Queen. It includes part of the coast as well as many villages and farms.

You enter the gardens through an entrance in the wall that surrounds the house. You have to pay to see it, of course. The gardens are very big and colourful, and you have to walk a long way through them to get to the house. You can just imagine the young princes and princesses playing games on the
20 grass or zooming around the paths on their bikes.

You don't see many rooms in the house but you do see how the Royal Family live as "normal" people. There're family photos everywhere with furniture and carpets that look used, just like yours or mine … but probably a lot more expensive and much older, too!

25 In the museum behind the house there is a lot of information about life at Sandringham and on the estate. What I like best is the collection of cars that the Royal Family have used privately and also officially. There are even ones which were specially built for the Royal Family – for example, one made

much longer so that it could take all their suitcases to the train station at King's Lynn. ... And here's a little secret – the Queen sits with normal passengers in a first-class coach on the train when she travels back to London! Although the Royal Family use Sandringham to relax in away from the public, Christmas Day always includes a walk to the church on the estate and many people come to see them then. The church is very small but it's also very beautiful and you can see where the members of the Royal Family sit. Old houses always have a ghost. So does Sandringham? The answer is "yes". No one knows what the ghost looks like but it throws books off shelves and alters the time on clocks. Even Prince Charles said that he felt something very strange and very cold in one room. I hope you enjoyed hearing about Sandringham House – it's really worth a visit.

Listening Test 11: The Super Bowl

Radio commentary: ... 1st and 10, good protection – and Brady finds a receiver – it's White. Nice move for a first down inside the 30.

(fade in)

Jeff: That's American football at its best – that's the Super Bowl.

Chelsea: Exactly. My name is Chelsea Morgan and with me in the studio today is football expert Jeff Donald. Jeff, can you tell us a bit more about the history of this great sporting event – how did it all begin?

Jeff: Well, for a long time the most important organisation for American football in the USA was the National Football League, – the NFL. But in 1960 a group of businessmen became dissatisfied with the organisation, so they started another one, the American Football League, – the AFL.

Chelsea: Were there enough players to have two different leagues?

Jeff: Yes, but there were constant fights over who got the best players, and of course also over who attracted the most fans. So in 1966, the two leagues eventually gave up their rivalry and decided to merge into one common league. But until this new league could start, in 1970, the winners of the NFL and the AFL were meant to play against each other in a sort of "super final".

Chelsea: ... and so the idea for the Super Bowl was born. But where did the name "Super Bowl" come from?

Jeff: Well, a club owner jokingly named the final the "Super Bowl" after one of his children's toys, the "Super Ball". It was meant as a suggestion until a better name was found, but eventually the media started using it and so it stuck.

Chelsea: But why the word "bowl"?

Jeff: In American football, the term "bowl" was traditionally used for the last game each college team played in their league. Also, when a new stadium was built at Yale University in 1913, it was called the "Yale Bowl" because of its shape. After that many other stadiums and competitions included the word "bowl".

Chelsea: So when did the first Super Bowl game take place? 1966 or 1967?

Jeff: In 1967, between the Green Bay Packers and Kansas City Chiefs. And guess what? They couldn't sell all the tickets!

Chelsea: That wouldn't happen now, would it?

Jeff: Definitely not! But at the time, a lot of supporters didn't want to travel to a "neutral" football stadium, so they simply stayed at home. However, more than 50 million people watched the game on TV.

Chelsea: How did the Super Bowl grow into what it is today?

Jeff: After the two leagues had merged, the new one was then divided again, into the American Football Conference and the National Football Conference. And the winners of those leagues again played each other in the Super Bowl.

Chelsea: When does the Super Bowl take place and where?

Jeff: It's always on the first Sunday in February and different cities compete to hold it. However, they must have a stadium with at least 70,000 seats and of course a good infrastructure. Strangely, no team has ever played in its home stadium so far – but that's just coincidence.

Chelsea: Nowadays the Super Bowl is a huge event, isn't it?

Jeff: That's right. The Super Bowl is usually the most watched sporting event in the USA and the game is broadcast live around the world. Major pop stars perform before the game and during half-time. For most Americans, the day feels almost like a national holiday …

Chelsea: Well, who knows – maybe someday it'll be one! Thanks, Jeff, for the interesting information and we'll be right back after the break …

Listening Test 12: Sundae Girl

Nobody likes Parents' Night, do they? It's when the truth comes out. Your parents discover that you haven't been wearing your nice maroon St Joseph's blazer, you've only handed in one maths homework since September and you're hanging out with a gang of scary Year Tens who have LOVE and HATE written across their knuckles in black marker pen.

That's the kind of stuff most kids are stressing about, anyhow. Not me. […] I'm not worried that my family will find out the truth about school – I'm more anxious that school will find out the truth about my family.

And now they are here for Parents' Night – all of them. Nightmare.

I'm here too, watching the whole thing, fascinated, horrified. Being here is a kind of torture, obviously, but when Mr McGrath asked for volunteers to make the tea and coffee, my hand shot up instantly like the good Year Eight teacher-pleaser that I am. It's a bit like the way moths get drawn to a flame. I can't help myself, even though I know it will end in disaster […]. […]

"Tea?" I ask brightly.

"Ah, Jude, […] your form teacher Miss Devlin was just telling me that she runs the school drama club. Why ever didn't you tell her I was in show business?"

"You're a hairdresser, Mum," I mumble.

20 "Now I am," Mum says, exasperated. "But what about my musical past? I've played all the top venues – Filey, Minehead, Clacton-on-Sea." [...]

"Mum," I hiss [...]. "I thought I'd better tell you that Dad and Victoria are here. They're in the queue behind you."

"They are?" Mum squeaks. "Oh! Nice chatting to you, Miss Devlin. I have to 25 go now."

Mum and Dad are no longer together – they haven't been for 12 years, but that doesn't stop Mum from turning all drama-queen if she happens to spot Dad with his girlfriend.

Mum leans across the desk, lending Miss Devlin [...] her brightest showbiz 30 smile. "If you ever need some professional input with the drama club, I'd be only too pleased to offer my expertise!" Miss Devlin shuffles some papers.

"Well ... thanks, Ms Reilly," she says, weakly. "I'll be sure to let you know if we need any ... um, professional input."

Back at the tea-urn, Kevin Carter from my English class is sipping a cup of tea. 35 [...] "Are your parents here?" [...]

"I think they're around somewhere," I say vaguely.

"Will you look at that?" he suddenly explodes with laughter, looking out across the hall. "Who does he think he is, Elvis Presley?"

Dad and Victoria have reached the head of the line for Miss Devlin. Victoria 40 looks neat in a dark city suit, but Dad is wearing a grey raincoat over his white rhinestone catsuit. He has a gig later, an 80th birthday party at some old folks' home. He smoothes his black quiff and sideburns as he sits down. I should explain – Dad is an Elvis impersonator. This is not a fact I tell many people. I have no intention of telling Kevin Carter, obviously. [...]

45 "Think he's really someone's dad, or the entertainment programme?" Kevin Carter muses.

"No idea." I let my hair swing forward to hide my blushes, and Carter lets out a low whistle as Year Eight beauty Kristina Kowalski walks past. She is wearing something that might have once belonged to a Barbie doll, but has now 50 shrunk in the wash. Scary.

"Kristina Kowalski is hot!" Carter breathes [...]. Hot is not a word I'd use to describe Kristina. She is wearing so little, she may be in danger of freezing.

Just as I think Kevin Carter is safely distracted from my family, Gran and Grandad join the end of Miss Devlin's queue. Grandad is wearing his yellow 55 tartan waistcoat with the Marilyn Monroe tie, and Gran is knitting as she waits. It's the green scarf, today. At only three metres long, it's the easiest one for her to carry.

"Who are they?" Carter gawps, following my gaze. "Unreal! I wonder what poor kid has got grandparents like that?"

60 My heart plummets. Carter is going to guess the exact identity of that poor kid, unless I come up with a good idea – and fast.

"Actually," I tell him, "They're Kristina Kowalski's mum and dad." [...]

Adapted from: Cassidy, Cathy. Sundae Girl. London: Puffin Books 2007.

Listening Test 13: Mary Robinson

Presenter: Welcome to the "Irish Idol" podcast. To all of you who are listening to us for the first time, in each of our episodes, young people present their personal heroes, people they find particularly inspiring. My guest today is Brenna from Dublin. Brenna, who are you going to present to us today?

Brenna: Well, my idol is Mary Robinson. I think she is an amazing woman and a role model for young people worldwide.

Presenter: Can you tell us a bit about her?

Brenna: Mary Robinson was president of Ireland between 1990 and 1997, and she was also the first woman to hold that office. Later, she had leading positions within the United Nations, where she dealt with human rights issues and climate change, for example.

Presenter: Could you elaborate a bit more on her career?

Brenna: Well, from what I read and what my parents told me, Mary Robinson has always been an outspoken woman and strong advocate for human rights. Already in the 1970s, when she was working as a lawyer, she fought for the rights of women to get access to the contraceptive pill and demanded that same-sex relationships should no longer be regarded as a crime. At the time, this was a very brave thing to do because the Church still had a very strong influence and society was very conservative.

I think the modern, more liberal Ireland in which we live now, and in which same-sex couples have the possibility to marry, for instance, is something that would have been impossible without people like Mary Robinson.

Presenter: What would you say are the qualities you admire the most about her?

Brenna: For one thing, her capacity to build bridges. For example, as the Irish president, she always tried to promote tolerance between Catholics and Protestants and to seek a dialogue between the United Kingdom and the Republic of Ireland. And secondly, her willingness to stand up for marginalised groups. Both as president of Ireland and while working for the UN, she gave a voice to those who are usually not heard. She has raised awareness about African communities who were affected by hunger or war, for migrants who were exploited, for prisoners who were awaiting their death sentence in the USA, and so on. Her memoir is entitled *Everybody Matters*, and I think this is a good message, also for young people, you know, to broaden their perspective and show solidarity with others.

Presenter: I suppose Mary Robinson is not the kind of woman to simply lie back and enjoy her retirement. What has she been up to in recent years?

Brenna: Well, she is a member of the so-called "Elders". This is a group founded by Nelson Mandela which consists of leaders who are known for their wisdom and strong moral convictions. But above all, she has tried to draw attention to the issue of climate change. She says it is very important to reduce the burning of fossil fuels and eat fewer animal products in order to prevent temperatures from rising further. Because for her, climate change also concerns human rights: If the weather becomes more extreme, people will lose their homes and often their lives, and although rich countries produce the most greenhouse gas emissions, it is the poor that suffer the worst from changing weather conditions. And of course she is also thinking about the future generations who will have to deal with the effects of climate change.

Presenter: That would be us then, I suppose.

Brenna: That would be us.

Presenter: So, a big thank you to Mary Robinson for her strong commitment to human rights, and also to you, Brenna, for presenting this inspiring woman to us today.

Listening Test 14: New Zealand Tips

Janet: Hi there, and welcome to our podcast "Discover New Zealand". My name is Janet...

Jack: ...and I'm Jack...

Janet: ...and every week we're taking you on an exciting trip to the land of the kiwis.

Jack: Let's start with some facts today. Did you know that a lot of the rivers in New Zealand are used for commercial purposes?

Janet: What exactly is meant by that – are these rivers sold?

Jack: Well, they aren't "sold" really, but money is made with them. For example, they're used for tourism and for activities such as rafting, canoeing or bungy jumping.

Janet: Interesting! I've got another fact for you. Bungy jumping was invented... you may have guessed it... in New Zealand! There are some really amazing bungy jumping spots on bridges crossing rivers. Have you ever tried it, Jack?

Jack: No, actually, I'm not so much for jumping off bridges – I prefer kayaking and rafting. One of my favourite places is Waikato River, which is a hotspot for these activities.

Janet: Waikato is not an English name, is it?

Jack: No, it's not. It's a Māori term, meaning "flowing river". It's the longest river in New Zealand. New Zealand generally offers so much to do in terms of water sports, especially during the summer months. December to February is the best time of the year for snorkelling in the sea and surfing.

Janet: But I must say I also really like the winter months from June to August when the mountains are covered in snow and you can go skiing or snowboarding. My favourite season is spring, though. It's the time of year when most visitors come to New Zealand to experience the famous "Lord of the Rings" tours.

Jack: "Lord of the Rings" has become a phenomenon all over the world. Everyone knows the trilogy, most people have watched the movies... it's been such an amazing success. And the shootings of these films have brought millions to the country's economy. Good for us!

Janet: How many times have you participated in a "Lord of the Rings" tour?

Jack: Me? Several times. This year, I want to go and see the famous Hobbit holes in Matamata in Waikato. But there are guided tours all over the country.

Janet: Well, talking about the Waikato region, I've got another tip for you. Why not go on a cave exploration tour?

Jack: Sounds like a real adventure!

Janet: It is! Imagine being in a cave and abseiling down. There's an instructor giving you all the necessary security information. But then it's you and the cave, you are free-hanging and bouncing and roping down, which is a really thrilling experience. The view is awesome, there are enormous stone and rock formations and you can even see glowworms. The first time I did it I thought I'd never have the courage to abseil. But I did! And it's probably even better than bungy jumping.

Jack: Even better than bungy jumping... well, I don't know if that sounds so good to my ears, but I'm sure our listeners will enjoy it. So bye for today and I hope you guys will join us again next week!

▶ **Original-Aufgaben der zentralen Prüfung in NRW**

Zentrale Prüfungen 2017 – Englisch
Anforderungen für den Mittleren Schulabschluss (MSA)

2017-1

Erster Prüfungsteil: Hörverstehen – Leseverstehen

1 Hörverstehen Teil 1: *Mama Africa*

Penny Vale from BCC radio regularly chats with people about topics and people that should not be forgotten. With the help of today's guest Dorothy Masuku, Penny Vale remembers the famous South African musician Miriam Makeba.

- First read the tasks.
- Then listen to the interview.
- While you are listening, tick the correct box.
- At the end you will hear the interview again.
- Now read the tasks. You have **90 seconds** to do this.
- Now listen to the interview and do the tasks.

1. Miriam gained international celebrity …
   a) ☐ after a long career.
   b) ☐ thanks to a TV broadcast.
   c) ☐ with a hit in her home country.

2. Miriam Makeba spent her early life …
   a) ☐ in prison.
   b) ☐ without her mother.
   c) ☐ in a family of alcoholics.

3. Miriam's great voice was recognized by …
   a) ☐ her musical family.
   b) ☐ a South African band.
   c) ☐ two American relatives.

4. Miriam's musical style is …
   a) ☐ African-American.
   b) ☐ typically South African.
   c) ☐ a mixture of different influences.

5. Miriam got foreign attention through …
   a) ☐ a politically critical film.
   b) ☐ her production of an illegal film.
   c) ☐ her leading part in a film on Apartheid.

6. Because of her success in the US, Miriam …
   a) ☐ wanted to stay in America.
   b) ☐ was declared a criminal outcast.
   c) ☐ lost permission to enter her country.

7. Miriam got her nickname "Mama Africa" …
   a) ☐ for her life as a singer.
   b) ☐ for her sacrifice to South Africa.
   c) ☐ for her work as a pioneer and role model.

8. Later, the US let Makeba down because of her …
   a) ☐ relationship with a political rebel.
   b) ☐ political views concerning South Africa.
   c) ☐ commitment in American political affairs.

9. Miriam Makeba died …
   a) ☐ in US exile.
   b) ☐ as a free woman.
   c) ☐ after a long illness.

2 Hörverstehen Teil 2: *Mamohato Children's Centre*

Prince Harry, who lost his mother at a very young age, opened a children's care centre during his South African tour in 2015. Listen to his opening speech.

- *First read the tasks.*
- *Then listen to the speech.*
- *While you are listening, tick the correct box or write down the information needed.*
- *At the end you will hear the speech again.*
- *Now read the tasks. You have **90 seconds** to do this.*
- *Now listen to the speech and do the tasks.*

1. When Prince Harry first came to Africa he …
   a) ☐ realised the needs of the children.
   b) ☐ saw how independent the children were.
   c) ☐ was shocked by the high rate of youth crime.

2. Harry points out that he and the children ...
   a) ☐ suffered the same fate.
   b) ☐ had people to help them.
   c) ☐ knew that time would heal.

3. When Prince Harry saw the children in 2004 he ...
   a) ☐ helped at once.
   b) ☐ wanted to help fast.
   c) ☐ wondered when to help.

4. Back then, Prince Harry already ...
   a) ☐ saw the lack of money.
   b) ☐ asked volunteers to sign up.
   c) ☐ wished for more local support.

5. Today's scientific reports show that ...
   a) ☐ HIV children suffer from loneliness.
   b) ☐ infected children need better medicine.
   c) ☐ people are more open-minded towards sick people.

6. At the centre children learn how to live with their illness.
   Give **two** examples.
   a) _____
   b) _____

7. The charity organisation Sentebale has ...
   a) ☐ organised medical exams.
   b) ☐ built new homes for families.
   c) ☐ spent hours talking to politicians.

8. Talking about challenges, Prince Harry states that ...
   a) ☐ Mamohato has to learn about HIV.
   b) ☐ most African teenagers die of HIV.
   c) ☐ Africa is important in fighting HIV.

3 Leseverstehen

New, Multiracial Beginning in Story of "Madam & Eve" John Murphy (Baltimore Sun)

JOHANNESBURG, South Africa – The doorbell rings at the home of Madam Gwen, but Eve, the black maid, refuses to answer it. Madam reluctantly pulls herself up from the sofa and opens the door. "I don't think I've ever seen you answer the door before," says the startled[1] visitor, a neighbor.

"I wouldn't let Eve have time off to see her Uncle Joe, so now she's getting back at me," says Madam.
"By making you answer the door?"
"Forget about the door. She's protesting by not doing her work. She's on a go-slow."
"A go-slow? How slow is she going to go?"
Eve enters from the kitchen, walking at an exaggeratedly slow pace as if her feet are stuck in glue. She delivers tea to a displeased Madam and her guest.
"Well, at least she made you tea," says the visitor.
"I asked her last night," Madam says wryly[2].

So goes the first episode of "Madam & Eve," a popular South African sitcom to hit television screens. Based on a popular comic strip of the same name, "Madam & Eve" explores the awkward relationship between a wealthy white woman and her black maid as they try to make their way in post-apartheid South Africa.

Signs of political and social change are everywhere in the new South Africa, but there are few places like television to understand how South Africans see themselves – or would like to see themselves. Under Apartheid, a show such as "Madam & Eve" would have had no chance of getting on the air. But since the democratic elections in 1994, television producers are turning to multiracial sitcoms as an entertaining way to deal with the country's uncomfortable past and perhaps show a path to the future. South Africans want to look at South African life comically. They like to laugh at themselves. But behind the laughter, "Madam & Eve" delivers its share of social commentary.

Sitcoms are allowed to play with cultural stereotypes, such as the rich madam, the poor maid, the old racist Afrikaner and the Zulu grandmother, freeing the show's writers and viewers to explore the contradictions and complexities of South Africa today.

What sets South African television apart from its American and British counterparts is that by law, all shows must include as many of the country's 11 official languages as possible.

To an outsider, it makes for strange, often confusing, viewing. In "Madam & Eve," for instance, Eve speaks Zulu with the family's black gardener but will talk with the Madam in English. Sometimes viewers are provided subtitles; other times, viewers are expected to understand the conversation within context or with repetition.

Some critics view the visual humor – the funny faces, the objects falling on people's heads and toes – as a way of reaching across a multilingual audience.

Fearing that it would be a dangerous, perhaps revolutionary technology, television was banned by Apartheid leaders until 1976, when the first government-owned station, the South African Broadcasting Corp., went on the air with tightly controlled news, sports and entertainment programs.

Early on, a black person could not appear in the same frame as a white person. Half of the programs were in English and half were in Afrikaans. Native African languages were rarely heard. But over the years, the restrictions were relaxed somewhat as the government launched two more stations broadcasting in black tribal languages.

In 1994, South African television was liberated from its Apartheid restrictions. Viewers now have their choice of the state-run South African Broadcasting Corp.'s three channels with programming in all 11 languages, independent e-TV[3] and several pay channels with home-grown shows. American, British and other foreign imports make up nearly half of all shows on television. Audiences, however, still prefer anything made in South Africa, because the shows reflect their own experiences.

Adapted from: http://articles.latimes.com/2001/mar/07/entertainment/ca-34178

Annotations
1 startled – here: confused, surprised
2 wryly – showing that you are both amused and disappointed or annoyed
3 e-TV – South Africa's biggest independent TV channel

"Madam & Eve" is based around the theme of a middle-class white woman and her black maid. Theirs is a relationship of friendly quarrelling.

- *Tick the correct box **and** give evidence from the text.*

1. The introductory scene of *Madam & Eve* is funny because …
   a) ☐ the maid is on strike.
   b) ☐ a stranger opens the door.
   c) ☐ Madam treats her guest rudely.
   Evidence from the text:

2. The storyline of *Madam & Eve* was invented for a TV series.
   This statement is … ☐ true ☐ false
   Evidence from the text:

3. TV is seen as a good way to reflect on South African identity.
   This statement is… ☐ true   ☐ false
   Evidence from the text:
   _____

4. Today's South African TV productions…
   a) ☐ limit satirical programmes.
   b) ☐ treat Apartheid with humor.
   c) ☐ favour sensitive over funny broadcasts.
   Evidence from the text:
   _____

5. Shows like *Madam & Eve* work with clichés to help understand South Africa.
   This statement is… ☐ true   ☐ false
   Evidence from the text:
   _____

6. South African TV must represent several African languages.
   This statement is… ☐ true   ☐ false
   Evidence from the text:
   _____

7. During Apartheid, watching TV was restricted because of…
   a) ☐ poor financial resources.
   b) ☐ outdated technical equipment.
   c) ☐ concerns about bad influences.
   Evidence from the text:
   _____

8. Discrimination on TV showed in the underrepresentation of…
   a) ☐ black people.
   b) ☐ African languages.
   c) ☐ native programmes.
   Evidence from the text:
   _____

9. Today, South African viewers give priority to international TV imports.
   This statement is… ☐ true   ☐ false
   Evidence from the text:
   _____

Zweiter Prüfungsteil: Wortschatz – Schreiben

The gun

4 Wortschatz: "A South African experience"

Michelle Faul and her mixed-race family experienced racist incidents in South Africa in the early 60s, forcing them to leave the country for England. Today Michelle Faul is Chief Africa correspondent for "The Associated Press". She looks back at what life was like in South Africa during Apartheid.

- Fill in suitable words or tick the correct box.

1. My widowed mother had driven us from our _____ in Zimbabwe, which was then called Rhodesia, to visit family in her native South Africa.

2. There was racism in Rhodesia, too, but it was nothing like the laws in South Africa that made blacks subhuman because they had to …

    a) ☐ suffer   b) ☐ hurt
    c) ☐ experience   d) ☐ feel

    in the most horrible ways.

3. We did not take the train because halfway through the trip, passengers would have to get out of the Rhodesian Railway compartment and _____ to old and run-down black-only South African carriages.

4. The car trip presented its own challenges. Hotels _____ only whites and everywhere you could see signs declaring places and facilities "for whites only".

5. Only whites were allowed inside the stores. So we had to carry piles of food and drinks from home because our mother _____ to go to the back door of shops.

6. Being white meant you could live where you wanted. However, …

    a) ☐ circles of   b) ☐ crowds of
    c) ☐ cliques of   d) ☐ clouds of

    blacks were caged in townships, if they could get jobs in the city.

7. If they didn't get jobs, their urban shacks – poor homes – were _____ so that black South Africans had nowhere to live. They were then moved by force to unproductive "homelands".

8. My experience was more of absurd trivialities of Apartheid, rather than brutal ...
    a) ☐ attack   b) ☐ strike
    c) ☐ violence   d) ☐ storm
    used to uphold it.

9. If you were white, you had ...
    a) ☐ access to   b) ☐ entrance to
    c) ☐ arrival to   d) ☐ reception to
    jobs denied to blacks.

10. The only black professionals were teachers, like my mother, lawyers like Mandela and nurses and doctors, who could only _____ black patients.

11. My mother spoke English. But to guarantee white superiority even at school, black learners should be taught to speak Afrikaans, the _____ of the Apartheid regime.

12. Today, South Africa is a democratic country where everybody has the right to ...
    a) ☐ choose   b) ☐ elect
    c) ☐ vote   d) ☐ select
    so that their voices may be heard.

13. It is a tribute to Mandela's efforts that today, I and others forgive but do not ...
    a) ☐ forget.   b) ☐ lose.
    c) ☐ remember.   d) ☐ suppress.

5 Schreiben

The gun by Beverly Naidoo

Esi and his parents are faithful and valued employees at the Mackay game farm[1] at the time of the South African Apartheid regime. When their boss Mackay has to leave one day, he asks his future son-in-law Williams to take charge until Mackay's return.

1 Early the following afternoon, there was the familiar sound of Mackay's Land Rover entering the camp. Esi saw immediately that it was being driven by the young man Williams – and he was alone. When he jumped down from the driver's seat, he was carrying Mackay's gun. Although he could only be a few
5 years older than Esi, there was something in his manner that reminded Esi of the sneering[2] officer in the Mapoteng[3] attack. His bush-green eyes narrowed on their target.
"What're you staring at? You've seen me before, haven't you? Go get your boss-boy[4] for me. Be quick about it, jong[5]!"
10 Esi could feel his face going hot, but he turned rapidly and sprinted off. Even Mackay never spoke to him like that, always calling him by his name.
Esi accompanied his father as he walked forward to greet the white man. He wanted to see how Papa would react.
"You remember me? ... Boss Williams. Boss Mackay has asked me to come and
15 look after his place, so we better get on, you and me. I don't want any trouble from the other boys either, OK?" He turned to Esi.
"You can get my bags out the back and carry them to my room." Papa simply gave a little nod. It was impossible to tell what he was thinking. His lined face remained quite passive as father and son carried the young white man's cases.
20 Before long it was clear that Williams assumed Esi to be his personal servant. Up till now Esi had taken instructions either from his father or Mackay, who had known him since he was little. But this man's manner was different. He didn't seem to care at all who Esi was. It was as if he was just a thing to be used. Much of the time Williams would sit on the veranda outside Mackay's room,
25 legs stretched out on a stool, a can of beer at his side, while cleaning or playing with Mackay's gun.
"Hey, come clean my boots!"
"You can wash the truck now!"
"Make my bed properly, jong! Don't just pull the sheets up like that!"
30 "Do you call these boots clean? If you were in the army I'd donder[6] you! Do them again!"
"Go call the girl! I want her to do my washing this morning."
At the last order, Esi had to fight to control himself. Who did this man think he was? Didn't he know that "the girl" was Esi's own mother, old enough to
35 be the white man's mother? When Esi found her, busy collecting wild spinach, his anger spilled out.
She tried to calm him. His temper would get him into trouble. He should try to be like his father. "Papa just lets them push him around. I don't want to be like that!"

⁴⁰ "Ha! What else can you do my young man?"
And with that his mother began walking slowly, steadily, toward the camp to collect the dirty washing.

from OUT OF BOUNDS by Beverly Naidoo (Penguin Books, 2011). Copyright © Beverly Naidoo, 2001. Reproduced by permission of Penguin Books Ltd..

Annotations
1 game farm – a farm with wild animals
2 sneering – unpleasant, arrogant
3 Mapoteng – a South African village
4 boss-boy – insulting expression for an adult man who is in charge of something
5 jong – expression from Afrikaans meaning 'boy'
6 donder – expression from Afrikaans meaning 'hit' or 'bully'

> - *Read the tasks carefully.*
> - *Make sure to write about **all** the aspects presented in each task.*

1. **Describe** Williams' behaviour towards Esi and his parents and how it compares to that of Boss Mackay.

2. **Explain** how Williams' behaviour is reflected in the language he uses and the reaction it causes in Esi.

3. You have a choice here. Choose **one** of the following tasks.

   a) Esi's mother tolerates Williams' behaviour and states: "What else can you do?"
   Comment on this statement and remember that this story is set during the Apartheid regime.

   or

   b) Esi cannot accept his mother's attitude. When Williams calls Esi again and bosses him around, Esi cannot control himself any longer. **Write down** how the story goes on.
   Include the following aspects:
   - Esi's reaction
   - Williams' reaction
   - the consequences for everybody

Hörverstehen – Transkripte

Zentrale Prüfung 10 – 2017: Englisch

Mittlerer Schulabschluss – Haupttermin

Wichtige Hinweise: Alle Texte, die im Folgenden zu hören sind, werden zweimal vorgespielt. Vor dem ersten Hören wird Zeit gegeben, sich mit den Aufgaben vertraut zu machen. Der Hörverstehenstest besteht aus zwei Teilen.

1 Hörverstehen Teil 1: *Mama Africa*

Penny Vale from BCC radio regularly chats with people about topics and people that should not be forgotten. With the help of today's guest Dorothy Masuku, Penny Vale remembers the famous South African musician Miriam Makeba.

- First read the tasks.
- Then listen to the interview.
- While you are listening, tick the correct box.
- At the end you will hear the interview again.
- Now read the tasks. You have **90 seconds** to do this.
- Now listen to the interview and do the tasks.

1 **Penny Vale:** Today is part of our music month and I'll be using the BCC archives to take us back to 1959. And in the days when just arriving in the United States a young female singer from South Africa called Miriam Makeba was catapulted into stardom literally overnight.

5 **Miriam Makeba:** I did one song on the Steve Allan Show and that was it, because he had 60 million viewers.

Penny Vale: Dorothy, tell us about the young Miriam.

Dorothy Masuku: Miriam Makeba's start in life in Johannesburg in 1932 was dramatic. It was hard for her father to get a job. And so her mother brewed
10 some beer. And it was illegal for Africans to drink alcohol at any time, and her mother was caught and she was arrested. Miriam Makeba was 18 days old and her mother spent 16 months in jail with her.

Penny Vale: Oh no. How was Miriam's talent for singing discovered?

Dorothy Masuku: In Makeba's family there was always music. Her mum, her
15 grandmother, her sister and brother used to sing on Sundays and just get together and sing. Miriam got her big breakthrough when she was still a teenager after she was asked to sing with one of South Africa's most popular bands, the Manhattan Brothers. She went on to form the Skylarks, an all-woman group which sang a blend of jazz and traditional melodies of
20 South Africa.

Penny Vale: So how come she became an international star?

Dorothy Masuku: Miriam became known first outside South Africa after a small role in the film "Come back Africa". The film secretly exposed the brutalities of Apartheid and it was an instant hit.

Penny Vale: But Miriam paid a high price for her fame abroad.

Dorothy Masuku: Mhm. A year after taking the US by storm she tried to return to South Africa but the Apartheid regime said no. Her mother died. It was then that she woke up to the fact that she couldn't come back home. Her papers were no longer valid.

Miriam had to spend 30 extraordinary years in exile. Miriam became known affectionately as Mama Africa, not just because she was the first singer to take the melodies of Africa to the rest of the world, but also because she was a symbol of the struggle against Apartheid. In 1963 she even called for action against Apartheid before the United Nations.

Penny Vale: But in 1968 the US establishment's love affair with Mama Africa came to an abrupt end because of another love affair.

Dorothy Masuku: Mhm. Concerts and recording contracts were cancelled when she married Stokely Carmichael, a leading and controversial civil rights activist and a member of the Black Panthers. She didn't know why this was thrown at her. She wasn't involved in the politics of the United States. She'd simply picked a man, not his politics. Only after the release of Nelson Mandela in 1994 was Mama Africa finally free to return to her homeland.

In 2008 Miriam Makeba died at the age of 76 doing what she most loved. She had just finished a concert with her signature tune "Pata Pata" when she suffered a heart attack as she came off stage.

Now listen to the interview again and check your answers.

2 Hörverstehen Teil 2: *Mamohato Children's Centre*

Prince Harry, who lost his mother at a very young age, opened a children's care centre during his South African tour in 2015. Listen to his opening speech.

- First read the tasks.
- Then listen to the speech.
- While you are listening, tick the correct box or write down the information needed.
- At the end you will hear the speech again.
- Now read the tasks. You have **90 seconds** to do this.
- Now listen to the speech and do the tasks.

1 "Eleven years ago I made my first visit to Lesotho, with the help of Prince Seeiso. I couldn't believe that so many children had been robbed of their childhoods by extreme poverty and the ravages of HIV and AIDS. Behind those smiles it was clear they desperately needed care, attention and above all, love.
5 Although our situations couldn't have been more different, I felt a strong connection to many of the children I met. They were far younger than me, and of course, their situation was a great deal more challenging than my own. But we shared a similar feeling of loss, having a loved one, in my case a parent, snatched away so suddenly. I, like them, knew there would always be a gaping hole
10 which could never be filled.
Experiencing this first hand in 2004 put all my experiences and worries into perspective. From that moment, it wasn't a question of when but how quickly we could put something in place which could help these children, robbed of the carefree childhood many other children across the world enjoy.
15 It was already obvious to me that a great deal of valuable work was being done by local people across these communities. But it was also clear that the volunteers and organisations weren't able to attract the financial support they needed. Prince Seeiso and I felt that we could make a meaningful and long-term difference to these children.
20 Research showed us that children living with HIV received little support to help them deal with the social and psychological challenges of their condition. As a result they felt isolated and afraid to face up to their illness.
The theory of our Mamohato camp is simple – if children have the chance to share with each other how HIV affects them and how they cope with it in a
25 safe and accepting environment, they will lead healthier, more well-adjusted lives. Through these camps, children learn about their condition and can then share this knowledge with their peers once they return home. HIV-focused games, sports, arts, crafts and drama all help to inform while boosting self-confidence.
30 This centre is now the heart of Sentebale; it represents how far we have come as a charity but more importantly how much more we want to achieve.

Much has already been accomplished. Sentebale and its partners have provided care for 5,000 orphans, delivered 1/4 million hours of psychosocial support and, this year alone, tested 13,000 adults and children for HIV – 62 % of whom were women and girls.

Many countries face the challenge of HIV and AIDS, particularly across Southern Africa. In fact, according to UNAIDS, HIV remains the number 1 cause of death amongst adolescents in Africa. We hope the Mamohato Children's Centre will become a centre of excellence for the region; allowing us to share this valuable local knowledge and experience with partners in other countries.

Quelle: https://www.royal.uk/speech-prince-harry-official-opening-sentebales-mamohato-childrens-centre-lesotho
(zu Prüfungszwecken gekürzt und adaptiert, nachgesprochen von Daniel Holzberg)

Now listen to the speech again and check your answers.

Ende des Hörverstehenstests.

Zentrale Prüfungen 2018 – Englisch
Anforderungen für den Mittleren Schulabschluss (MSA)

2018-1

Erster Prüfungsteil: Hörverstehen

Hörverstehen Teil 1: *67 blankets for Mandela Day*

Carolyn Steyn is the founder of the charity project "67 blankets for Mandela Day". Each year, Steyn and her followers produce handmade woollen quilts which they give to people in need on Mandela Day on July 18th. Find out how it all began.

- *First read the tasks.*
- *Then listen to the broadcast.*
- *While you are listening, tick the correct box.*
- *At the end you will hear the broadcast again.*
- *Now read the tasks. You have **90 seconds** to do this.*
- *Now listen to the broadcast and do the tasks.*

1. Steyn started *67 blankets* because of …
   a) ☐ a new hobby.
   b) ☐ a tricky challenge.
   c) ☐ a funny birthday present.

2. Steyn soon understood that she needed …
   a) ☐ help.
   b) ☐ the tools.
   c) ☐ the know-how.

3. Support for *67 blankets* comes from …
   a) ☐ around the world.
   b) ☐ 55 different countries.
   c) ☐ 600,000 South Africans.

4. *67 blankets* is so successful thanks to …
   a) ☐ celebrity support.
   b) ☐ political attention.
   c) ☐ modern communication.

5. Compared to last year's result, *67 blankets* wants to …
   a) ☐ top the success.
   b) ☐ repeat the success.
   c) ☐ get near the success.

6. Steyn found extra support …
   a) ☐ in schools.
   b) ☐ in prisons.
   c) ☐ in old people's homes.

7. The success of *67 blankets* also shows in …
   a) ☐ the winning of important awards.
   b) ☐ the support of famous companies.
   c) ☐ the respect for its efforts through the years.

8. With *67 blankets* Steyn has already managed to …
   a) ☐ fight against poverty.
   b) ☐ get political attention.
   c) ☐ create a feeling of togetherness.

9. Do this task **after** you have listened to the whole broadcast.
   With her broadcast, Steyn wants to …
   a) ☐ criticise inequality.
   b) ☐ win more supporters.
   c) ☐ remind us of Mandela.

In 30 seconds you will hear the text again so you can check your answers.

Hörverstehen Teil 2: *Teen fiction*

BBC 4 radio journalist Lynne Jassem takes her audience on a literary journey talking to famous South African author Beverley Naidoo. Find out about Naidoo's interest in teen fiction and her new book "No turning back".

- *First read the tasks.*
- *Then listen to the interview.*
- *While you are listening, tick the correct box.*
- *At the end you will hear the interview again.*
- *Now read the tasks. You have **90 seconds** to do this.*
- *Now listen to the interview and do the tasks.*

1. For Naidoo, Apartheid meant …
   a) ☐ limitations of freedom.
   b) ☐ violation against rights.
   c) ☐ separation from close relatives.

2. Above all, Naidoo writes her books for …
   a) ☐ political reasons.
   b) ☐ personal reasons.
   c) ☐ educational reasons.

3. Naidoo's books …
   a) ☐ have no thematic limits.
   b) ☐ focus on Apartheid issues.
   c) ☐ pick up on teenage problems.

4. The book *No turning back* is about …
   a) ☐ the life of a homeless child.
   b) ☐ the development of Apartheid.
   c) ☐ Naidoo's childhood experiences.

5. Sipho's story is about …
   a) ☐ the reasons for family violence.
   b) ☐ the injustice of racial segregation.
   c) ☐ the strength of an unusual friendship.

6. Sipho's story takes place …
   a) ☐ after Apartheid.
   b) ☐ during Apartheid.
   c) ☐ before Apartheid.

7. As a teenager, Naidoo was fascinated by a girl's …
   a) ☐ sense of survival.
   b) ☐ disrespect for adults.
   c) ☐ sense of right and wrong.

8. Thinking about her childhood, Naidoo admits she …
   a) ☐ accepted racist behaviour.
   b) ☐ was blind to racial injustice.
   c) ☐ was upset about racial discrimination.

In 30 seconds you will hear the text again so you can check your answers.

Zweiter Prüfungsteil: Leseverstehen – Wortschatz – Schreiben

Leseverstehen

The Great British Bake Off by Melissa Clark

In the six years it has been on air, *The Great British Bake Off* has very much changed the way the British see baking, dessert-eating and even their own culture of sweets. The *Bake Off Effect*, as it is known, has made home baking popular again and has led to an increase in the quality of baked goods sold all over the country.

The show, with its multicultural number of contestants[1], has created a modern vision of Britishness. About 8,000 hobby bakers apply for each season. After sorting out the best, the producers then decide on a mix of contestants that stands for British diversity from range of ages, races and professions from different parts of Britain.

Famous British chef and host of the show Mary Berry said that the main reason for the show's success is that baking has a universal, healthy charm. "You have whole families from all different cultures and across the generations, who can sit down to watch it and know that there will be no swearing, that it's a family show," she said. "The children especially love it because it's full of sweet things. They can't wait to run home after school and have a go at making them themselves."

Before *Bake Off*, it was nearly impossible to find classic British sweets like Victoria sponge sandwiches, Eccles cakes and Bakewell tarts[2] unless you or your granny made them at home.

As the show's audience grew, interest in home baking rose. Masses of people who had never held a whisk[3] were now convinced that making complicated marzipan-covered cakes was the most fulfilling way they could spend their weekend.

Younger people show more and more interest in careers in pastry and are looking for apprenticeships in ever-growing numbers since the show started. In a way *The Great British Bake Off* makes people rethink everything that British baking can be. Chetna Makan, a semi-finalist in 2014 who moved from Mumbai to Kent in 2004, charmed the audience with her inspired use of typical Indian spices. She called being on the show "the opposite of 'Brexit[4]'". "It's so different from the picture 'Brexit' painted, that the British want their nation back and that they want us out," she said. That's not how it actually feels, Ms. Makan said. "It was the most welcoming, warm place, that showed unity and love among the contestants," she said. "*Bake Off* has had such a positive effect on people's lives, certainly for the people on the show, but also for the people watching."

Annotations
1 contestant – a person who is taking part in a competition
2 sponge sandwich, Eccles cake, Bakewell tart – famous English cakes
3 whisk – kitchen tool
4 Brexit – in June 2016 the UK voted in favour of leaving the EU

Basic baking rules
Finalists of *The Great British Bake Off* share their secrets for the perfect cake.

Tip 1: Be sure you have all the ingredients and that you understand the recipe clearly.
Tip 2: Missing concentration leads to mistakes. If the telephone rings, let it ring!
Tip 3: Before starting, assemble all the bowls, pans and other kitchen things you will need.
Tip 4: Be sure your ingredients are fresh and are of a good standard.
Tip 5: This is a baking must! You can use the best ingredients in the world, but if you do not measure correctly, the recipe will not come out properly.
Tip 6: Never increase a cooking temperature because you are in a hurry. If the recipe needs a preheated oven, preheat it!
Tip 7: Be patient and let your cake cool down completely before you enjoy it!

Quelle: Zusammenstellung nach https://www.nytimes.com/2016/10/19/dining/great-british-bake-off-recipes.html;
https://www.buzzfeed.com/kristatorres/build-the-perfect-child-and-well-tell-you-what-type-of-mom,
https://www.bbcgoodfood.com/howto/guide/mary-berrys-top-10-baking-tips

You are doing some research for a school paper on "British food". You have come across the article "The Great British Bake Off" and want to present the main points.

- *Tick the correct box and give **one** piece of evidence from the text.*

1. Because of the *Bake Off Effect* ...
   a) ☐ British bakery products have a bad image.
   b) ☐ lots of British bakeries had to close down.
   c) ☐ the British have developed a new interest in sweet food.
   One piece of evidence from the text:
   _____

2. The participants of the TV show represent ...
   a) ☐ a range of British society.
   b) ☐ young members of British society.
   c) ☐ the best professional bakers in Britain.
   One piece of evidence from the text:
   _____

3. The TV show is very popular because baking attracts a great number of different viewers.
   This statement is ... ☐ true   ☐ false
   One piece of evidence the text:
   _____

4. Thanks to the show, a lot of things have developed positively in Britain:
   a) ☐ traditional cakes have been rediscovered.
   b) ☐ people spend money on fine bakery products again.
   c) ☐ grandmothers introduce their grandchildren to baking again.
   One piece of evidence from the text:
   _____

5. Despite the general positive trend, today's young adults don't want to start a baking career.
   This statement is … ☐ true ☐ false
   One piece of evidence from the text:
   _____

6. Thanks to the TV show, people's view on British baking is changing.
   This statement is … ☐ true ☐ false
   One piece of evidence from the text:
   _____

7. According to Chetna Makan, the TV show is a good example of …
   a) ☐ the present political trend.
   b) ☐ acceptance and togetherness.
   c) ☐ popular modern entertainment.
   One piece of evidence from the text:
   _____

8. You want to impress your friends with the perfect cake? The following rules guarantee a delicious surprise.

   - *Match the titles (A–G) to the 7 tips from the text.*
     There is one more title than you need.

	Title	Tip
0	**Example:** Use the perfect heat.	6
A	Be exact.	
B	Quality matters.	
C	Prepare your worktable.	
D	Pay attention only to baking.	
E	A good thing is worth waiting for.	
F	Don't get demotivated. Keep on trying.	
G	Read your recipe carefully before starting.	

Wortschatz: *The Rights of the Child*

All children have the same rights. These rights are listed in the UN "Convention on the Rights of the Child". It is very important that each child knows about his or her rights, so have a look below.

- *Fill in suitable words **or** tick the correct box.*

1. As you grow up, you have more responsibility to make …
   - a) ☐ options
   - b) ☐ choices
   - c) ☐ opportunities
   - d) ☐ selections

   and exercise your rights.

Here are some excerpts from the UN Convention:

2. All children under 18 have these rights. No child should be treated _____ no matter who they are, where they live or whether they are a boy or a girl.

3. All adults should do what is best for you. When adults make decisions, they should think about how their decisions will …
   - a) ☐ affect children.
   - b) ☐ look after children.
   - c) ☐ care for children.
   - d) ☐ see after children.

4. The government has the _____ to make sure your rights are protected.

5. You have the right to have a name. Your name should be …
   - a) ☐ proudly
   - b) ☐ sensibly
   - c) ☐ secretly
   - d) ☐ officially

   recognized by the government.

6. You have the right to find out things and share what you think with others, by talking, drawing, writing or in any other way unless it harms or _____ other people.

7. You have the right to the best care possible, to drink safe water, to eat …
   - a) ☐ fast
   - b) ☐ modified
   - c) ☐ healthy
   - d) ☐ low-calorie

   food, a clean and safe environment, and information to help you stay well.

8. You have the right to a good education. You should be _____ to go to a school and learn.

9. Your education should help you discover and develop your talents and …
   a) ☐ certificates.　　b) ☐ abilities.
   c) ☐ subjects.　　　d) ☐ grades.

10. You have the right to express your _____: say what you think! Adults should listen to you and take you seriously.

11. You have the right to protection from any kind of _____. Nobody has the right to act against your will.

12. You have the right to legal …
    a) ☐ organisations　　b) ☐ consequences
    c) ☐ development　　　d) ☐ help
    and fair treatment in the justice system that respects your rights.

13. You have the right to know your rights! Adults should know about these rights and help you to _____ about them too, so that you are well informed.

Quelle: UNICEF, https://downloads.unicef.org.uk/wp-content/uploads/2010/05/UNCRC_summary-1.pdf

Schreiben

First earning extract from *No turning back* by Beverley Naidoo

Sipho is a 12-year-old black South African boy who runs away from home and now lives on the streets in Hillbrow, a poor neighbourhood of Johannesburg, South Africa.

1 A few of his new friends, all homeless like himself, were hanging out near the supermarket. When someone came out of the shop, each boy held out an open hand. Another boy was pushing a trolley and another was loading boxes into a car.

5 Sipho's new friend Jabu led the way inside the supermarket.
"Sometimes security people chase us like dogs. But other times they let us right in."
He took Sipho towards a till[1]. "Watch me," he whispered.
There were packers helping the customers load their trolleys at the tills. A lady
10 was ready to leave and Jabu moved forward.
"Ma'am?" he offered, putting a hand out towards the trolley.
The lady shook her head with a frown[2], almost hitting him with the trolley. Jabu jumped back. A man was next in the queue. Sipho thought he too would send Jabu away, but instead he let the boy take the trolley from him and push
15 it out. Jabu winked[3] across at Sipho as he left.
Sipho stood back for a minute, looking into the shop. Here were white people, black people, everybody. It was like that outside but suddenly, inside the shop, he noticed it more. In the township there were very few white people.
At one of the tills, a small boy was crying to his mother that he wanted
20 'sweeties'.
"Still here?" Jabu was back already. "You have to move quickly if you want a job", he said.
Jabu kept his eyes on the tills and soon enough he was again in charge of a trolley. Sipho gave himself a little shake, now ready to follow Jabu's example.
25 The lady with the little boy was paying and about to leave. The child had slipped through the tills and was beginning to run around. "Robbie! Come back here!" his mother called angrily.
But the little boy took no notice and as the mother let go of the trolley to get him by the hand, Sipho stepped forward to take hold of the trolley.
30 "All right! You can take it to the car for me," said the woman.
"I want to push the trolley!" cried the little boy.
Sipho had to smile as the child tried to reach the handlebar. He pushed the trolley slowly so the little boy didn't trip over. When they reached the car Sipho helped unload the shopping, then stood waiting by the trolley as the
35 mother put the child into the car. With her back to Sipho, she looked in her bag before turning around and holding out a twenty-cent coin.
"You were very helpful," she said with a smile.

Sipho shyly murmured his thanks as she dropped the coin into his open hand. It wouldn't buy much but it was the first coin he had earned in Hillbrow. He was learning fast. He didn't wait to see the car drive off, but quickly pushed the trolley back down the hill, ready to find another customer.

Quelle: © Beverley Naidoo, 1995.

Annotations
1 till – a cash desk in a supermarket
2 a frown – a look of dislike
3 to wink at somebody – to quickly close and open one's eye

- *Read the tasks carefully.*
- *Make sure to write about* **all** *the aspects presented in each task.*

1. **Describe** the situation Sipho is in and how he deals with it one day.

2. **Explain** how Sipho's behaviour changes in this situation and what it tells you about him.

3. You have a choice here. Choose **one** of the following tasks.

    a) The UN Convention on the Rights of the Child says that *"all children have the right to care and protection, no matter who they are and where they live"*.
    Comment on this right.
    Also include your thoughts on …
    - Sipho's situation as a homeless black child,
    - why support from adults is or is not important for young people.

    or

    b) At the end of an exciting day, Sipho settles down in the evening and thinks about what he has experienced that day. Imagine you are Sipho.
    Write Sipho's **diary entry**.
    Include …
    - his feelings and thoughts about living on the street and earning money,
    - his relationship with Jabu,
    - his aims/wishes for the next day.

Hörverstehen – Transkripte

Zentrale Prüfung 10 – 2018: Englisch

Mittlerer Schulabschluss – Haupttermin

Wichtige Hinweise: Alle Texte, die im Folgenden zu hören sind, werden zweimal vorgespielt. Vor dem ersten Hören wird Zeit gegeben, sich mit den Aufgaben vertraut zu machen. Nach dem ersten Hören wird Zeit gegeben, die Antworten zu überprüfen. Der Hörverstehenstest besteht aus zwei Teilen.

Hörverstehen Teil 1: *67 blankets for Mandela Day*

Carolyn Steyn is the founder of the charity project "67 blankets for Mandela Day". Each year, Steyn and her followers produce handmade woollen quilts which they give to people in need on Mandela Day on July 18th. Find out how it all began.

- First read the tasks.
- Then listen to the broadcast.
- While you are listening, tick the correct box.
- At the end you will hear the broadcast again.
- Now read the tasks. You have **90 seconds** to do this.
- Now listen to the broadcast and do the tasks.

voiceover: Take a red, pink, green or blue thread of wool,
   Make a blanket and help keep people warm.

Carolyn Steyn: The blanket project was a gift to me. It started on my husband's birthday, December 19th, 2013. Joking around, my sister wanted to test me. She suggested I should make 67 blankets by Mandela Day, believing, of course, it would be impossible for me to make so many blankets by July 18th. So I said "Sure, no problem" because I had learned how to knit at school and make pullovers, cardigans and scarves from wool. Then on Christmas Day my sister arrived with a bag of wool and two knitting needles. This was my present. So, I started right away making blankets on Christmas Day. But I quickly realised: I can't do it on my own. I don't have so many friends. So I went on Facebook and created this group called *67 blankets for Nelson Mandela Day*.

voiceover: There are already over 6,000 South African members and many more in about 15 other countries including Canada, Australia, Germany, the United States and India. So come and join in!

Carolyn Steyn: It's really exploded into a movement. I do know that it's Nelson Mandela's magic and the power of social media combined that has created this explosion of energy. It's becoming a creative revolution in Mandela's name.

voiceover: Last year alone, 7,000 blankets were made and given to the people in need by *67 blankets for Mandela Day*. This year, we hope to break this record and beat it with 15,000 blankets. So everybody join in and help us give these blankets to people in need on Mandela Day, July 18th.

25 **Carolyn Steyn:** Taking this project to people in jail is very important for me in particular. It started out because we wanted to get as many blankets as possible. I wondered: Who has time on their hands? So, I came up with the idea of taking this project to people in jail. I believe that this project is changing their lives.

30 **voiceover:** After only nine months the project won *Campaign of the Year* beating huge brands like *Coca Cola* and *KFC*. And on April 21st, 2015, celebrating 21 years of South African democracy, *67 blankets for Nelson Mandela Day* broke the *Guinness Book of Records* with the biggest woollen blanket in the world.

35 **Carolyn Steyn:** It was unbelievable! Such a sense of unity! We are getting together as a nation through bright colourful thread in Mandela's name because we want to hold on to what he left behind. So don't hesitate to join in: the greatest gift that you can give is your time.

Quelle: Zusammenstellung nach https://67blankets.co.za/about/; https://www.nelsonmandela.org/news/entry/67-blankets-for-nelson-mandela-day-celebrates-its-first-birthday; http://67blankets.co.za/67-blankets-for-nelson-mandela-day-breaks-guiness-world-record/
Hinweis: Carolyn Steyn ist eine reale Person – der vorliegende Radiobericht ist jedoch fiktiv und wurde zu Prüfungszwecken von anderen Sprecher*innen eingesprochen.

> *In 30 seconds you will hear the text again so you can check your answers.*

Hörverstehen Teil 2: *Teen fiction*

BBC 4 radio journalist Lynne Jassem takes her audience on a literary journey talking to famous South African author Beverley Naidoo. Find out about Naidoo's interest in teen fiction and her new book "No turning back".

- *First read the tasks.*
- *Then listen to the interview.*
- *While you are listening, tick the correct box.*
- *At the end you will hear the interview again.*
- *Now read the tasks. You have* **90 seconds** *to do this.*
- *Now listen to the interview and do the tasks.*

1 **Lynne Jassem:** Beverley, I know you're originally from South Africa and had some problems there before you came to the UK because of your criticism of Apartheid. How did you experience Apartheid?

Beverley Naidoo: Well, Apartheid, one of its major crimes was a crime against 5 family, it divided family. It tore families apart. I joined the anti-apartheid movement. So I was part of the problem. That's why I was arrested.

Lynne Jassem: Why do you choose to write for young readers? You seem to enjoy meeting young people and telling them about the importance of justice and tolerance.

Beverley Naidoo: I write the kind of books that I wish I could have had as a young white person growing up in South Africa under Apartheid. Most of the books that I read as a teenager came from Europe and had a very narrow perspective. But I think first of all I'm probably writing, I'm writing for myself.

Lynne Jassem: Right. What are the topics you especially deal with in your books?

Beverley Naidoo: I think there's no strict rule ... I grew up in a society of racial segregation, one of the most unjust in the world. For me, writing has been a way of crossing borders. It's freedom.

Lynne Jassem: I see. The main character of your book *No turning back* is Sipho, he's in Johannesburg. What inspired his story?

Beverley Naidoo: When I returned to South Africa again in 1993, I was working with street children and young people who weren't street children. And I immediately knew that I wanted to tell the story of a street child and get into that life story.

Lynne Jassem: Mmh ... I see. So, what is Sipho's story?

Beverley Naidoo: Sipho is a black teenage boy who is angry at his mother because she hasn't protected him against his father who regularly beats him. So he runs away to the streets of Johannesburg where he gets to know a young white girl. Right from the start there is a strong connection between them and they become close friends. I wanted to find out for myself how possible it is that a strong friendship like this could develop ... in this society, which is still deeply divided between black and white people although racial segregation is officially over.

Lynne Jassem: Beverley, is there one book from your age as a young adult that you remember having a really big influence on you?

Beverley Naidoo: It would have to be more than one because there's a story connecting them. The first book that really told me that literature could be about real life was the *Diary of Anne Frank*. I was fascinated by Anne Frank's strong voice and her speaking out against injustice, whether it was the behaviour of the Nazis or whether it was when she felt an injustice from her parents.

When I look back, I realize that I didn't see the reality of Apartheid all around me at the time. And so it was a little bit later on, perhaps, at 17 or 18, when I was given a couple of books that had been banned by the Apartheid regime that really began to open my eyes. All the stories of those illegal books took place not very far from where I had grown up, but it could have been on another planet.

Quelle: Zusammenstellung nach https://www.bbc.co.uk/programmes/b07m4d53
Hinweis: Lynne Jassem und Beverley Naidoo sind reale Personen – das Interview wurde jedoch zu Prüfungszwecken umformuliert und von anderen Sprecher*innen neu eingesprochen.

In 30 seconds you will hear the text again so you can check your answers.

Ende des ersten Prüfungsteils.

Zentrale Prüfungen 2019 – Englisch
Anforderungen für den Mittleren Schulabschluss (MSA)

Erster Prüfungsteil: Hörverstehen

Hörverstehen Teil 1: *Lighthouse Walk*

You have decided to visit Cape Point, a cliff at the southwestern tip of the African continent. Start your walking tour at the visitor centre at the foot of the hill. Climb up the hill while listening to interesting facts about this wonderful part of the earth in this audio guide.

- First read the tasks.
- Then listen to the audio guide.
- While you are listening, tick the correct box.
- At the end you will hear the audio guide again.
- Now read the tasks. You have **90 seconds** to do this.
- Now listen to the audio guide and do the tasks.

Stop 1

1. On the tour you may …
   a) ☐ leave the path.
   b) ☐ have a barbecue.
   c) ☒ take photographs.

2. Monkeys find their food on …
   a) ☒ the cliffs.
   b) ☒ the trees.
   c) ☐ the bottom of the sea.

3. Giving food to the monkeys is …
   a) ☒ against the law.
   b) ☐ dangerous for you.
   c) ☐ a special attraction.

Stop 2

4. People believe a ship sank near Cape Point …
   a) ☒ during bad weather.
   b) ☐ for mysterious reasons.
   c) ☐ due to crew members fighting.

5. According to a story the sailors …
   a) [x] killed the captain.
   b) [ ] saved themselves.
   c) [x] still travel the oceans.

6. Cape Point is known for its …
   a) [x] rough sea.
   b) [ ] warm wind.
   c) [ ] sandy beach.

Stop 3

7. You might fall off the cliffs because of …
   a) [ ] slippery rocks.
   b) [ ] missing fences.
   c) [x] stormy weather.

8. Unfortunately, the first lighthouse was …
   a) [ ] burnt down.
   b) [x] in the wrong place.
   c) [x] not powerful enough.

9. The new lighthouse …
   a) [ ] is 87 meters high.
   b) [x] was finished in 1919.
   c) [ ] attracts 10 million visitors each year.

In 30 seconds you will hear the text again so you can check your answers.

Hörverstehen Teil 2: #YourChoice

You are doing a project on "School Life in other Countries" in your English class. You have come across a radio interview in which 17-year-old Mandisa, a South African student, is talking to Bongi Louma, host of the show, about a conflict she had at school in Pretoria in September 2016.

- *First read the tasks.*
- *Then listen to the interview.*
- *While you are listening, tick the correct box.*
- *At the end you will hear the interview again.*
- *Now read the tasks. You have **90 seconds** to do this.*
- *Now listen to the interview and do the tasks.*

1. At Mandisa's school it is forbidden to have …
   a) ☐ short hair.
   b) ☐ hair accessories.
   c) ☒ African hairstyles.

2. For Mandisa, hairstyle is an expression of …
   a) ☐ school identity.
   b) ☐ fashion identity.
   c) ☒ cultural identity.

3. The rule at Mandisa's school is …
   a) ☐ an exception.
   b) ☒ an educational trend.
   c) ☐ a government decision.

4. In reaction to the protests, Mandisa's school …
   a) ☒ stopped the rule.
   b) ☐ modified the rule.
   c) ☐ tightened the rule.

5. South Africans showed their criticism through …
   a) ☒ Internet protests.
   b) ☐ letters of complaint.
   c) ☐ street demonstrations.

6. Some teachers say: Controlling students' looks improves ...
   a) ☐ the school's reputation.
   b) ☐ the pupils' social equality.
   c) ☒ the learners' concentration.

7. Breaking the school rule could lead to ...
   a) ☐ financial punishments.
   b) ☒ exclusion from school.
   c) ☐ extra hours after lessons.

8. The movement was the inspiration for a ...
   a) ☐ flash mob.
   b) ☐ conference.
   c) ☒ media report.

9. The rule is even considered to be ...
   a) ☐ sexist.
   b) ☐ old-fashioned.
   c) ☒ discriminating.

In 30 seconds you will hear the text again so you can check your answers.

Zweiter Prüfungsteil: Leseverstehen – Wortschatz – Schreiben

Leseverstehen

Please, Sir – sit! The story of a learning support dog

More and more schools now employ furry little helpers.

When rubbish at Huntington School in York got out of control recently, staff managed to solve the problem pretty much overnight – not by replacing detentions with collecting rubbish, but by employing their newest, cuddliest colleague: Rolo, the school dog. They made a short video for assembly, showing what a state the schoolyard was in. "Rubbish, isn't it?" was the headline, followed by: "Do you know what would be really rubbish? If Rolo had to leave because of rubbish." This clever tactic of emotional blackmail[1] pictured the five-month-old, chocolate-brown Labrador. He was chewing on a plastic bottle and sniffing other rubbish in the schoolyard, while looking up into the camera with big brown eyes.

"The effect was incredible," says the headteacher, John Tomsett. Within a week of 'Operation Rolo Says No', the school grounds were spotless, as the 1,500 students had worked together to clean it up.

Just as a flag is raised when the Queen is at Buckingham Palace, a sign on top of one of the bookshelves in the school library shows when the puppy is at school. The words 'Rolo is in' create a lot of excitement among pupils who would never normally be seen in the library. "People stand in a queue to see him – he's like a celebrity," says Abbie Watson, 13. He has his own name tag, 'Mr Rolo', just like any other member of the staff.

Rolo's job title is "learning support dog" – a phenomenon which can be found more and more in modern classrooms, states Tracey Berridge of the charity *Dogs Helping Kids (DHK)*, which trains school dogs. "In the last two or three years the number of dogs in schools has exploded in a really big way," she says.

Tracey Berridge is convinced of the benefits for pupils, but she is worried that too many dogs are unprepared for classroom life and have no proper training. "It is not right for all dogs," she warns. "There are probably hundreds and hundreds of dogs in schools across the country now, many not properly trained." The *Department for Education* has no idea how many dogs are currently working in classrooms and does not require schools to register or train their animals. Classroom dogs not only improve pupils' reading and writing skills, but also have a calming effect, *DHK* claims – something headmaster Tomsett says is true. Sometimes Rolo follows Tomsett to small classes, and Tomsett settles him in a corner on his blanket. "He's fabulous. He just goes to sleep and the children don't want to wake him so they are really quiet," he says.

Rolo is learning how to become a "listening dog" who will help children read aloud more confidently. He will put his head on their knees and listen without judgement, encouraging them to turn a page.

Quelle: Helen Pidd: Please, Sir – sit! The tale of a learning support dog, https://www.theguardian.com/education/2017/mar/28/teaching-support-dog-school-teach-read. Copyright Guardian News & Media Ltd 2019; Foto © Can Stock Photo / ijdema

Annotation: 1 blackmail – the act of putting pressure on a person

Your British partner school employs a dog to create a better learning environment. You really like this idea and want to convince the school community to introduce a school dog programme at your school, too. The following text provides you with the necessary background information.

> - Tick the correct box **and** give evidence from the text by quoting short passages from the text.

1. Thanks to Rolo, a difficult school situation could be stopped very quickly.
   This statement is ... ☐ true ☐ false
   One piece of evidence from the text:
   _____

2. Rolo raised the pupils' awareness of the situation because he ...
   a) ☐ had to leave to stay safe.
   b) ☐ swallowed trash and became ill.
   c) ☐ made them feel badly about their behaviour.
   One piece of evidence from the text:
   _____

3. Rolo managed to create a feeling of common responsibility among the pupils.
   This statement is ... ☐ true ☐ false
   One piece of evidence from the text:
   _____

4. Rolo's presence at school is ...
   a) ☐ indicated by a notice.
   b) ☐ announced in advance.
   c) ☐ organised by fixed schedules.
   One piece of evidence from the text:
   _____

5. Rolo hasn't become a real part of the educational team yet.
   This statement is ... ☐ true ☐ false
   One piece of evidence from the text:
   _____

6. Having a dog at school is …
   a) ☐ a recent trend in the UK.
   b) ☐ still an exception in the UK.
   c) ☐ usually forbidden in the UK.
   One piece of evidence from the text:
   _____

7. Dog trainers are concerned about …
   a) ☐ the dogs' well-being.
   b) ☐ the pupils' behaviour.
   c) ☐ the teachers' qualifications.
   One piece of evidence from the text:
   _____

8. The ministry is observing the school dog situation very closely.
   This statement is … ☐ true   ☐ false
   One piece of evidence from the text:
   _____

9. School dogs encourage an atmosphere of silence during lessons.
   This statement is … ☐ true   ☐ false
   One piece of evidence from the text:
   _____

10. School dogs help pupils to …
    a) ☐ make friends.
    b) ☐ accept criticism.
    c) ☐ believe in their abilities.
    One piece of evidence from the text:
    _____

Wortschatz: *The British school system*

Spending some time in a school in the UK is a once-in-a-lifetime experience and guarantees life-long memories. Check out this basic information on the British school system.

- *Fill in suitable words* **or** *tick the correct box.*
- *Give only one solution.*

1. Children's education in the UK is normally ...
   a) ☐ isolated into   b) ☐ divided into
   c) ☐ segregated into   d) ☐ cut into

   two separate stages: primary education at the age of five, and secondary school where they stay until they reach sixteen, seventeen or eighteen years of age.

2. In the UK, 93 % of children in England and Wales _____ "state schools". Although state schools are free, parents are expected to pay for their child's school uniform and items of sports wear.

3. Schools in the UK are almost always ...
   a) ☐ diverse,   b) ☐ varied,
   c) ☐ different,   d) ☐ mixed,

   i. e. for both girls and boys.

4. Nearly 88 % of secondary school pupils in the UK go to comprehensive schools, as do all pupils in Wales. These take children of all ...
   a) ☐ abilities   b) ☐ skills
   c) ☐ know-how   d) ☐ gifts

   and provide a wide range of secondary education.

5. Grammar schools are ...
   a) ☐ open   b) ☐ free
   c) ☐ selective   d) ☐ undemanding

   and only take the best-qualified pupils in their academically oriented education.

6. This is why entrance is based on a/an _____ to find out if the children are up to the standards the schools expect. It's called CE, the Common Entrance.

7. Children have to _____ the Common Entrance (CE) at the age of 11 (girls) or 13 (boys). Without it pupils don't get accepted.

8. Most schools in England require uniforms. The British government believes that uniforms play an important role in supporting the school's …
   a) ☐ identity.
   b) ☐ character.
   c) ☐ recognition.
   d) ☐ identification.

9. However, there are many _____ for school uniforms. They must be fair for both genders, available at a reasonably low cost, and respect religious freedoms (such as wearing a turban).

10. Most secondary schools in the UK …
    a) ☐ work from
    b) ☐ run from
    c) ☐ continue from
    d) ☐ go on from
    8.30 a.m. to 3.30 p.m., Monday through Friday.

11. Most teachers in British schools offer time before or after school when students can ask questions or _____ extra help.

12. Almost all British secondary schools offer a wide range of _____ including sport teams, music and art clubs, cultural clubs, and academic groups.

13. In addition, most secondary schools have many artistic programmes including music, dance, theatre, and visual arts that students can …
    a) ☐ carry out.
    b) ☐ complete.
    c) ☐ exercise.
    d) ☐ participate in.

14. In the UK, PE is _____ for all students until the age of sixteen, after which time they can quit. Sports culture is very strong in boarding and independent schools in the UK.

Quelle: adapted from http://projectbritain.com/education/schools.html

Schreiben

Jessica's speech extract from *Separation* by Babette Brown

In the early 1990s, 15-year-old Jessica is sent to live with her granny in London by her parents because of the situation in Cape Town, South Africa. There is a lot of violence between anti-apartheid activists and supporters of the regime.

1 "Jessica. Mr Herbert wants to see you right away."
With everyone staring at me, I rushed from the room. Mr Herbert was the principal and only called people to his office if they'd done something really bad.
5 I knocked at the door.
"Come in."
"You wanted to see me, Sir?"
"Yes. Sit down, relax, no need to look like a frightened rabbit. I'm going to ask you to do me a favour."
10 How weird was that? What could he possibly want me to do?
"I would like the pupils in this school to have the opportunity to hear about South Africa from somebody who has lived there. At next Friday's assembly I was wondering if you would tell them about what's happening to your friends."
15 I wouldn't know what to say, I'd never done anything like it in my life. I was going to refuse, when a thought hit me: Ben and Daisy would want me to do it.
"Sounds really scary, but I'll have a go."
The time flew by. I was scared, but I'd thought a lot about what I was going to
20 say. It would be good to get it over with.
Mr Herbert invited me to come on to the platform and introduced me. Hundreds of eyes looked up expectantly. My heart thundered, my legs shook and my mind went blank[1]. Words tumbled out of my mouth.
"One of the hardest things about leaving South Africa was leaving my best
25 friend, Daisy, and the love of my life, Ben. We didn't even get the chance to say goodbye. He's in prison, in solitary confinement which means he's all alone in a very small and empty cell."
A shocked murmur echoed around the hall. "I have no idea where Daisy is because she's in hiding. The cops want to arrest her not because she's stolen
30 anything, hurt anyone, been in a fight or anything like that. Her 'crime' and Ben's is that they, like millions of others, want to get rid of[2] the government and its apartheid laws. Because of these laws Daisy and I have never travelled together on a bus, tram or train. We've never been to a cinema, theatre, pub, restaurant, café, or park. Do you know why? All those places, and many
35 others, are for whites only and Daisy's black."
My words provoked gasps[3] and shaking heads. "Ben and I are white. Our comfortable homes are in tree-lined suburbs; all our neighbours are white. I visited the township where Daisy and hundreds of black families are forced to live. They don't have running water or electricity in their homes.

⁴⁰ On my first day at this school, I was really surprised. Black and white pupils in the same class! It couldn't happen in South Africa, but Daisy and Ben are hoping it will one day. The good news is that we can do something to help it happen. The black people in South Africa are asking us and our parents, family and friends, to stop buying fruit, cigarettes, wine, anything that is grown or
⁴⁵ made in South Africa. If people in this country and in lots of other countries boycott South African goods, we will all be helping to get rid of apartheid sooner rather than later."

Dead silence and then a loud burst of applause. A smiling Mr Herbert came over and congratulated me. "Thank you Jessica. I think I speak for everyone in
⁵⁰ this hall when I say you have given us a most interesting and moving account of what is happening to your friends and others in apartheid South Africa." Turning to face the rest of the school he said, "I want you all to remember what Jessica told us about the boycott." More supportive clapping. I returned to my seat feeling rather pleased with myself.

Quelle: Babette Brown: *Separation*. London: Whitefox Publishing 2014. [Hinweis des Verlags: In Babette Browns Roman findet die beschriebene Szene im Jahr 1966 statt.]

Annotations
1 to go blank – to be suddenly unable to think
2 to get rid of sth – to make yourself free of sth that you do not want
3 a gasp – a quick deep breath, usually caused by a strong emotion

---

- *Read the tasks carefully.*
- *Make sure to write about **all** the aspects presented in each task.*

---

1. **Summarize** what you get to know about Jessica's life and the political situation in South Africa. (8 Punkte)

2. **Explain** what you get to know about Jessica's character. Look at her behaviour and her relationship to her friends. (10 Punkte)

3. You have a choice here. Choose **one** of the following tasks.

   a) The text is an extract from the book *Separation* by Babette Brown.
      Comment on why the title *Separation* fits.
      Base your comment on the following questions:
      - Who is separated from whom in the text?
      - Why are these people separated?
      - Why do you think the author has chosen this title? (12 Punkte)

   or

   b) Back in the classroom, Jessica is surrounded by her classmates.
      Write the **continuation** of the story.
      Include …
      - how the classmates behave towards Jessica after her speech,
      - their ideas to raise awareness about apartheid,
      - what they want to do to fight apartheid,
      - how Jessica experiences the situation.

      Start like this: *I was really surprised – everybody …* (12 Punkte)

Hörverstehen – Transkripte

Zentrale Prüfung 10 – 2019: Englisch

Mittlerer Schulabschluss – Haupttermin

Wichtige Hinweise: Alle Texte, die im Folgenden zu hören sind, werden zweimal vorgespielt. Vor dem ersten Hören wird Zeit gegeben, sich mit den Aufgaben vertraut zu machen. Nach dem ersten Hören wird Zeit gegeben, die Antworten zu überprüfen. Der Hörverstehenstest besteht aus zwei Teilen.

Hörverstehen Teil 1: *Lighthouse Walk*

You have decided to visit Cape Point, a cliff at the southwestern tip of the African continent. Start your walking tour at the visitor centre at the foot of the hill. Climb up the hill while listening to interesting facts about this wonderful part of the earth in this audio guide.

- *First read the tasks.*
- *Then listen to the audio guide.*
- *While you are listening, tick the correct box.*
- *At the end you will hear the audio guide again.*
- *Now read the tasks. You have **90 seconds** to do this.*
- *Now listen to the audio guide and do the tasks.*

1 You're about to explore the fascinating landscape and history of Cape Point. So, let's get going. Turn, so that the visitor centre is on your left and follow the track up the hill, past the sign that says "Cape Point – Lighthouse". Keep your earphones in. You'll hear from me again in a moment.

5 **Stop 1**
Keep going up the hill. As you walk, let's talk about some important rules:
Firstly, please don't smoke outside the clearly marked smoking areas. Fires can start easily, and are hard to put out.
Secondly, please make sure you stay on the tracks. This is for your own safety,
10 and that of the animals and plants that make Cape Point so special.
Finally, the old saying: take nothing but pictures and leave nothing but footprints.
Don't be alarmed if you see some of South Africa's largest monkeys, called baboons, but please be careful.
15 Did you know about 60 % of baboon food is made up of grass? And did you know that Cape Point baboons are the only monkeys in the world that also eat seafood? That's why you can see them sitting along the rocky areas, eating straight off the rocks.
Feeding baboons is illegal in any national park. If you feed them, you have to
20 pay a fine. So don't do it! When tourists feed baboons it can be deadly for the monkeys.
Keep on climbing up the track. You'll hear from me again in a moment.

Stop 2

Continue up the hill, with the cliffs on your right.

Look around carefully. You might be able to see the *Flying Dutchman*, a sailing ship that sank near the coast in 1680. The ship came from Amsterdam, and was on its way to Indonesia. Legend says that a terrible storm hit the ship. The crew wanted to get safely on land, but the captain forced them to sail around Cape Point. It was his last decision. The ship hit the rocks and sank ... leaving no survivors. People say that the captain and the crew were guilty of a terrible crime. And this is why they have to sail the seas forever as ghosts. So, if you are lucky, you might spot the ghostly shape of the *Flying Dutchman*.

Even today sailors have to be very careful around the Cape. The waters here are quite wild and strong storms often hit the coast. No wonder the coastline is full of shipwrecks. So a lighthouse is a must to guide ships safely around the Cape.

We're now on our way to the lighthouse which was built in the mid-1800s. Okay, carry on along the track.

Stop 3

Well done. You've made it to the top! But I must warn you not to climb over the barriers to get the perfect photo. It's against park rules, and it's extremely dangerous. The wind up here is very strong and it could blow you right off the cliff.

You're now standing 249 m above sea level. The lighthouse was the first to be built on Cape Point. That's why people around here call it the 'Old Lighthouse'. It has a candle power of 2000 candles, and was first lit in 1860. You would think this would be the perfect location for a lighthouse, but actually it's too high! That's why the light is often hidden by fog.

A new lighthouse was built lower down, at 87 m above sea level and nearly at the very tip of Cape Point. It was completed in 1919 and has a powerful light beam. It shines as strongly as 10 million candles.

I'll leave you in silence for a while, to enjoy the view. When you're ready to move on, leave the lighthouse area and go down the stairs along the stone wall.

Quelle: based on: https://voicemap.me/tour/cape-point/cape-point-audio-guide-lighthouse-walk

In 30 seconds you will hear the text again so you can check your answers.

Hörverstehen Teil 2: #YourChoice

You are doing a project on "School Life in other Countries" in your English class. You have come across a radio interview in which 17-year-old Mandisa, a South African student, is talking to Bongi Louma, host of the show, about a conflict she had at school in Pretoria in September 2016.

- *First read the tasks.*
- *Then listen to the interview.*
- *While you are listening, tick the correct box.*
- *At the end you will hear the interview again.*
- *Now read the tasks. You have **90 seconds** to do this.*
- *Now listen to the interview and do the tasks.*

Presenter: For many teenagers, nothing is more emotional than the way they feel about their looks. Now South African schools are under attack over hairstyle rules. We have Mandisa on the line, creator of the hashtag *#Your choice*.

Mandisa: Hi.

Presenter: Thanks for being on the show, Mandisa.

Mandisa: You're welcome.

Presenter: So Mandisa, you and a whole lot of other students have walked out in protest against your school's policy on certain hairstyles. What's the story?

Mandisa: What actually happened is that our school rules banned all Afro hair fashion like rasta hairstyle, braids and dreadlocks last month. In short ... you have to keep your hair tidy. All styles have to be conservative, neat, and in line with the school uniform.

Presenter: And obviously, you were not very happy with that decision.

Mandisa: Of course not! This is Africa, and we can't be naturally who we are? It's one thing for you to decide if you like to wear your hair natural or straighten it. But it's a completely different thing if someone else decides for you what kind of hairstyle you have to wear.

Presenter: As it turned out, your school was not the only one that had this policy?

Mandisa: Yeah. Many South African schools have introduced similar rules before. *[Presenter: Wow.]* But this time, girls protested – and our complaints touched a nerve. Our school dropped the restrictions a few days later ...

Presenter: ... but not before starting a debate throughout South Africa, right?

Mandisa: Yes, obviously we hit a nerve because thousands of people signed an online petition supporting our protest. Even South Africa's minister of arts and culture tweeted that "Schools should not be used as a platform to stop students from openly showing their African identity".

Presenter: So true. But why would schools set up such stupid hair policies?

Mandisa: Some South African teachers argue that the reason for hair and dress codes is that personal expression can take the focus away from learning.

Uniforms are worn in schools across the country. And when it comes to hair, teachers insist on tidy hair. They defend this standard and say it's race-neutral.

Presenter: Yeah, but what about students who didn't wear their hair according to the code?

Mandisa: Those who didn't stick to the rule were told to cut their hair or else be banned from school.

Presenter: Unbelievable! What about parents and the public? Didn't they sort of ... step in?

Mandisa: Yeah. Thousands of people have tweeted with our hashtag *#Your choice* on Twitter. They called the school rule "disrespectful" and "stupid". *[Presenter: Quite right.]* A famous journalist wasn't surprised at all that so many women joined this protest. That's why she has decided to work on a documentary about hair and black identity that will be released next year. *[Presenter: Interesting.]* And the education minister even ordered an investigation because some people said that the school rule was racist.

Presenter: Incredible story ... South African students demand "To Be Naturally Who We Are" ... this is Radio SA FM ...

In 30 seconds you will hear the text again so you can check your answers.

Ende des ersten Prüfungsteils.

Zentrale Prüfungen 2021 – Englisch
Anforderungen für den Mittleren Schulabschluss (MSA)

2021-1

Erster Prüfungsteil: Hörverstehen

Hörverstehen Teil 1: *The summer plans of Danny Boyle*

Danny Boyle, the teenage hero of William Graham's book "Danny Boyle and the ghosts of Ireland", is looking forward to carrying out his plans for the summer. Find out more about Danny from the beginning of the audiobook.

- *First read the tasks.*
- *Then listen to the extract.*
- *While you are listening, tick the correct box.*
- *At the end you will hear the extract again.*
- *Now read the tasks. You have **90 seconds** to do this.*
- *Now listen to the extract and do the tasks.*

1. Danny and his family are about to ...
   a) ☐ move to Ireland.
   b) ☒ go on a trip to Ireland.
   c) ☐ get visitors from Ireland.

2. Dany is very interested in ...
   a) ☐ science fiction.
   b) ☒ other countries.
   c) ☒ flying vehicles.

3. Dany is the kind of person who is rather ...
   a) ☐ shy.
   b) ☐ patient.
   c) ☒ adventurous.

4. Danny dislikes the fact that Melinda is ...
   a) ☐ the first-born.
   b) ☒ in his school year.
   c) ☐ an athletic person.

5. Danny reacts to Melinda with ...
   a) ☐ anger.
   b) ☐ laughter.
   c) ☒ disinterest.

6. Melinda behaves like a ...
   a) ☐ bully.
   b) ☒ know-it-all.
   c) ☐ helpful person.

7. Danny is excited about ...
   a) ☐ magical stories.
   b) ☒ strange locations.
   c) ☐ the Irish language.

8. Danny ends the conversation so he can ...
   a) ☐ learn new vocabulary.
   b) ☐ get his suitcase ready.
   c) ☒ continue his earlier activity.

9. Danny connects Ireland with ...
   a) ☒ bad weather.
   b) ☐ grassy fields.
   c) ☐ traditional clothes.

10. In the end, Danny has a terrible ...
    a) ☐ accident.
    b) ☐ argument.
    c) ☒ nightmare.

In 30 seconds you will hear the extract again so you can check your answers.

Hörverstehen Teil 2: *Thomas Caffrey's chocolate world*

Thomas Caffrey's sweet creations are loved by many Irish people. Joe Duffy from RTÉ Radio 1 is talking to his guest Neville about the famous Irish chocolate maker.

- First read the tasks.
- Then listen to the interview.
- While you are listening, tick the correct box.
- At the end you will hear the interview again.
- Now read the tasks. You have **90 seconds** to do this.

- Now listen to the interview and do the tasks.

1. The reason for the interview is …
   a) [x] an unhappy event.
   b) [ ] a new sweet creation.
   c) [ ] a company's anniversary.

2. Neville is one of Thomas Caffrey's …
   a) [ ] faithful clients.
   b) [x] close relatives.
   c) [ ] former employees.

3. Making chocolates at Caffrey's is a …
   a) [x] family affair.
   b) [ ] new business.
   c) [ ] modern industry.

4. Thomas Caffrey went into the chocolate business thanks to a …
   a) [ ] holiday job.
   b) [ ] close friend.
   c) [x] creative talent.

5. Caffrey's big success came thanks to a …
   a) [ ] new location.
   b) [ ] big wedding.
   c) [x] business deal.

6. Irish chocolate fans really like …
   a) ☐ Caffrey's crunchy sweets.
   b) ☐ anything made by Caffrey's.
   c) ☒ one of Caffrey's creations in particular.

7. Inspiration for one of Caffrey's creations came from a …
   a) ☒ child's pet.
   b) ☐ children's story.
   c) ☒ child's plaything.

8. Today one of Thomas Caffrey's early creations …
   a) ☐ has a modernised recipe.
   b) ☒ exists in several varieties.
   c) ☒ has completely disappeared.

9. Thomas Caffrey is described as …
   a) ☐ strict.
   b) ☒ big hearted.
   c) ☐ money focused.

10. Caffrey's creations are on offer …
    a) ☐ only in Ireland.
    b) ☒ in some countries.
    c) ☒ anywhere in the world.

In 30 seconds you will hear the interview again so you can check your answers.

Zweiter Prüfungsteil: Leseverstehen – Wortschatz – Schreiben

Leseverstehen

The family that is enough by Juliet Rix

"If you want to hang out with my brothers you have to be in top form or you'll be destroyed," says Eoin (pronounced 'Owen') Colfer, the second of five boys and author of the hugely successful *Artemis Fowl* books (often described as James Bond with fairies). His relationship with his brothers, he believes, explains the quick, dry humour in his books. His writing style has put his books at the top of many bestseller lists, and so Eoin, who used to work as an Irish primary school teacher, became an international celebrity.

Born in 1965, Eoin grew up in the seaside town of Wexford, Ireland. The household was large, loving and loud. Eoin's father used to take his sons on historical trips. "To keep us from fighting, my dad would tell us all stories about fairies and dragons. He had to keep going because whenever he stopped, me and my brothers were at each other's throats[1]."

Eoin loved comic books, invented his own characters and drew and wrote his own comics when he was young. His interest in writing continued as a love of drama: He used to help his mother (a drama teacher and local actress), learned her lines with her and had parts in Wexford Opera Festival productions.

It is perhaps not surprising that when Eoin started to write books, his brothers became the characters. All five boys are part of the story. In the second *Artemis Fowl* book, four goblins[2] have a fight. Their names are almost identical to those of Eoin's brothers.

Eoin had written three other children's books while teaching at the local primary school in Wexford. He thought that his *Artemis* books would also become successful but only in Ireland. But when his wife Jackie read the manuscript, she knew it was different. She asked Eoin's brothers to take him to a pub and make him promise to get an agent[3]. Convincing their brother was really difficult, but it paid off.

The money was not as big as has been reported, but fame came fast and bigger money followed later. Didn't that change things? "Not as much as you would expect," says Eoin. In Ireland everyone is a writer and people in Wexford aren't interested in wealth and fame: "They've known me for decades, so they don't care." The brothers keep his feet on the ground too, Eoin adds.

Colfer's kids have changed his writing. "My son Finn, for example, is very funny," says Eoin. "He comes up with some great funny remarks and I get a lot of material straight from him." When Finn argues in the back of the car, Eoin doesn't tell stories to stop him. Instead, he tries to remember it for his books.

The realisation that his children would one day read his books also made him think about the violence. "There is a huge fight in the first book. I decided there was no need for that really ... Now there are struggles but not much

actual violence." The amorality⁴ of his hero – the criminal boy *Artemis Fowl* – worried the new father in him too. Over the next four books, Artemis dev-
45 elops a feeling for right and wrong. "I don't know how much longer he will stay interesting as a character," admits Eoin. "Once he turns completely good, that's it."

Quelle: Juliet Rix: The family that is enough, *Guardian* 14 Oct 2006, https://www.theguardian.com/lifeandstyle/2006/oct/14/familyandrelationships.booksforchildrenandteenagers © Guardian News & Media Ltd 2021

Annotations
1 to be at each other's throat – to argue angrily
2 goblin – a small scary, fantastical creature
3 agent – here: a person who is paid to advertise and sell someone's books
4 amorality – a lack of moral principles

You are doing a reading project in your English class. All the students have to present a famous English-speaking author who writes books for young adults. You have come across Irish author Eoin Colfer, creator of the famous Artemis Fowl *books. Who is this man? Find out more about him in the online article.*

- *Tick the correct box* **and** *give evidence from the text by quoting short passages from the text.*

1. Eoin Colfer grew up as an only child.
   This statement is ...   ☐ true   ☐ false
   One piece of evidence from the text:
   _____

2. Colfer's way of writing is influenced by his ...
   a) ☐ family.
   b) ☐ former job.
   c) ☐ favourite book.
   One piece of evidence from the text:
   _____

3. Colfer grew up in a household with ...
   a) ☐ peace and quiet.
   b) ☐ little entertainment.
   c) ☐ lots of fantastic tales.
   One piece of evidence from the text:
   _____

4. Growing up, Colfer showed little creative talent.
   This statement is ...   ☐ true   ☐ false
   One piece of evidence from the text:
   _____

5. Figures in the *Artemis Fowl* books are based on family members.
   This statement is ... ☐ true ☐ false
   One piece of evidence from the text:
   _____

6. When Colfer wrote the *Artemis Fowl* books he ...
   a) ☐ kept them secret from his family.
   b) ☐ already had some experience in the job.
   c) ☐ hoped they would become an international hit.
   One piece of evidence from the text:
   _____

7. The *Artemis Fowl* books made Colfer rich overnight.
   This statement is ... ☐ true ☐ false
   One piece of evidence from the text:
   _____

8. Because of Colfer's success the people in his town ...
   a) ☐ began to ask him for money.
   b) ☐ kept their distance from him.
   c) ☐ behaved like they had before.
   One piece of evidence from the text:
   _____

9. Despite his success as a writer, Colfer has remained a fairly normal person.
   This statement is ... ☐ true ☐ false
   One piece of evidence from the text:
   _____

10. Daily-life situations with his children are an inspiration for Colfer's books.
    This statement is ... ☐ true ☐ false
    One piece of evidence from the text:
    _____

11. Because of his children, Colfer's stories have become ...
    a) ☐ gentler.
    b) ☐ simpler.
    c) ☐ more exciting.
    One piece of evidence from the text:
    _____

12. Colfer plans to stop writing the series once *Artemis Fowl* is too ...
    a) ☐ old.
    b) ☐ nice.
    c) ☐ strict.
    One piece of evidence from the text:
    _____

Wortschatz: *Welcome to "Thinkuknow"*

Using the Internet can be very helpful but it can sometimes also be dangerous. Explore the advice of the "Thinkuknow" websites about staying safe when you're on a phone, tablet or computer.

> - Fill in suitable words **or** tick the correct box.
> - Give only one solution.

1. With every new photo or comment we _____ on the Internet, we add lots of information about ourselves which stays online.

2. This is called a ...
    a) ☐ numerical   b) ☐ statistical
    c) ☐ digital   d) ☐ valued
    footprint. People who know us, and people who don't, can see and learn more about us.

3. These footprints can show us in our most positive moments – but sometimes they reflect thoughts or experiences that we later wish had been kept _____ and not visible for everyone.

4. When you put something online, who can see it? Think about who you're ...
    a) ☐ parting   b) ☐ dividing
    c) ☐ splitting   d) ☐ sharing
    the information with.

5. Don't forget: it's easy for other people to copy, change and _____ _____ that information to others without you knowing it.

6. Most apps and social networks have 'privacy settings'. These help you to ...
    a) ☐ control   b) ☐ govern
    c) ☐ direct   d) ☐ command
    who can see what.

7. It's easy to lie online. Some people set up _____ profiles on social networks.

8. If you use social networks, always think about what personal information your footprints ...
   a) ☐ give away. b) ☐ let out.
   c) ☐ carry out. d) ☐ show off.

9. If you _____ to someone via social media, don't tell them anything which could help them find you in the real world – things like your full name, school, email address or even photos.

10. Be careful! It can be _____ when you meet people online: Some people could threaten you if you don't do what they say.

11. If you stop using an app or a social network, remember to delete your ...
    a) ☐ organisation. b) ☐ participation.
    c) ☐ account.   d) ☐ society.

12. Are you worried about something that's happened on the Internet? Most sites will let you ...
    a) ☐ guard   b) ☐ block
    c) ☐ arrest d) ☐ catch
    people if you don't want to talk to them online anymore.

13. *The Mix* is a service which provides free, personal support for young people 24/7. If you're experiencing any painful emotion or are in crisis, you can send a _____ to *The Mix*.

Quelle: nach: https://www.thinkuknow.co.uk/11_13/need-advice/digital-footprint/

Schreiben

Click'd by Tamara Ireland Stone

Teenager Allie Navarro has participated in a special summer camp on computers: Code Girls Camp. At the end of the summer camp, she presents her result to a jury, parents and participants.

1 She took a deep breath.
And then she began.
"On the first morning here at Code Girls Camp, our instructor told us we had a whole summer to create any kind of app or game we wanted. Anything.
5 Something just for fun. Something that would solve a real-life problem. I loved that."
"But I admit," Allie continued, "on that first morning, I wasn't sure I was ready for that kind of challenge. I was much too terrified. Because I didn't know a single person."
10 Allie began walking up and down the stage. Her legs were shaky and she hoped the audience wouldn't notice.
"I kept looking around the room at these girls – nineteen total strangers I'd be spending my whole summer with – and wondering who they were. Did we like the same music? Did we read the same books? Did they have sisters or
15 brothers?"
"And that's when the idea hit me. Why not an app that could help you make new friends?"
Allie waved her phone in the air. "For my summer project, I created a game called *Click'd*."
20 "Let me demonstrate how it works. This auditorium[1] seats two hundred and twenty people. I assume most of you don't know each other," she said jokingly, and she could see people looking around and shaking their heads.
"What if I told you there was one person in this room right now who had more in common with you than with anyone else? Of course, you could leave
25 this room and never know who that person is, but..." Allie leaned forward. "Wouldn't it be more fun to find out?"
"We're going to use that *Click'd* app you installed when you came in, so, everyone, please pull out your phones and play along."
Allie took a deep breath. "Ready, everyone?" she asked as the screen behind
30 her filled with four scenic[2] photographs. "Which do you prefer: the ocean, the forest, the desert, or the mountains? Select A, B, C, or D."
Allie looked down at her screen. She could see the data collecting in the app she'd built specifically for this demonstration. It used the same system as *Click'd*, taking all the information the audience entered and immediately
35 matching people with similar interests.
"Let's do some more so we have lots of information to work with," Allie said, and she clicked through seven more slides.
"When you're done with the quiz, *Click'd* figures out how you scored against

each person, but it doesn't immediately tell you who your top friends are,
40 because that wouldn't be as much fun," she said with a wink[3]. "Instead, *Click'd* uses sounds, lights, and clues to help you find your top ten friends."

As she walked across the stage, she noticed her legs weren't shaking anymore. Allie tapped on her screen, and one of the phones in the back of the room let out a sound that startled[4] its owner. "Sir, would you please stand?" She tapped
45 another button, and a phone in the front row on the opposite side of the auditorium sounded. A woman held her phone in the air and then stood and turned around.

"Congratulations! If you two were playing *Click'd*, you'd be in each other's high score lists." They waved at each other from across the auditorium.
50 "That's basically how my game works."

Everyone clapped as the man and woman took their seats.

Allie looked back at the audience, feeling on top of the world!

Quelle: Tamara Ireland Stone: *Click'd*, Disney Book Group 2017

Annotations
1 auditorium – a room for a large audience
2 scenic – showing beautiful countryside
3 with a wink – to shut one eye briefly as a signal
4 to startle – to surprise s.o. suddenly

- *Read the tasks carefully.*
- *Make sure to write about* **all** *the aspects presented in each task.*

---

1. **Describe** Allie's product, how it works and why she has created it. (8 Punkte)

2. **Explain** how Allie's feelings change during the presentation.
   To do this, look at how she acts and speaks at the beginning, in the middle and at the end of her presentation. (10 Punkte)

3. Here you can choose between three different options.
   Do only ONE of them!

   a) What do you think about *Click'd*? **Comment** on Allie's product.

   Include the following aspects:
   - risks or chances of Allie's product,
   - the role social media play in your life,
   - your opinion on personally using *Click'd*. (12 Punkte)

   or

   b) Imagine you were in the audience and listened to Allie's presentation. You have to write an article on it for the summer camp's magazine.

   Write this article.

   Include the following aspects:
   - things to know about *Click'd*,
   - the audience's possible reactions to *Click'd*,
   - your view on computer summer camps for teenagers.

   You can start like this:

Have you been "Click'd" yet?
16-year-old Allie Navarro is the winner of this year's Code Girls Camp. She has demonstrated her product in a convincing presentation to ... (12 Punkte)

or

c) Imagine that Allie is the first speaker at the *Code Girls Camp*'s opening event one year later. She is talking to the new participants about her experiences over the last year.

Write Allie's speech.

Include the following aspects:
- how *Click'd* has changed her and her life,
- how she feels about the summer camp in general,
- her advice for the new participants.

You can start like this:
Hi everyone, I'm happy to be back here at Code Girls Camp. I can't believe it's already been a year. So much has happened since ... (12 Punkte)

Hörverstehen – Transkripte

Zentrale Prüfung 10 – 2021: Englisch

Mittlerer Schulabschluss – Haupttermin

Wichtige Hinweise: Alle Texte, die im Folgenden zu hören sind, werden zweimal vorgespielt. Vor dem ersten Hören wird Zeit gegeben, sich mit den Aufgaben vertraut zu machen. Nach dem ersten Hören wird Zeit gegeben, die Antworten zu überprüfen. Der Hörverstehenstest besteht aus zwei Teilen.

Hörverstehen Teil 1: *The summer plans of Danny Boyle*

Danny Boyle, the teenage hero of William Graham's book "Danny Boyle and the ghosts of Ireland", is looking forward to carrying out his plans for the summer. Find out more about Danny from the beginning of the audiobook.

- *First read the tasks.*
- *Then listen to the extract.*
- *While you are listening, tick the correct box.*
- *At the end you will hear the extract again.*
- *Now read the tasks. You have **90 seconds** to do this.*
- *Now listen to the extract and do the tasks.*

1 Danny Boyle sat in his room with a map of Ireland lying on his bed. He was carefully circling all the destinations where he and his family would be going on their summer vacation. He had circled Dublin, Galway, and other places with magical names like Connemara. Danny carefully ran his fingers across the
5 map like it was a piece of treasure.
   Danny loved to read about distant locations, but this was the first time that he would be getting on a plane and travelling to a place that he had only read about or had stared at on a map.
   He thought he had been waiting long enough. Danny lived in Rivertown, a
10 small town near the Mississippi River. Not much happened in Rivertown, so Danny was always looking for adventure wherever he could find it.
   Ireland was far away. It was a foreign country and that made all the difference to Danny.
   Danny was interrupted by his younger sister Melinda. Even though Danny was
15 two years older than Melinda, they were in the same grade. This fact annoyed Danny but amused Melinda who told everyone she met that she had jumped ahead two grades because she was special.
   "Are you still staring at that old map? I've been doing something practical," Melinda said.
20 "Go away," Danny said, keeping his eyes on the map.
   "Don't you want to know what I've been doing?"
   "Does it look like it?"

"Well, I'll tell you anyway. I've been learning some words in the native Irish language," Melinda said proudly.

"But people in Ireland speak English," Danny reminded her. "Here's one," Melinda continued. "In Irish, Ireland is called 'Eire'. A river is known as 'abhainn'." Melinda said ignoring Danny's response completely.

"Well, you can talk to the fairies there," Danny said.

"There are no such things as fairies. They're just a legend. You know, something that isn't real," Melinda said.

"I know what a legend is," Danny said. "But there are some dark and mysterious places in Ireland that I want to explore. You never know what you might find."

"We'll go wherever Mom and Dad take us," Melinda said. "And that's that."

"Yeah, yeah," Danny said. "Now can I go back to what I was doing?"

"Fine. I'm going to look up more words and begin packing," Melinda said, turned around and went to her room.

Danny had already packed. Even though it was summer, Ireland can be cool and wet, so he had packed a rain jacket and pants and his waterproof hiking shoes. Danny hadn't slept well the night before he and his family went to the airport. He dreamed that he was alone on a windy island surrounded by fireballs that were leading him to the edge of a cliff. He then began falling down towards the ocean below. Just as he was about to hit the rocks at the bottom of the cliffs, he heard his mother telling him to wake up because it was time to get ready.

His adventure was about to begin.

Quelle: William Graham: *Danny Boyle and the Ghosts of Ireland*, GreatUnpublished.com 2002

In 30 seconds you will hear the extract again so you can check your answers.

Hörverstehen Teil 2: *Thomas Caffrey's chocolate world*

Thomas Caffrey's sweet creations are loved by many Irish people. Joe Duffy from RTÉ Radio 1 is talking to his guest Neville about the famous Irish chocolate maker.

- First read the tasks.
- Then listen to the interview.
- While you are listening, tick the correct box.
- At the end you will hear the interview again.
- Now read the tasks. You have **90 seconds** to do this.
- Now listen to the interview and do the tasks.

1 **Joe:** Hello and good afternoon and welcome to Culture of Ireland. Sad news for the children of Ireland and chocolate lovers everywhere: Dublin's favourite chocolate creator, the legendary Thomas Caffrey, died yesterday. He will be sadly missed by his family and the children around
5 the country. We have Neville Caffrey, who is Thomas Caffrey's son, on the line. First of all let me say that I am really sorry about the death of your dad, Neville.
Neville: Thank you very much, Joe, and thanks a lot for talking to me.
Joe: Your business is now in its third generation.
10 **Neville:** Yeah, that's right. Thomas Caffrey, my dad, had been there making chocolate since 1930, which is incredible.
Joe: How old was he? May I ask?
Neville: 92. He was 92, the last traditional sugar baker. He was born here in Dublin.
15 **Joe:** And when did he get involved in chocolate making, Neville?
Neville: Well, it goes back quite a bit. During summers as a little boy he worked in the chocolate factory of his brother William. William was the chocolate maker and manager for a company called Browns. My dad loved making things…
20 **Joe:** Mmh.
Neville: His great breakthrough came when he got a contract with a huge chain of shops in the 1950s. And in 1953, he was asked to make the chocolate confections for the crowning ceremony of Elizabeth II in the UK.
Joe: Wow, incredible. Among the many of Caffrey's creations are Ireland's all-
25 time favourite, the Chocolate Snowball. Did your dad invent the coconut kind of creamy ball we love so much?
Neville: Yeah, he did. It's amazing really so many people haven't forgotten. I remember when I was little I was on the floor with my little toy mouse, and my dad picked it up and said, "Can I borrow this?" He went away with it
30 and used it as a model for his Marshmallow Mice. That was the start of the Marshmallow Mice… they were a sensation! They had two eyes in them and a little tail…
Joe: Are they still a big sell?

Neville: The Marshmallow Mice are no longer sold. But the Snowball still is,
35   yeah. It's one that people come in for. It's a nice sweet to have with a cup of tea or coffee.

Joe: So true ... What memories do you have of your father?

Neville: I remember that we were a small business in town. I remember as a kid I used to go to the company and my father, who was a very fine man, used
40   to give a few sweets to me, and my brothers and sisters and to other kids. We loved that.

Joe: Oh, I would have liked that, too. So, how is business going?

Neville: Great! We make a wide range of products really. You can also buy our products in Australia, Canada and in the United States. And people often
45   write asking, "Please, could you also send a box of chocolates or marshmallows to other places."

Joe: Brilliant. Tell us, what was your father's favourite product?

Quelle: nach: http://www.caffreyschocolates.com/thomas-caffrey.html

In 30 seconds you will hear the interview again so you can check your answers.

Ende des ersten Prüfungsteils.

Bildnachweis:
2021-1: © Natalia Chuen / Shutterstock.com
2021-3: © Can Stock Photo / photography33
2021-5: Artemis Fowl (2001), https://www.artemis-fowl.com/the-books/artemis-fowl/

Zentrale Prüfungen 2022 – Englisch
Anforderungen für den Mittleren Schulabschluss (MSA)

Um dir die Prüfung 2022 schnellstmöglich zur Verfügung stellen zu können, bringen wir sie in digitaler Form heraus.
Sobald die Original-Prüfungsaufgaben 2022 freigegeben sind, können sie als PDF auf der Plattform **MyStark** heruntergeladen werden. Deinen persönlichen Zugangscode findest du auf den Farbseiten vorne im Buch.

Prüfung 2022

www.stark-verlag.de/mystark